"The Chameleon Diaries is a l
self-discovery and acceptan

Brown's *'The Gifts of Imperfection,'* offering readers an opportunity to confront their fears and doubts head-on. Amanda's rich experiences, from establishing a successful interior design firm to her journey of personal growth, lend credibility to her vulnerable narrative."

— *Tony Dufresne, PhD*
Women's Confidence Coach and host of *She Talks Confidence Podcast*

"You would never think a woman who dresses in black leather and drives a Harley Davidson would struggle with having boundaries, but too many strong, powerful women do. In Amanda's writing, we discover we are not alone when it comes to betraying ourselves in our effort to be loved, and we are lovingly reminded the journey to self-love takes time and follows a very windy road."

— *Renee Linnell,*
author of *The Burn Zone* and *Still On Fire*

"A courageous and unflinching look at the world of people pleasing. Amanda writes with gripping honesty and a keen insight into the chemistry of toxic relationships, leading the reader on an incredible journey that serves as a powerful reminder: greatness comes from within. A must-read for anyone who believes they're not enough."

—*David Richards,*
international best-selling author of *Whiskey and Yoga*

This book is a work of creative nonfiction/memoir. The events are portrayed to the best of the author's memory, and some names and identifying details have been changed to protect the privacy of the people involved.

The material in this book is of the nature of general advice and is designed to provide information and motivation to the reader. The author does not claim to be certified in therapies or coaching modalities aside from their life experiences. Neither the author nor the publisher is entitled to engage in any type of psychological, legal, financial, or any other kind of professional advice. In any and all cases, the author suggests seeking the advice of a licensed professional whenever possible or pertinent to the reader's situation.

When desired, readers can obtain additional understanding of the content of this book by connecting with the publisher at info@two29publishing.com.

Published by Two 29 Publishing, LLC
ISBN: 979-8-9895737-0-7 First edition.

For resources that accompany this book, please scan the QR Code, or visit www.amandagreaves.com/book-bundle/ to get access to *The Chameleon Diaries* bonus bundles.

There you will find:

— *PDF of The Chameleon Diaries: Reader Transformation and Chapter Guide*
— *PDF of the compiled "Dear Diary" Journal*
— *Links to join Amanda Greaves' community, learn about upcoming speaking engagements, podcasts, and much more...*

Let's design *your* life worth changing for together.

The Chameleon Diaries

Designing A Life Worth Changing For

A Memoir and Guide to Self-Discovery

Amanda Greaves

For all of you that fit in, stand out,
hold on, and let go
—all at the same time.
For the old you. The new you.
And all the yous in between
then and now.

Table of Contents

Foreword

trans·for·ma·tion

/ˌtran(t)sfərˈmāSH(ə)n/

noun

1. a thorough or dramatic change in form or appearance

Amanda's transformation over the last five years can only be described as night and day. When I first met her, I was a Tony Robbins Results Coach and a twenty-year veteran life and business coach. I had seen it all. Amanda was the classic participant who returned home from the fire-walking UPW experience—high on life, ready for radical change. Only, Amanda found herself standing in the middle of a life she no longer recognized or wanted.

After our first call, I knew Amanda's passion for understanding life at the soul level and her deep desire to shift the perils of our human conditioning would make her a dream client and one day a dear friend. What Amanda didn't know was she was standing on the precipice of a five-year journey that would rip her open and transform her life from the inside out.

This book you are holding is the result of that uneven journey. It is her invitation to you to break the chains of shame and unworthiness, share your hidden parts and false starts, and to foster healing. It gives language and context to the thoughts, beliefs, feelings, and actions we don't understand and never want to expose. This book is a gift to you from a woman strong and brave enough to offer it. Amanda's words are that of a coach, mentor, sister, and best friend willing to share with you the things we desperately try to hide, in order to help you open up a world where healing is possible for everyone.

I invite you to follow Amanda's journey and uncover the parts and stories in your own life you don't think others would approve of and sit with them. Give them a voice, share with others, and allow them to be seen, heard, and healed. These parts hold your greatest truths, stories, passions, and your soul's purpose.

Transformation is hard. It is work. It is commitment. It is looking at the stuff you don't want to look at and diving deep over and over again. What Amanda's story helps us understand is that healing and sharing our truest selves with the world *is* our work.

Kerri Krell, *CEO Soul Solutions Inc.*
Master Certified Integrative Coach
Master Leadership Coach
Tony Robbins Business Coach

Introduction

"Our deepest fear is not that we are inadequate. Our deepest fear is that we are powerful beyond measure. It is our light, not our darkness, that most frightens us. Your playing small does not serve the world. There is nothing enlightened about shrinking so that other people won't feel insecure around you. We are all meant to shine, as children do. ... It's not just in some of us; it's in everyone. And as we let our own light shine, we unconsciously give other people permission to do the same. As we are liberated from our own fear, our presence automatically liberates others."

~*Marianne Williamson*

DESIGNING YOUR JOURNEY

I am going to take you on a journey through some incredible experiences that left me crying in my spaghetti, traveling halfway around the world, walking on fire, and begging for forgiveness. There have been times in my life when I was so full of love I was bursting at the seams. And times when I have suffered heartache so baffling, I felt broken into teeny tiny little pieces, wondering how I would ever pull myself back together.

This book is a collection of honest, raw, and vulnerable stories about my adventures, the lessons I've learned along the way, and how I eventually applied my knowledge to cracking my own life's code, turning the corner from victim to victor and embarking on a true journey of self-discovery.

As a child, I found the outlet of writing took me to many magical and imaginary places that no one else around me seemed to understand.

I filled books and books with pages of notes, love letters, song lyrics, and poetry. Silent words that were a part of my history, kept hidden under the mattress of my bed, then followed me around the planet, and eventually landed in the basement of my current home.

In the process of writing this book, I spent a year digging into whatever diaries still remained in my possession. Some of my collection had been lost over the years by way of inadvertently leaving books behind in a move, and others got burned in a fire. But as I read through the words, I found myself reaching through my memories—going as far back as necessary to find the reasons for the lost loves, anguish, and explanations of why I stayed or why I had to go.

I stumbled across educational exposures, entries that sent me back to high school like a slingshot, humorous accounts of ridiculousness, and nightmares of me running away from it all like a movie on double speed. I found vision boards that displayed the hopes of now-actualized dreams of which I congratulated myself for, and ones that never materialized for which I offered myself grace. I laughed out loud. I cried. And then I cried again. I remembered what I had intentionally forgotten, and I discovered new truths amongst the lies that had been buried years and years ago.

The stories rediscovered on those pages, coupled with the experiences etched in my memory, are the stories that are about to unfold on the pages before you. As I wrote this book, I pushed and I pulled. I expanded and contracted. I forced myself into cathartic exercises of reliving my past and preparing for my future as I poured my heart and soul into every sentence within every story. It has been a fascinating, messy, and sometimes discouraging process where a lot of painful tears gave way to moments of joyous clarity.

But through it all, the realization that I was on a greater journey than just writing a book came to light. My soul started to shift. I discovered myself within the depths of these stories and found a deep-rooted sense of pride emerge while I scrawled the words onto these pages and lovingly crafted the masterpiece of this book. The ratchet strap around my heart started to loosen. I now understand that I had initially embarked on a mission to capture the facts of my life, but the process evolved into a spiritual journey instead. The more I wrote, the more I evolved and the more confident I became in my ability to overcome my own limiting belief of not being enough for some, and my contradicting fears of being too much for most.

A primary theme throughout these stories focuses on these limiting beliefs, getting out of toxic and abusive relationships, and about healing from the inside. I talk about defining your core values so you can end decades of frustration as you sync your new reality and unleash your beauty from within. Unencumbered and empowered.

Life takes us on a journey through various ups and downs, through and around things, beneath obstacles and over hurdles. We experience events that ideally help us learn how to fine-tune our emotional compass and navigate our lives. And these messages are about encouraging you, creating relentless resiliency and contagious courage.

By recounting the steps in my quest, working through the chapters of my life, revisiting both the pains and the pleasures again (and again, and again), documenting where I veered left when I should have turned right, and celebrating those instances when I bravely leapt forward instead of shrinking back, I've uncovered the genuine me hiding beneath the many faces I've presented to the world. And it's through this process I've begun to embrace self-love for the very first time, realizing that my life is truly worth changing for.

THIS BOOK IS FOR YOU

Even though these are stories of my journey of self-discovery, I hope by sharing them, they help you consider where you've come from, where you are now, and where you want to go. As you possibly recognize yourself in the characters (both good and bad) and see via the stories of my life that you are not alone, you will learn there are people who understand and want to be there for you with support and encouragement. These stories may be told from the perspective of my experiences, but they could possibly echo similar versions of you that you've once been and that you dream of becoming.

Who is this book for exactly? Well, it's for …

— The younger versions of you that are still holding on to limiting beliefs of not being enough or unlovable;

— The rebellious teenager who is masking their pain with defiance and chaos;

— Anyone who has considered going to therapy because you know you *aren't* fine, even though you keep saying you are;

— The woman who's suffocating in an unhealthy relationship, feeling stuck, afraid, and upset, and putting up with things she shouldn't have to;

— All of us who have battled or are currently battling depression, or who feel hopeless, helpless, and alone;

— Those of us who keep repeating the same patterns over and over again, hoping for different results but unsure how to change our own habits;

— The woman searching for her purpose and yearning for connection and faith;

— The woman who knows her energy and spirit have a deeper calling;

— And the loving, empowered, creative, unstoppable force of beautiful nature that you've always dreamed of being.

You are who I have written this book for. The old you. The current you. The future you. The you that is designing a life worth changing for because you know, in this very moment, whoever you are, you are worth it.

YOUR STRATEGY

My aim is to give you guidance on how to uncover your true self and overcome your limiting beliefs by telling you about some of my own. Within each chapter, there are direct messages and underlying lessons. And I make suggestions on how you can apply the lessons to your own life through a journaling process and thought-provoking exercises at the end of each chapter.

How you approach this book and the potential process within it is totally up to you. My hope is that you are entertained while also feeling empowered and inspired to rewrite your own story as you (hopefully) learn through my mistakes. It's about uncovering *your* truth and *your* most powerful self. It's an inside job, so dig deep! Trust the process and know with a little shift here and there, you'll be able to reach new heights, use your voice with strength and conviction, and shine your own virtue like never before.

I've opened myself up wide in here and created a vulnerability I never knew I was capable of. I found that even though it can be a frightening place, vulnerability is where the good stuff lives and grows. It's where your soul gets ignited, and sometimes catches fire. Vulnerability is where you will find empowerment, and that empowerment can very well be the first step to finding the path of self-discovery.

So don't be afraid to be vulnerable. Peel back your layers, and evaluate your life with an intention to create some change. Become that person you've always wanted to be.

No one who has ever done any of this is going to tell you it's easy. But my good God, it's totally worth it. It's going to take discipline. Emotional, spiritual, physical, and psychological discipline. It's going to take time—as much time as you are willing or able to devote. And remember, no matter what happens, you are exactly where you are meant to be, and you're doing an amazing job. Congratulations on making it this far. You're doing great.

So, get on with it! Go have fun. Explore the corners of your soul and your psyche, and ideally you will uncover everything you've ever been, all that you will become, and fall in love with *you* unconditionally.

The more you seek, the more you will find.

The greater the seeker, the greater the journey.

"I fell in love with her courage, her sincerity, and her flaming self-respect. And it's these things I'd believe in, even if the whole world indulged in wild suspicions that she wasn't all she should be. I love her, and it is the beginning of everything."

~ *F. Scott Fitzgerald*

What Happened?

Part 1

PIVOTAL MOMENTS

"When something happens to you, you have
two choices in how to deal with it.
You can either get bitter or get better."

~ *Donald Miller*

Pivotal moments can be defined by words like "very important, critical, consequential, and climactic." **Pivotal** means the precise moment in time that provides us distinct clarity and offers new perspectives or opportunities that drastically change our lives.

These **moments** are ones that you remember vividly and can recall easily at any given time. They can be the absolute greatest event in your life or the worst possible experience you could ever imagine. Major events like buying your first home, starting a new job or career, the end of a relationship, or getting married. Or they might be smaller instances like bumping into an old friend or waking up on the floor of your living room and not recalling how you got home. When these moments happen, they create a shift in your perspective. You get redirected. You change. And your life is never the same.

Think about moments in your life that have shifted your energy and thoughts so much that you made a pivot and never looked back. What may have happened if you didn't pivot? What if you stayed exactly where you were and kept living as if nothing had happened?

1

PIVOT POINT, Part 2–CONNECTING THE DOTS

Your Defining Moment in Time When Everything Changes

"Healing opportunities can be disguised as people who really piss you off. Pay attention because they could be your greatest teachers."

~ Gabrielle Bernstein

When I was in high school, I made the career choice to become an interior designer. Since then, I have been working in the industry for over two decades, running my own firm for thirteen of those years.

My company's mission statement has been to "enhance people's lives through design…" as we "...skillfully practice the art of turning our client's dreams into reality." Our portfolio includes the interiors of houses, restaurants, offices, and hotels, and at times, I have had over twenty projects on the boards and in process simultaneously.

But while I was working towards turning other people's dreams into reality, I was failing at enhancing my own life. The irony of my company's mission statement being totally misaligned with who I had become in my own personal life became a clear reality when I started to realize I was having more nightmares of poorly procured wallpaper patterns rather than dreams of perfectly presented projects.

For years, I had been in the habit of using my work as an escape from anything else that was happening in my life, so the following particular Sunday/Monday combination was not unusual. Until it was…

SUNDAY, DECEMBER 11, 2022

Sundays have historically been my opportunity to play catch-up from the week before and attempt to get a jump start on the week ahead. The office was always quiet, and it was a great time to get all my thoughts in order.

This Sunday was no different. As I sat in the quiet, working on a bathroom tile scheme for a new client, I got a text from my cousin, Melanie.

"Can you talk?"

I didn't think anything of it. I had just seen her for the first time in three years at Thanksgiving and was excited to have reconnected after the pandemic. Hoping she was going to invite me to dinner, I quickly replied.

"Yes," then I went back to tile selections until the phone rang.

"Hey, Mel," I answered.

"You remember my friend Larissa, right?" she immediately began. For some reason the combination of her tone, the slight hesitation in her voice, and her strange question made my stomach sink. Something wasn't right; I could just feel it.

Mel and I attended the same high school, but she was four years older than me so we didn't hang out with the same people. In our small-ish town, everyone kind of knew who everyone was, so yeah, I remembered her friend, Larissa. Her younger sister was in my class.

Initially she stumbled over her words, unsure how to approach the subject. Eventually, she asked a few specific questions about some of the vacations I took with my most recent boyfriend, Jay.

Why was she asking about where I was last Fourth of July? How did she know I had gone to Florida in March?

My answers were quick and to the point because I was super curious about why she was probing. Finally, after enough conversation, she shared her assumptions and told me something that made my knees buckle. As I collapsed on the floor I heard myself say, "I'm sorry, can you repeat that?" And for the next thirty minutes, I stayed crumpled in a ball while we went through the strange back-and-forth process of her asking questions based on her assumptions and me affirming everything she thought she knew.

It was a totally fucked-up conversation, but one that had to happen.

As we talked, answers to two years of questions confirmed a truth I had feared. My mind was a tornado of chaos. Feelings of confusion, disgust, and rage swirled through me. I didn't know if I should laugh, cry, or scream.

Mel shared that her friend Larissa had been telling her some really strange stories about her boyfriend, his aggressive behavior, and his random disappearing acts. When Mel and I saw each other at Thanksgiving, she found it odd that the stories I was telling her about my on-again/off-again boyfriend sounded oddly similar to Larissa's. So after turkey day, Mel did some research of her own through social media channels and online resources, and when her concerned hunches started to line up, she texted me.

Halfway through our call, she forwarded me the photo. It was Jay and Larissa from last summer. I didn't want to believe it, but deep down, I knew I had to. I couldn't unsee or unknow what I had just learned. The photo qualified the nonsense of our conversation, and suddenly it was all too real.

Before we hung up, I said, "Please have Larissa call me...if she wants to."

I was able to keep my shit together while talking to Mel, but I could feel a sickness erupting in my gut during our conversation. The second we hung up, my body started shaking. I rushed to the bathroom, then got violently ill. It all happened so fast I felt like I had been poisoned. My neurological system shut down, and my body went into shock.

Ten minutes later, with nothing left for my body to purge, I lay on the floor of my office in silence as the emotional devastation continued to wash over me. I knew that if Larissa called me, so many of my suspicions and questions that had accumulated over the past couple years were going to be answered. I felt like I was about to step into a bad movie full of ghosts and deceptive manipulation. But it wasn't a movie; it was reality. The worst part was that I was one of the main characters in the nightmare, and even though I believed what Mel had just told me, **I didn't want to believe it was actually happening to me.**

—

I managed to peel myself off the floor and grab some water before the phone rang again. This time, I was better prepared for the upcoming conversation. Through the dark, mysterious haze that consumed my attention, I quickly found a chair to sit in before the shaking ensued again.

"Hello, this is Amanda."

"Hi, Mandi, this is Larissa. Do you have time to talk?"

Time was the only thing I had right now. "Yes, I have all night."

Once the initial niceties passed, we both apologized to each other, then immediately consoled the other by saying, "It's not your fault," and "Yes, I know, but I feel horrible..."

She would start a story, then pause, and I would fill in the missing details, and vice versa. This went on and on. Just when I thought I had heard it all, she'd mention something else that knocked me off my feet again. Just when I desperately wanted the nightmare to be over, she would bring something else up, and the emotional hell would start again. And then I would do the same thing to her.

A vast pathetic cauldron of lies, deceit, and manipulation was boiling over the top, exposing a deep but long-overdue understanding of what we had both been dealing with for far too long. Lost time was now being found. Months of mysterious, unexplained ghosting and heartbreak sagas, sudden availability and love-bombing, gas-lighting and puzzles were being solved in seconds. The darkness and mystery that surrounded Jay, the guy I had dated for the past two-and-a-half years, faded and gave way to the source of all his shadows, finally having me seeing the light.

I asked her if the lingerie, make-up remover, and toothbrushes belonged to her. Yup.

She asked if the sweatshirt and sneakers were mine. Yup.

I asked if she had joined him on the boat with wine and dinner on a specific night. Yup.

She wanted to know if I was the one he was with on the Fourth of July. Yup.

I told her I was the one who designed his condo in Charlestown.

She told me she had decorated his house in New Hampshire.

How he had choreographed our calendars to overlap the way they did was so illusive and disgusting. Neither one of us could comprehend the depths to which we had been played and manipulated so intensely. We weren't mad at each other, nor did we use any harsh words. We shared a mutual discernment that connected the dots to uncover that Larissa and I had been dating the same man for almost three years.

When she asked if I was still seeing him, I confessed that after not talking to him since the middle of July, we had reconnected in early November. He and I had planned to attend UPW[i], a Tony Robbins event in Florida, together, but after a big blowout, I had written him off completely and moved forward with the intention of going alone. The day before I flew to West Palm for the event he had reached out with a "sincere" apology and told me he had really wanted to go but wasn't going to make it because he had COVID. I reluctantly succumbed to his pathetic situation, felt bad he was going to miss the event, and agreed to meet for dinner upon my return home.

"Hmmm," she said. "Of course. He disappeared on me in May, came back in July for a whirlwind summer of boating and trips to New Hampshire, then went quiet again in November."

Pausing for a second, I thought about what to say next, then confessed, "We are supposed to have dinner Monday night."

Laughing, she replied, "We have a dinner date set for Tuesday."

After about an hour, we hung up, and I felt like I had had my yearly fill of shock and surprise. I never wanted to experience that kind of bullshit ever again.

I wasn't sad. I had already made peace with the huge blow-up Jay and I had back in July and started healing from a lot of his mysterious nonsense and emotional abuse. I wasn't really angry either. I actually felt relief and closure when I got off the phone with Larissa (although the shock of it all had residual effects on my psyche). Because for me, the

---

i Tony Robbins' four-day event, Unleash the Power Within. This is more fully explained in Chapter 9 of this book.

revelation of his bullshit wasn't about an ending—it actually triggered a new beginning inside of me.

You see, heartbreak isn't always sad. Sometimes it can open the door to becoming more emotionally mature. And sometimes it can redirect you to learning how to heal and love yourself more fully without the cover of someone else's crap getting in your way.

MONDAY, DECEMBER 12, 2022

The morning after my phone calls with Melanie and Larissa, I was a disaster. Even though I finally understood the reasonings behind all of Jay's shenanigans, it didn't help me sleep any better. It had been such a huge revelation that it put my subconscious into overdrive, exhausting me both emotionally and physically so much that I was unable to sleep.

A recurring nightmare kept me awake all night as I watched puzzle pieces of information fall like snow all around me. As soon as I would attempt to put the pieces together, they would melt, and I would be left lying in a puddle of mud. Desperately searching for help, I would look up to see a conniving, tormenting gremlin sitting at the end of my bed, teasing me with a life ring that he would pull away each time I reached for help.

After watching this scene repeat itself three times, I decided I would rather stay awake than watch the horror story again and again. So, I got up ridiculously early and went into the office to get my mind off of everything.

—

As I began going through my inbox, I saw Howard's email at the top. Since May, I had been chasing him for payment on outstanding invoices for design and installation services we had been provided earlier that spring, so initially I was pleased to finally hear from him. Then I started reading.

"Amanda, I am on a seven-week vacation in South America but had to find the time to show you why our relationship has deteriorated by responding to the most bizarre of all of your confounding invoices..."

What?

As the owner of a large resort development in New Hampshire that just keeps getting bigger and bigger, Howard had been one of my company's top clients for over six years. My firm had completed over a dozen houses, more than fifty hotel suites, and multiple restaurant renovations throughout the five-hundred-acre campus. But, by the end of 2022, he was five months behind in payment and owed us a lot of money.

So my last email to him in late November had been straight and to the point. I told him I needed payment, or I wasn't going to deliver the rest of the furniture for the restaurant in time for their holiday party. I didn't have many other options, and since he owed me close to $8,000, I figured using the furniture as a leveraging technique was reasonable and would get his attention.

But it seems Howard didn't agree with me.

His response to my payment request resulted in him picking apart every single word and every single minute of time, effort, and energy I had poured into his development over the past six years. Words like "confounding, befuddled, ineffective," and "amusing" filled his email. He accused me of double-billing him, being overpriced, and called me childish and ludicrous for "holding his furniture hostage."

His tirade went on for six pages. By the time I finished reading his twisted, preposterous account of perceptions and his audacity of undervaluing my company, which he had praised tremendously while he was trying to get in my pants, flames were spewing out of my eyes. I felt my head spin around a few times, and I let out a screeching, "He's such a FUCKING DOUCHE BAG!"

I couldn't take it anymore. First the drama of Larissa and Jay, and now this?! What was happening?

I was about to toss my computer out the second-story window when one of my employees came flying into my office at the sound of my wailing. Staring at me, not sure what to do, she calmly told me to put the computer down. As I looked up and made eye contact, I was brought back to planet Earth and lowered the monitor back onto the desk. I slid off my chair, melting onto the floor like the snowflakes from my nightmare.

Crying hot tears of frustration, anxiety, and rage, I let out a pathetic, victimized scream until I almost couldn't breathe.

Then after a few moments, I realized I had just lost my shit in front of my employee and quickly tried to gain some composure.

Pulling myself together, I started writing a draft rebuttal. It took me over two hours to really stick it to him. But when an employee read it for me (always proofread your work), she sheepishly suggested I may end up getting sued if I sent it. Heeding her review, I read it again and agreed with her assessment. I realized my emotions and energy were totally fractured, and I should probably sleep on it before replying. So, instead of raging around the office like a bull, I packed myself up and went home to take my anger and aggression out on cleaning my house and wrapping Christmas presents.

—

The following day, when I returned to the office and reread my initial response, I realized just how valuable my decision to sleep on it was. My first draft was littered with profanity and spelling mistakes. If I was going to tell this guy what I *really* thought about him, I wanted my message to be clear and concise, not full of blunders and immaturity. And I wanted to make sure it was just as much of a kick in the balls as his message was to me.

The general essence of my response was that I was done dealing with his disrespectful and insidious business practices and that he didn't need to find time on his sabbatical to show me why our relationship had deteriorated. However, I was thankful that he did since it created the opportunity for me to lay into his delinquency.

Reminding him of all the work my company had completed over the past six years, I explained how we had turned ourselves inside out to accommodate his unrealistic and chaotic timeframes, and that working for his development company was the most stressful and tiresome circus I had ever been a part of. I then pointed out that, at his request, I had lowered my billing rates with the falsified belief that he was actually going to follow through on all of the deals we had agreed upon. He had already been getting a massive discount for the past three years.

I gained the courage to tell him he was disrespectful to women, ignorant to reality, and abusive in his undermining approach to managing a project and the people associated with it. I was done subjecting myself to his sexual harassment advances and had determined that I wasn't going to lower my personal standards or tolerances any more, thinking he was "just a nice guy" and I should just deal with it for the sake of keeping the client happy.

I never wanted to work for him again.

The revised version was a little softer, but still very strong and laden with anger. I took out all but one of the "fucks" and believe I communicated my severing message very clearly with pride and precision. With an honorable sense of closure and self-respect, I signed it, "Merry F'ing Christmas, Howard. Regards, Amanda" and pressed send as a smile of relief and triumph crept across my face.

Then, I stood up, walked away from my desk, raised my hand high in the air, and patted myself on the back. Even though I felt in my gut that it was the right thing to do, I knew that with one click I had just severed fifty percent of my company's future projects and skewed all our financial projections for the following year. Trying to not let the overwhelming stress take over, I pulled forth the belief that I had a strong team, and I knew that we would find a way to figure it out. With an invisible weight lifted off my shoulders, I tabled the concern of next year and skipped down the street to celebrate what I considered a win by ironically treating myself to a ridiculously expensive latte and chocolate croissant.

That week I got a few phone calls from other members of the development team congratulating me on finally telling Howard where to go. One of the guys even shared, "Amanda, that email was EPIC! All of us in the office have read it at least twice. It's amazing! Well done!" Any "atta girl" after telling your biggest client to go screw himself is always welcomed encouragement.

Though it was something that had to be done, none of it was easy. It was actually one of the most difficult emails I have ever written. After dealing with the emotional turmoil from Jay and Larissa, I really had to dig deep to believe that my decision to fire this client wasn't coming from a place of emotion, but from a place of respect, self-discipline, and growth.

I certainly don't recommend responding to emails immediately when there is emotion involved; if not thought through, the repercussions can be treacherous. However, sometimes the only way to win a fight with a bully is to use their own techniques and fire back at them. My one piece of advice for something like this is give yourself time away to evaluate the possible consequences of your actions. **Only send what you are willing to receive.**

THE NEXT FEW WEEKS

When the frightening realization that everything I had been working towards for the past few years both personally and professionally was now gone, I felt my emotional and mental capacity for bullshit break down more than I ever had before. I had previously chosen to ignore the confusion and anxiety that had been building all around me for months, but I wasn't completely dense to the fact that my entire relationship with Jay had been inconsistent and emotionally abusive and that Howard was creating more stress than any other client we had ever had.

However, rather than take ownership of either situation, I had been doing my best to stay in my lane and let the men lead. The dramatic crescendo of Larissa's phone call and Howard's email happening one right after the other was the clearest indication that I had lost control of most things and revealed just how chaotic and unpredictable *all* aspects of my life had become.

After a few bottles of wine and many, many boxes of tissues, I was able to pull my head out from underneath the blanket of my fear of being alone and fear of failing and push through the holidays with a fake smile and a broken heart. Whenever anyone would ask how things were, I deflected and turned the conversation back to them. Even though I was typically the one jockeying for attention and center stage, after all that just happened, I found more solace in stepping back and becoming more of an observer rather than an active participant. Oddly, with this shift, I found more comfort and support than I had ever experienced before.

A couple of weeks passed before the visions of Jay and Larissa subsided and the thoughts of potentially going bankrupt stopped waking me up in the middle of the night. At that point, the holidays were also over, and the ringing in of a new year of prospects and resolutions took the place of relationship dilemmas and raw feelings of failure. Somehow, I tapped back into the lessons I had been accumulating for years and figured out how to remove my love-struck and ignorant blinders, allowing me to see how much better off I was without Jay.

When I returned to the office in January, I also saw that in my emotional absence, my amazing design team had been able to overcome the bad decisions of one greedy client and had already confirmed a few new projects to fill in the blanks where Howard once stood.

The drama and chaos turned me around a hundred and eighty degrees causing my energy to abruptly redirect in ways I could literally feel happening, and I pivoted. It was my "ah-ha" moment. I felt myself change, and as I stopped running towards what I thought I wanted, I began walking towards what I now knew I needed.

With the massive intention of healing and generating more self-respect and self-love than ever before, I started 2023 with a fresh perspective of refocused values and deliberately adjusted priorities. I reassessed my dreams, my understanding of life, and how I wanted to live, and could feel that my soul was in search of joy, truth, and a more meaningful life. So I started digging in and doing the deeper work, knowing it was time for me to recreate my life's story with fulfillment and love.

And, as I embarked on writing this book, I subsequently felt my new, unique life's purpose evolving.

DEAR DIARY

As we embark on this life-designing journey together, I encourage you to reflect on your life and keep a journal or diary of sorts while you read and work your way through this book. Each section will contain exercises where I will encourage you to write your thoughts or answer some questions, so having a designated journal or diary (and a great pen!) will be helpful.

As you've read this first chapter, you may have remembered your own "ah-ha" moments or pivotal points where decisions or drama have subsequently shaped your next move.

Let's take some time to work through them:

1. What events in your own life have left a significant impact and helped shape who you are today?
2. What are one or two pivotal moments in your life that you can recall in a flash? Can you see where adjustments could have been made before things got totally out of control? How did these events change your thoughts, movements, beliefs, or life overall?
3. What has happened since that moment (or moments)? Can you now recognize what needs (or needed) more of your attention? Define how you want your story to pan out before you are forced to react rather than plan, and see how your life is happening *for* you. It may just be a matter of pivoting in a different direction to change the entire storyline.

Who Are You?

Part 2

SUM and SUBSTANCE

"Sometimes you gotta go back to go forward. And I don't mean goin' back to reminisce or chase ghosts. I mean go back to see where you came from, where you've been, how you got there."

~ *Matthew McConaughey, Lincoln Ad 2014*

Recognizing yourself isn't just about looking in the mirror and saying, "Hey, I know you!" It's about paying attention to *who you are today*. Reflection and recognition of your life can give you the opportunity to see things through more mature lenses, aiding in creating a different perspective and mindset moving forward. Looking back also helps you to decipher what you like (and don't like) about yourself—your habits, patterns, and journey to date—and potentially how you can change moving forward.

Throughout this section of the book, you'll get to look back at your life's experiences and hopefully start to see *who* you are, but more importantly, understand *why* you are. You are the ultimate **sum** of all your parts, and once you understand that, you can start setting intentions that could potentially weave the threads of your life into an entirely new fabric of dreams. The **substances** you choose to include in that fabric and those dreams are endless. You just need to figure out which ones—people, things, thoughts, experiences—are best for your intended final equation, and then adjust the quantity and quality accordingly by adding or subtracting a little more of "this" or a lot less of "that."

It's about understanding and owning who you are at your core. The point is to evaluate yourself, as best you can, so you can grow into the most authentic version of yourself.

"Knowledge without mileage = Bullshit."

~ *H. Rollins*

2

FITTING IN and STANDING OUT

Recognize and Define Your Limiting Beliefs

"True belonging never asks us to change who we are.
True belonging requires us to ***be*** *who we are."*

~ *Brené Brown*

EIGHTH GRADE, 1989

With his body pressed up against mine, I could smell, feel, and hear his sweet, warm, excited breath panting on my cheek. We had squeezed into this two-by-six closet by folding ourselves up like pretzels. There was no wiggle room, and certainly no extra space for two thirteen-year-old kids. We couldn't even move. And aside from his panting, I was convinced all the oxygen had been sucked out of this black hole as soon as the door shut behind us. We had to stay in there for seven minutes, and I feared it would be the longest seven minutes of my life.

And then, I don't know how it was possible, but he got closer…

I didn't want this. I had just wanted to be liked by the "cool kids." I wasn't ready for all these pre-teen fooling around antics and every time I felt pressured into doing something, I would get a stomach ache.

The 80s were strange enough with the iconic and far-out fashion faux-pas like big hair and high-waisted jeans. But add in the radical explosion of the heavy metal rock bands, MTV, and video games, and that unique decade created quite an unsettling platform of "anything goes" that filtered down into the concepts of what us kids were "supposed to be" doing and what we weren't. It was a time when I didn't know which direction I could or should be heading, so I constantly looked around to see what everyone else was doing and did what they were.

I hated the high hair, but I crimped, curled, and sprayed anyway. I couldn't stand listening to lengthy, strung-out electric guitar solos, but I pretended to get into the groove and jam along with my fellow wanna-bes anyway. **My fear of being laughed at or being different started to rule my psyche, so I played along whenever I could and tried to follow the leaders.**

—

We had been playing "Spin the Bottle" when one of the guys upped the ante and shouted, "Seven Minutes in Heaven," as soon as I had spun my turn. As the neck of the bottle stopped and faced Tim, my insides did a backflip. I immediately turned to his girlfriend, my friend Nina, for her reaction. They had been dating for a few months, but she didn't seem to care about what was about to happen and gave me a reassuring look. Feeling sick to my stomach, I looked at Donny, my boyfriend, hoping he would step in and say he didn't like the idea. But all he did was shrug his shoulders and look away.

A week prior Donny had wanted to go to second base with me, but I said, "No." I knew the other girls were letting their boyfriends feel them up (and a whole lot more), but I wasn't ready. My body had been changing a lot during this time, and I always felt uncomfortable. But by not performing the same way the other girls were, I felt like I was losing in the competition to grow up fast, and I hated it.

Desperately wanting to prove I was cool like them, I ignored my stomach ache and crammed myself into the closet with Tim. Right before the door closed, Donny blurted out, "Good luck, Tim! She never lets me do anything. I bet you don't even get to kiss her!"

Everyone laughed. My face turned crimson red, and I was temporarily thankful for the darkness that swallowed us when the door closed. Even my own boyfriend was betting against me, which cut through my heart like a hot knife through butter. I interpreted his teasing as betrayal and just wanted to hide my disappointment in the closet with all my other uncertainties and confusion.

The closet was suffocating, filled with shards of fear of the unknown and my silent screams for help. My lungs felt like they may burst if I didn't take a breath, and I could feel the stabs of speculation piercing through the door. As a tiny beam of light forced its way through a crack in the door, my eyes finally adjusted. I was barely able to make out the side angle of Tim's chiseled jawline, but being able to see his face gave me some level of recognizable comfort, so I let out a soft sigh.

My relief was short-lived. As he began fumbling for my hand with his clammy fingers, I could feel myself start to sweat as my stomach ache got worse and my nerves made me tremble with performance anxiety. We had been friends since the fifth grade (a whopping three years that felt like a lifetime), and although I had always thought Tim was cute, I didn't want this. So I whispered, "We don't have to do anything, right? It's just a silly game, right?"

Completely ignoring my plea, he leaned in and tried to French kiss me. I turned my head quickly, causing him to slobber all over my cheek. He tried again. This time he managed to soak my ear with his wet, wide tongue before I squirmed out of his grasp and pressed myself into the back corner of the closet. A sweatshirt fell off a hanger like a guardian angel falling from heaven, creating a natural block between me and this over-eager, salivating, hormonal man-child.

He giggled and tried for a third time. Except, I wasn't giggling. I was scared and started to cry.

"Tim, STOP!"

Quivering, I pushed him away. Reluctantly, he obliged, and with a defeated mumble said, "Come on, Mandi. At least just stay in here with me and pretend. We can just lie and tell everyone we fooled around. No one needs to know the truth."

He clearly only cared about his reputation and didn't give a shit about mine. He wanted me to lie about messing around with him, which made me feel even more sick. The longer I sat there, the more my anxiety increased. My insides tied themselves in knots, and finally, I just had to get out. I wanted nothing to do with this stupid fucking game anymore and didn't care if anyone liked me or not. After what felt like an eternity (but was probably only ninety seconds), I lost my cool, fumbled for the handle, shoved open the door, and fell onto the basement floor.

Everyone stopped talking. The only sound that could be heard was the Poison song "Every Rose Has Its Thorn" playing in the background. I looked up and briefly froze as I realized everyone was staring at me, then quickly ran upstairs.

Crying from embarrassment and shame, I called my mom to come get me, but she said her friends were over, so I would have to wait. I grabbed my jacket and sat outside. I couldn't stay in that house. I had to get away from the thoughts, the sounds, the humiliation.

No one came to check on me. Not even Donny. So, I sat at the end of the driveway and cried.

When my mom finally arrived, she didn't notice my tears. As I got in the car, she was irritated and told me I messed up her night by making her come get me, then asked why I couldn't have gotten a ride home with Nina's parents like we had planned. I told her the party sucked, then added that I got my period and didn't feel well (which wasn't a complete lie). She let it go, and we rode home in silence.

—

By the time puberty hit, I had compared myself with so many of the magazine models and music television pop stars that my reality got totally warped. I was convinced I needed to change everything about myself in order to fit in with everyone else because I was afraid to do my own thing and stand out. **I thought that fitting in would make me happy, because if I fit in, then I would be enough, and being enough would mean I would be perfect, and if I was perfect then I would be loved.** It became a never-ending cycle that I wasn't able to stop before it got out of control because I didn't feel like I had the right kind of positive guidance to help me figure it out.

The stomach aches, or "niggling feelings," happened a lot. Sometimes it would feel like happy fluttering butterflies that made me smile; sometimes it was like food poisoning that made me nauseous. Whenever I asked my mom about them, she would ignore my curiosity and tell me I was fine, attributing whatever I was feeling to tween jitters, PMS, or period cramps.

Feeling dismissed, and not having a clear understanding of the flutter or the poison, despite knowing damn well they weren't cramps or PMS, I eventually stopped asking for help trying to understand the niggling and convinced myself these aches were just part of growing up.

I had no idea those feelings were my soul trying to guide me in healthy directions—that it was my intuition trying to tell me I was enough. Instead, I ignored whatever messages my intuition was trying to tell me, and created a pattern of bad and harmful habits over time that perpetuated deep into my life, and once discovered, took years to understand and decades to navigate out of.

A few weeks after the Seven Minutes in Heaven incident, Donny and I were upstairs in one of the bedrooms at another party. He wanted me to put my hands down his pants, and I just couldn't do it. There were a million things I wanted to do, but touching his dick was not one of them. With my intuition now screaming at me to get out, I stood my ground and said, "No," a few more times than I thought I needed to. He got aggravated and called me a prude. Once again, I left the party early. This time I walked home.

The following Monday at school, Donny broke up with me. By Tuesday, none of those "friends" from the parties were talking to me, and on Wednesday morning, I found a note taped to my locker that officially uninvited me to the party of the year that upcoming weekend. Thursday, between classes, I walked past a few of the girls and could hear their intentionally loud conversation: "Mandi is such a goody-two-shoes. I can't believe she wouldn't let Tim kiss her." And, "Yeah, Donny told me about what *didn't* happen at the party. He says she barely even has a chest, and he doesn't want to be with her because she thinks she's better than everyone else."

I tried to make myself invisible, but they knew exactly where I was and that I heard every word they said. I held it together as I raced towards the exit doors, but when I got outside, I burst into tears and sprinted home.

My mom let me stay home from school Friday. I told her I had cramps.

"Your need for acceptance can make you invisible in this world. Don't let anything stand in the way of the light that shines through this form. Risk being seen in all of your glory."

~Jim Carrey

LIMITING BELIEFS

Limiting beliefs live within all of us. Many of us don't even know they exist because they mask themselves as allies pretending to create some sort of balance in the grand scheme of things. But I have discovered that, in reality, they can create a stronghold on our true potential, anchoring us down and keeping us in places of "lack" and "less than."

Feelings of not being enough will make you think you aren't smart enough, pretty enough, or good enough. They can cause you to get stuck in competition mode, adjusting your boundaries and tolerances all the time in an effort to equate yourself with everyone else.

Conversely, feeling like you are too much for people may cause you to condense your impact, quiet your voice, dim your light, or lower your intensity, when in reality, your drive is just stronger than theirs.

But whether you feel like you're not enough or too much, when you combine any of this with bullying, cruel actions from others, and a lack of support from the people you think you can rely on, it can create an ugly narrative of limiting self-beliefs that plague you and hamper your potential for greatness.

These deeply ingrained thought patterns typically come from past experiences (both positive and negative) and can cause us to hold ourselves back from our own forward momentum. Our upbringing and the society we are raised in can have a direct impact on the type and severity of these thoughts which may keep us from going after and achieving our wildest dreams. Tack on the unhealthy, sociological fear that if we stand out, if we are different, if we speak up and take action, then we just might make everyone else feel less-than, and we create our own recipe for mental, emotional, financial, and relationship barriers that prevent us from exploring new opportunities, pursuing our passions, or taking risks.[1]

So, we limit our power. We limit our grace. We limit our natural belief about who we truly are because one day someone once told us we weren't enough (for them). Or inversely, we were told that we were too much (for them), causing us to push and pull and stretch and shrink to fit in with the masses just to maintain a perception of harmony. We hold on to things that no longer serve us because maybe we grew up in scarcity and lack. Or, let go of things too fast because we get overwhelmed with unbalanced values of abundance and success.

Maybe, just maybe, it doesn't really matter how much or how little someone else perceives us to be. Because, God forbid, we do our own thing and let our light shine the way it was always meant to. That would simply make too much sense.

SPRING, 1990

Being bullied and consequently losing all of the things I thought mattered because I stood up for myself shaped my misguided understanding about what love and trust were all about. I was crushed after Donny broke up with me, and because of it, I developed the distorted perception that if I didn't do what the boys wanted then I'd end up by myself and no one would love me. It got to the point that I didn't know who I could trust, and with that lack of trust taking a stronghold on my psyche, I wasn't able to understand that love was about being accepted for who you are and included self-respect and integrity, not how far you would go with a guy at a party.

Not wanting to walk the halls of junior high alone with this cloud of self-loathing hanging over my head, I searched for souls to connect with and tried to be anything to anyone. Because I so desperately wanted to fit in, and discipline and self-worth weren't things I fully understood either, I got incredibly skilled at ignoring my gut (the intuition I didn't understand) and learned how to morph my personality in my efforts to be like everyone else. I changed how I dressed to be more preppy or hippie or sporty or goth. I shaved the back of my head trying to stand out and be cool and kept piercing my ears thinking the more holes in my head, the better. I pushed my shame and embarrassment of being dumped by one of the coolest kids in our class under my fake outward persona as far as possible. In a desperate attempt to not feel so alone, I grasped onto any common ground with whoever was around just so I could feel like I belonged somewhere.

Rather than go to the guidance counselor at school or seek out a mentor who might have helped me heal from the pain of being dismissed by my "friends," I ended up finding an upperclassman boyfriend who was the total opposite of me. He had bad grades, didn't play sports, skipped class, and subsequently spent a lot of time in detention. He became the ultimate distraction from the nonsense that had happened earlier that year because I turned all my attention towards trying to be a good influence on him in the hopes that if I did what he wanted, I'd get the attention and love I desired.

As it turned out, he was more of a bad influence on me. I did a complete 180-degree flip from the boundary-holding, value-seeking preteen I was in eighth grade to a ninth-grader who got pressured into having sex way too early and ended up picking up bad habits of drinking, smoking cigarettes, and getting high behind the church. In a short six months, I went from being a "goody-two-shoes" to a rebellious teenager who would try almost anything at least once, setting myself on a path of destruction and chaos. The fear of failing at another relationship constantly lingered over me, and I ended up doing whatever he wanted me to in an effort to keep him happy. Thus my people-pleasing pattern began.

"If they aren't reaching down to pull you up, they are reaching up to drag you down."

~AMANDA GREAVES

That summer, after coming home high and being late for curfew one too many times, the fighting with my parents reached a climax, and they grounded me for a few weeks with no phone, no TV, and no boyfriend. Something inside me didn't really mind the punishment, and in the absence of my bad-boy distraction, I poured my confused and broken heart into my journals. After a few very quiet weeks, I realized I was facing something bigger than my fourteen-year-old head and heart could handle and wanted to get some help.

One day while in the car with my mom heading to the mall for back-to-school clothes, I drummed up the courage and asked her if I could see a therapist.

"Why do you want to see a therapist? What are they going to tell you that I can't?" she objected, keeping her eyes on the road.

After a long, awkward, and threatening pause, I played defense and rebutted with a classic teen attitude, "Well, I've never been to one, so how the hell am I supposed to know? I just know I *need* to talk to someone."

Her eyes darted into the rearview mirror. Slamming on the brakes, she pulled over to the side of the road.

"Who *are* you? You haven't said a word about anything to me or your father in the past three weeks, and now you want to go talk to a therapist? Mandi, there is *nothing* wrong with you. Why do you think you need to talk to someone else when *I am right here*? No. *You're FINE.* You either talk to me, or you don't talk. ***Everything is just FINE.***"

Silenced and defeated, I sank into the seat. Tears welled in my eyes. Part of *my problem* was that I didn't know how to talk to her, so I wanted to get advice from someone else on avoiding these types of battles. Part of *her problem* was that she didn't know how to talk to me. I think she just accepted our repeated battles as part of the parenting role.

We didn't know how to communicate with each other on the meaningful level I was searching for, which left me feeling trapped in a world where I started to become an anxious, insecure wreck. I didn't know how to bring up the subject that my boyfriend had pressured me into having sex. I didn't know how to tell her I was feeling sad—a lot. I didn't know how to explain that I didn't feel like myself anymore and was uncomfortable in my own skin. And I had no idea how to explain that I didn't even know how to *pretend* to be happy anymore. I was totally confused and couldn't understand how, if she was actually paying attention, she thought I was fine when clearly I wasn't?!

She stared at me slumped in my seat. I said nothing. After a minute, she put the car in drive, pulled a U-turn, and drove home, abandoning the back-to-school shopping that day.

Throughout high school and most of college, I created the habit of "chameleonizing" myself for the sake of whatever relationship I was in, rather than stand out and be who I knew I was at my core. Eventually, I lost much of my true persona under all the variations of personalities I was changing in and out of, and at times, I wasn't sure who I was at all or where I belonged. My lack of self-confidence rose with the volume of my efforts to be free, seen, and heard, while my courage quietly hung out in the background, only coming out when I was alone or with my best girlfriends.

As my vocabulary and education expanded, I realized that my mother was 100% right about me being fine back in junior high. **FINE** is often used as an acronym meaning **F**reaked out, **I**nsecure, **N**eurotic, **E**motional.[2]

As an adult, I eventually sought out various therapies and communication strategies and now know how to connect on a very healthy level with my mom. Our relationship was strained when I was a teenager (who doesn't have challenges with teenagers?), but through it all, even without me realizing or understanding it, I think we fought because we loved each other, and that unconditional love has never wavered. (I just drove her crazy for a few years—and sometimes still do!)

DEAR DIARY

Writing and acrylic painting were some of the only saving graces I had when I was a kid. Without a verbal outlet (like a mentor or therapist), I let my fingers do the talking and poured my little heart out on paper and canvas.

To further your understanding of who you are and how the heck you got here, let's take the time to assess what limiting beliefs you have and where they may have stemmed from. It can be a difficult task to pinpoint emotions or beliefs that limit you, so be patient with yourself. Writing isn't always easy, and some of these questions aren't either. Digging in takes time, and learning to uncover these emotions takes practice.

1. Think back to a time in your life when you've felt out of place or misunderstood. What did you do? Did you change and adjust your personality or values to fit in? Or embrace your uniqueness and stand out?
2. Make a list of any of the limiting beliefs you may have been telling yourself over the years. Not enough? Too much? Too intense? Too quiet? This list will come in handy with some of the later exercises.
3. Is there someone in your life you wish you could have talked to more? Maybe you wish they understood you better. Is there any way you can communicate better with them now?

3

ALL ROADS LEAD to ROME

Clarify Your Intentions and Go After Your Dreams

"We travel, initially, to lose ourselves, and
we travel, next, to find ourselves.
We travel to open our hearts and eyes.
And we travel, in essence, to become young fools again —
to slow time down and get taken in and fall in love once more."

~ *Ray Bradbury*

FALL, 1993

I got that giddy, happy, butterfly feeling the instant we drove onto campus, and I knew I was in the right place. The weather was a warm 72 degrees, and the few puffy clouds in the sky made it feel like we were in a photo shoot for a postcard of our nation's capital. The recruiting tour guides presented the university perfectly, and the energy I felt when some of the athletes ran by had me undoubtedly knowing this was where I belonged.

At the age of seventeen, I was so ready to leave the drama of high school behind and had become very clear on what I wanted in a college experience. At the onset of my high school senior year, I considered and visited about a dozen different schools before I settled on the one that shaped the next four(ty) years of my life—Marymount University in Arlington, Virginia. It was the only school I applied to, and when I found out through early admissions that I was accepted, I finally felt like I knew where my future was headed.

Marymount hit all of the top four credentials on my "must-have" list. First, they had an accredited Interior Design program, a very important detail, since I wanted to be an interior designer. Second, Marymount, at the time, was a small school located near a big city (Washington, D.C.)—a dichotomy that teased me with just the right amount of opportunities for flirtatious shenanigans a few miles away, but kept the large Greek system parties mostly out of reach (MU didn't have fraternities or sororities in the 90s). Third, but somewhat the most significant part of the entire equation, they offered a study abroad program in London. And finally, it was located close enough that I could drive home in a day (about eight hours), but far enough away that my parents couldn't just pop in unexpectedly. Jackpot.

My dad had traveled a ton when I was little, sending postcards from abroad and gifting us with interesting foreign coins, T-shirts that said things like, "My dad went to Switzerland, and all I got was this silly T-shirt," and other little souvenirs whenever he would return home. Each time he left, I would long for him to come back while also living vicariously through his journeys. Fantasizing about all the places he had been and how I was going to travel like my dad when I grew up, I made a list of cities I wanted to go to and entertained the idea of backpacking around Europe. So, when I started learning what each college had to offer, it felt natural to only look at schools that included a semester abroad. I figured I was already going to be away at school, so I might as well be studying somewhere interesting.

SUMMER, 1996

To make my overseas adventures a reality, my summers home from college consisted of me working a ton and managing two, sometimes three, jobs. The summer right before I started traveling, I bounced between an insurance office, a Mex-American restaurant, and a boating supply/marine retail store every day of the week.

Tuesdays were typically the longest days. I would start as a secretary at 8 a.m., speed over to the restaurant, and clock a double waitressing shift from 11:30 a.m. until about 9 p.m., then finish out the evening by meeting the delivery truck at the marine store to stock shelves from 10 p.m. until about 3 or 4 a.m. More often than not, I would change uniforms in my car between shifts, praying that I had remembered to pack a clean shirt and that my hair didn't smell like a fajita.

On random days or nights off, I would hang with some of my less-motivated hippie friends from high school. I would typically arrive late, and they would immediately pass me a joint saying, "Hey, Mandi, we think you work too much. We never see you anymore."

Taking the hit, literally and figuratively, I would respond the same way each time as if I were a broken record. Holding in the smoke, with an airless whisper, I'd reply, "I'm saving my money so I can go to Europe." I'd then let out a long, slow exhale, blowing smoke in their direction, and add, **"Short-term sacrifices for long-term results.** I'm working for a living guys…" They'd laugh, and the conversation would end as soon as it began, which was alright with me because I much preferred to just get stoned and listen to Dave Matthews Band or Rusted Root than talk about work.

But what these stoners didn't realize was that, unlike how I had chased everyone else's dreams trying to fit in throughout junior high and high school, **I had finally found a deeper motivation and was working with intention toward my own dreams. I had big goals and was determined to not stop until I had achieved them all—beginning with making my vision of seeing the world a quick reality.**

Even though it sometimes felt like I was always working, I still found ways to enjoy my summer in the small pockets of time between shifts. Like on Wednesday mornings, after we were done stocking shelves, my retail buddies and I would take a daybreak boat cruise down the Essex River and watch the sun rise up over the Cranes Beach dunes. And sometimes, I would get out of the restaurant early enough to party with some of the waitstaff in a crowded apartment in downtown Peabody. Through these various jobs, I was constantly vacillating between different experiences with different groups of people, which I loved. It was like a warm-up to my next big adventure.

On the nights I came home too late (or too early, depending on which side of the clock you were viewing), I would catch a boatload of shit from my parents about how I was "burning the candle at both ends" and was "too irresponsible" to be allowed overseas.

The majority of it came from my mom since she was home more than my dad. She'd chuck statements at me like, "You are too lackadaisical to be trusted. You are only twenty, and if you don't stop partying, you are NOT going to London next year!" Then she would toss in a few accusations about me not having any common sense, which would make me fly off the handle in a defensive rage. Our desperately flawed communication style often left us both feeling misunderstood or disrespected, which would turn into us fighting until my dad came home, when he'd work his calm, reasoning wedge between us until we settled down. It was awful.

What I could not get either my mom or my dad to understand was that what they perceived as gallivanting was actually me racing from one job to the next, saving money for my trip. I didn't expect them to pay my way across Europe; I wanted to do it for myself. But it seemed no matter whether I was working, staying home, or staying out, it was never good enough for them. So, I just kept doing whatever I wanted (according to my parents) until it was time to go back to school in the fall, knowing I was only a few short months away from taking off to London and my goal of becoming a world traveler.

—

The sweetest thing about the summer of '96 was David. He was twenty-five, and the Assistant General Manager at the Mex-American restaurant. The restaurant rules stated that managers were not allowed to date waitstaff, but somehow we maneuvered our way around those boundaries and fell in love behind closed doors.

Initially, I kept him at arm's length because I didn't want to get involved in any kind of relationship before my big trip. But David was genuine, goofy, tall, handsome, well-traveled, and relentless in his pursuit. He started to win me over after sending a few dozen roses to my other jobs several days in a row. After one very long, deep, and meaningful conversation that lasted into the wee hours of the morning, his persistence paid off, and I started to fall in love with him.

Because I was intentionally not on the hunt for a boyfriend or a relationship, I had been acting more in line with who I really was. I wasn't trying to attract anyone because I didn't want to deal with the long-distance thing when I went overseas. So when I met David, I was caught off guard, and our consequential late-night encounter *almost* screwed up my long-term plans.

Once the summer started to heat up, so did our relationship.

We would rearrange our hectic schedules to accommodate days off and spend as much time together as possible. It was fun, fulfilling, honest, and true. He would often wait for me outside the marine store, then bombard me with flowers, hugs, and kisses. If he was working consecutive double shifts, I would bring him non-Mexican food and a change of clothes, and we'd make out on the back stoop for twenty minutes on his break, filling each other up with affection.

He promised me the moon and the stars, and I soaked it up any chance I could get. My parents adored him, and his ability to sweet talk my mom helped take some of the heat off the weekly battles of me not being home enough. When I went back to school in the fall, he would travel the eight hours just to watch a soccer game, then sneak into my dorm room at night and be gone before the sun came up the next day.

He showed me that **love is about the acceptance of who we are** and made it clear that it's not about performing or changing yourself for someone else. His statement of love being about aligning your soul with another was something I felt because I knew my soul had already recognized its counterpart within him. He was a good guy. One of the best, actually. I never felt like I had to hide who I was or pretend to please him. There was never any judgment, and I never felt the need to compromise. I was just being myself.

David would often say, "Amanda, I love you unconditionally."

And each time I would reply with, "I love you too," or something equally sweet. Love, in and of itself, was a magical, mystery tour that I was finally enjoying, but I didn't quite understand the whole "unconditional" thing, so I never said it back to him. Not even once.

One of the common bonds we had was our passion for traveling. However, long before I met him I had made up my mind that I was going to London and Europe on my own. On my own schedule. With no real responsibilities. And hopefully, end up without any debt. I also planned that I would be traveling as a single woman with no lingering relationship or extended commitments. One night in early November, we were on the phone, and I recall him saying, "Won't it be fun when I come visit you in London?" And, "Oh, I've always wanted to go to France. I hear there is a fast train from London straight to Paris. We could just hop over there for a weekend."

I shut him down instantly. "No. I'm traveling on my own. I didn't invite you. You can't come with me." I could practically feel his shock at this news through the phone. There was nothing nice or sugar-coated about my reaction to him trying to insert himself into my plans. And I wasn't about to start backpedaling on my own dreams of traveling solo.

I didn't want to mess up our amazing energy over the summer and early fall, so I never actually came directly out and told him I didn't want him to join me. But after that one particular curt and awkward phone call, he knew what my intentions were and was crushed to realize that he was not a part of them.

When I came home for Thanksgiving break, in an attempt to hold our romance together, he said he wanted to marry me. The heaviness of his love freaked me out; I was not ready, nor mature enough to handle that kind of commitment. So rather than lean into his encouragement and support, I backed away.

His unconditional dedication and strong desire to spend the rest of our lives together scared the crap out of me, and I had absolutely no idea how to balance his desires (which were kind of mine too) with my dreams (which were kind of his too). It was too much, too fast, and **I didn't think it was possible to have both a healthy relationship and my own agenda at the same time.**

My lack of understanding that I could have it all overshadowed what he was offering. I misunderstood the beautiful opportunity to embrace his partnership because I was too busy and focused on the perceived freedom of reaching my goals *by myself.* Overwhelmed with these new emotions of unconditional love as well as a desire to fight for my independence, I made the decision that I had to let something go, and it sure as shit wasn't gonna be Europe. So, rather than figure out how our relationship could work for a few months while I was away, we broke up right after Thanksgiving.

David refused to see me over Christmas break. I worked at the restaurant right up to the day before I left on January 6, 1997, but I didn't see him at all during that time. He had transferred to a different location for the four weeks I was home from school so he wouldn't have to see me before I took off for London.

My heart broke a lot when David and I split up, but rather than heal it properly with self-reflection, I covered it up with my European adventures and an attitude of safe distance when it came to future dating. Letting go of the healthy relationship I had with him for the sake of chasing my wild side and proclaiming my independence was the catalyst to a lengthy unhealthy cycle of attracting and dating unworthy and unavailable guys, and the early evolution of my "love 'em and leave 'em" attitude, since I made myself somewhat unavailable as well.

I was determined, now more than ever, to chase my dreams and not get hurt in the process. I would keep my heart open just enough but wouldn't let anyone in enough to truly understand me at my core or get to the point I had with David. But by denying my soul's ache for healing and unconditional support and love, I was unintentionally steering myself towards the chaos and roller coasters of dramatic and frustrating relationships. Foolish concepts now that I think of it, but it's who I became once I experienced a seriously broken heart for the first time.

SPRING, 1997

"Life isn't a destination, it's a journey. We all come upon unexpected curves and turning points, mountain tops and valleys. Everything that happens to us shapes who we become. And in the adventure of each day, we discover the best in ourselves."

~ *Anonymous*

My semester in London was rainy, dark, and cold. I was thrilled to be there, but the constant damp and gray weather was not what I had anticipated. It actually sucked a bit. Riding the underground tube and aboveground buses for a total of three hours a day back and forth to the super posh, snobby, high-end residential design firm I was interning at just added to the misery and feelings of seasonal depression that had me questioning my original reasoning for wanting to study abroad in the first place.

That internship showed me exactly what I *didn't* want in a career, or in a boss, and I decided that if working in residential design meant spending time with these kinds of people, I wanted nothing to do with it. But I pushed through the four months with a smile on my face because I was "living my dream" and just focused on my upcoming European traveling extravaganza.

I had planned it all out on paper since the internet was a commodity and smartphones hadn't been invented yet. When my route was confirmed and my itinerary set, I airmailed photocopies of everything to my parents back in the States so they had some sort of idea of where I would be over the next five weeks.

On May 1, 1997, the day after the semester was over, armed with a stack of calling cards and dozens of rolls of thirty-five-millimeter film, I set out to conquer more of my dreams wearing Birkenstocks, a jam-packed backpack, and my passport practically sewn into my underwear. With a paper map of Europe, train schedules and tickets, and American Express travelers' checks folded neatly in a stack held tight to my chest, I was on my way to becoming a world traveler.

I flew to Lisbon, Portugal, first, where I got my bearings straight and learned how to "ugly sign" as fast as possible—a phrase I coined to describe what tourists do when they don't speak the language: smile, point to the map or menu, and look like you are confused. I'm not sure if the locals understood my miming skills, felt bad for me, or were just used to young Americans wandering around hungry and lost, but most of them were relatively helpful.

I didn't speak a word of Portuguese (or Spanish, or Italian, or German for that matter), so verbal communication was a challenge. When I was hungry, I would rub my belly and make motions of feeding myself. I got better at communicating with charade gestures as the trip went on, but there were definitely blunders along the way—like the time I ended up with turtle soup when I thought I ordered a turkey sandwich. Thankfully though, I knew a little bit of French and dodged ordering lamb's tongue or snails because I stuck to words I knew like croissants and Croque Monsieur.

For the next five weeks, I meandered through various countrysides by train, bus, and foot, taking my chances on finding a youth hostel to stay at each night. I watched the sun come up through the grottos in Lagos, Portugal, with a cute guy from Ontario, Canada, and carved my name into a wall in an underground bar somewhere in Barcelona, Spain, with a kid from California who was headed to Australia and had some amazingly good weed. I burnt my boobs going topless in Nice, France, ran into the insurance guy I worked for back home on the steps of the Casino in Monte Carlo, Monaco, and was proposed to by a gondolier in Venice, Italy (he was very sweet, but the language barrier made things a little difficult). It was everything I had dreamed about and then some.

On May 18, I arrived in Rome, Italy, and called my bestie, Laura, to confirm her arrival in the city the next day. It was the only significant plan I had made for my entire trip—meet her in Rome. She was just as giddy as I was since we hadn't talked in three weeks nor seen each other since December. The thought of spending four days together in a foreign country was wild to us both and successfully kept me up all night in anticipation of the adventure we were about to embark on.

The following day, bursting with excitement, I practically knocked over a few old Italian ladies when I ran through the station at the arrival of Laura's train. Squealing like pigs in shit, we found each other amongst the crowd and hugged the best, tightest, and most loving embrace ever. I didn't want to let go. Stepping back, through tears of joy and a smile that lit up the platform, she said, "I brought a surprise!" On cue, my other best friend, Lori, stepped off the train, and my heart stopped. I screamed as if I had seen a ghost. My two best friends and I, together, in Rome, Italy! This was going to be EPIC!

The three of us walked every square inch of that city. We challenged our inner warriors at the archaeological ruins of the Colosseum and Roman Forum, then high-fived the statue of Julius Caesar on our way to the Pantheon. We tossed our wishes and dreams into the Trevi Fountain while being serenaded by three adorable young Italian stallions who gifted us each with a rose, and we casually picnicked on the Spanish Steps.

Vatican City took an entire day (as it should), and between St. Peter's Basilica and the Sistine Chapel, I learned more about religion and art in twenty-four hours than I had in the three years I had taken art history and religion classes at Marymount! I considered it a full immersion learning experience. The awestruck wonderment we felt through the centuries of myths and monuments, gods and goddesses, battles and bewilderment affected us all, and we knew it was the trip of a lifetime.

The three of us stretched our young, curious minds absorbing the sights, sounds, scents, and culture like no other trio had done before. Sauntering through the streets, we gawked at the magnificence of everything and respected the history. We roamed through piazzas while eating pizza and wandered through ruins while guzzling gallons of wine. And through it all, we became sisters—our connection exploding as we overlapped thousands of years of energy with our own personal and interwoven realities.

I was filled with outrageous amounts of love and fulfillment and deep feelings of pride and accomplishment while exploring this magical city with my two best friends. I had reached a pinnacle moment in my life by achieving an intentional goal and following a well-executed plan that had started four years earlier. It wasn't just the city and sights I became enamored with—**it was knowing that I went after what I wanted with relentless pursuit and made it all happen.** It was about sharing my dreams with the people I wanted to share them with and deepening friendships with the unconditional love that I had yearned for but also had abandoned six months earlier.

The four days went by in a flash, and before we knew it, it was time to go. Yet we were leaving as changed women. We had harnessed our desires and exploited our opportunities to expand our minds and nourish our souls. As we parted ways, Laura and Lori heading to Ireland while I took off towards Switzerland, I knew these two women would remain in my life forever, no matter what part of the world any of us ended up in.

I arrived at Balmers Youth Hostel in Interlaken, Switzerland, an iconic location for backpackers and travelers alike, at the end of May and was attacked at check-in.

"Amanda Greaves!"

I looked for the voice, and the next thing I knew, I was trapped in a bear hug by my friend Doug. We had met on a train from Seville to Barcelona three weeks earlier, traveled together for three days along the coasts of Spain and France, then parted ways when we reached Marseille. I was headed to Italy; he was flying out to Greece. Just like so many of the other amazing souls I met during my travels, I never thought I would see him again, but apparently, he had ditched his buddies and rerouted when the party scene tilted sideways in Mykonos. He claimed he needed more "solid ground" than island time and retreated to the Alps to sober up. I questioned his reasoning since I had heard that Balmers was the place to go for mountaintop mischief and riverside raves.

Two nights later, I was laughing hysterically (and praying to God that I wouldn't fall off), as two other girls and I heaved and hoed a mattress swing from side to side. Using our weight, we tried to get just a little bit higher to try to reach the barn rafters with our toes. We were suspended twenty feet in the air, sharing a joint, and having the time of our lives watching the party from above like a charm of finches floating above the music. I waved to my friend Doug, who smiled and ironically tossed me a beer. At the time, it was the most magical place on earth, and I felt like a flying princess (although, it might have been the weed).

I spent four days (two days longer than originally planned) at Balmers and continued to make more outrageous memories that are forever ingrained in my heart. The people, the energy, and the air were all so crisp and beautiful. I vacillated between screaming with excitement (and a little bit of fear) while white water rafting down class IV rapids with an enthusiastic crew of twelve, and singing Julie Andrews' "doe-a-deer" at the top of my lungs as I hiked solo up the mountainside amongst grazing cows clanking their joyous little bells. And one night, half a dozen of my new best friends (whom I haven't seen since and whose names I no longer remember) and I camped at the base of a white-capped mountain and woke with a light blanket of snow covering our sleeping bags and eyelashes. It was heavenly.

Despite wanting to stay, I knew when it was time to go and hopped a train to Munich, Germany, with Doug. Immediately upon arrival, we drank our way through a bike beer garden tour that lasted twelve hours, and a day or so later, I eventually caught my final flight back to London. After spending nearly a week with Doug, I made sure to exchange information with him before I left, but once I got on that plane, our connection was lost, and we've never spoken since.

Unique from every angle, those five weeks of travel opened my mind to the vast differences of cultures, religions, opportunities, and friendships that have continued to influence me ever since. I did whatever I wanted and saw the world through the lens of a free-spirited twenty-one-year-old, embracing whatever was in front of me with acceptance and excitement.

I felt like I had truly found myself—the real me who was the perfect amount of unfiltered and unedited personality. The loving and adventurous me who broke free from the limiting beliefs, criticism, and self-doubt I had grown into throughout high school and college. Each leg of that journey exposed a different side of myself that I leaned into and fell in love with. I even successfully completed my mission without having to manage a long-distance relationship and didn't get hurt or break anyone's heart along the way.

I was filled to the brim with accomplishments, but I was also ready to get back to London, then home, and back to school to finish my design studies and on with the rest of my life.

DEAR DIARY

"If you don't know where you are, a map won't help."

~ *Watts Humphrey*

One of the most important things when determining where you want to go is first understanding where you are. When you start your journey, figure out where you are physically, emotionally, and mentally. Not even Waze or a good GPS app is going to help with your navigation if you can't tell it where to begin. It would be like planning a trip around Europe but only using a map of the United States. Or trying to take the initiative without having clarity on the mission or goals. You won't get anywhere.

Figuring out exactly where you are right now is integral to the success of your intentionally created life. It will help you understand the path you must take to get from point A to point Z and the steps that need to happen along the way.

Here are a couple of things to consider as you dream about what you want:

1. Think of the top three dreams you would like to accomplish in your life. Write them down and get very, very clear on what they mean to you.
2. Imagine what your life will be like once you complete each of these dreams. Maybe it's finishing a marathon or climbing Mount Kilimanjaro. Maybe it's learning how to make the most amazing apple pie or how to salsa dance. Or maybe it's leaving your job and starting your own business. But imagine them as if they've already happened.
3. Now figure out what the first step is for each dream and write it down. Every journey begins with a single step. You just need to learn how to take it.

4

FLIP FLOPS and BOARD SHORTS

Realize Your Relationship Patterns

"I believe that everything happens for a reason. People change so that you can learn to let go, things go wrong so that you appreciate them when they're right, you believe lies so you eventually learn to trust no one but yourself, and sometimes good things fall apart so better things can fall together."

~ *Marilyn Monroe*

SUMMER, 1997

When I arrived back in London, the attitude and essence of the city were sunny, bright, and hot—an extreme contrast to the previous winter. Unknown to me, while I was wander-lusting around Europe, my dad had secured an internship for me at an international insurance company located in Central London in the hopes that I might broaden my understanding of international cultures and gain an extended education in business. Excited to stay in London for the summer, I accepted the opportunity immediately and let go of my plans of chilling at home that summer.

Since this company was situated smack dab in the middle of the largest international business and financial hub in the world, I found myself working with a group of incredibly intense, exceedingly intelligent, and voracious "suits," and they were all too interested in showing me, a young, hippie Yankee, what it was like to live in London in the summer. They liked to blow off steam often and party all night long in various watering holes throughout their famed city. Being polite, they would always invite me, and being me, I would always oblige.

The summer days in England don't get dark until 10 p.m., and it hardly ever rains, so I quickly adapted to the English businessmen's cultural habits of whipping through Lloyds of London first thing in the morning, then sneaking out of the office around noon for long outdoor lunches, that would often linger into early cocktails that would then finish up with late dinners. And we often turned thirsty Thursdays into Friday morning coffee with Baileys. Though I did learn a lot about insurance and various types of financial plans like my dad had wanted me to, my real education seemed to be mastering the art of catching the hair of the dog and deciphering which Indian restaurant served the best curry.

One Friday night, a large group of us landed in the rowdiest bar in all of Covent Garden to watch the Australia versus South Africa cricket match. I didn't really understand the game but was enthralled with hanging out with these power-hungry party animals, so I joined the boys with the goal of learning what it meant to "stroke well through the covers."[ii] But really, I had no idea what I was getting myself into.

In my slightly inebriated and take-charge kind of manner, I walked straight to the bar to order drinks. That's when a gorgeous, incredibly fit guy with a ponytail and beaming white smile, wearing flip flops and a pair of board shorts, came up next to me and said, "Hey, how's it goin'?" in a playful, Aussie accent.

His presence and confidence were totally unexpected. I thought it was clear I had just walked in with a bunch of professional guys but quickly realized how packed the place was and that he may not have noticed much of anything except the person standing in front of him, which was now me. Smiling coyly and feeling a little shy, I felt my cheeks turn pink when I replied, "Smashing," trying to sound as British as possible. Then I turned

---

ii To "stroke well through the covers"' is a term used in the sport of cricket. The cover drive is considered one of the most graceful shots playable in the sport and means to hit the ball perfectly towards a region of the field.

my attention back to the bartender, attempting to hide my interest in this jovial bloke who looked like he just came from the beach.

"Where ya from?" he persisted.

"Boston," I said quickly, not wanting to lead him on but not wanting to ignore him either.

"Boston? Oh!" he said, sounding a little confused. "I lived in San Diego fa' three years." His accent was extraordinary.

Realizing my short, indirect answers weren't going to deter him, I turned to face him in the hopes a more direct response would give him the hint that I wasn't interested (or at least I was going to try to tell him I wasn't interested).

That's when our gazes met, and he quickly undressed me with his dark sultry eyes. Instantly disarmed, I felt my face flush crimson from our energetic chemistry and heard myself blurt out a simple, "Good for you." Then I grabbed my drinks and nervously walked away with my future ex-husband hot on my tail.

I went to work on Monday in the same clothes I had worn on Friday and got some rather suspicious looks from my co-workers.

The last two weeks in London were an absolute whirlwind. Every night was a summer celebration, and every day was an effort to squeeze it all in. Rod, the smiling Aussie from the bar, had extended his walkabout to spend another week with me. We embraced a carefree lust with reckless abandon and complete disregard to the fact that we lived on opposite sides of the planet.

But even though I thought he was awesome, I missed the no-ties and no-boyfriend freedom I had enjoyed so much of the preceding six months. Yet I figured, "What the hell. He lives halfway around the world. I'll probably never see him again," and played the part of the doting, lovestruck girlfriend for the week.

What I didn't anticipate was coming home to Massachusetts in early August with a ring on my finger. Rod had proposed right before he left

London and gave me a small diamond ring he had bought at a pawnshop. Dumbfounded, I think I just nodded as he jumped for joy, grabbed his bag, and raced to catch his plane back to Australia. Obviously, I kept the ring, but I didn't take the time to fully digest the fact that a ring meant we were going to be together, and there were details associated with that. After all, I was only twenty-one and still in traveler mode, and he was this crazy dude on a walkabout, gleefully bouncing around the world. How serious could we possibly get?

But then, in pure Aussie fashion, he showed up in Boston, unannounced, two days after I had gotten home from London. I had been away for seven months and was looking forward to seeing my friends and family, but his arrival threw a wrench into those plans. He said he missed me terribly and wanted to whisk me away to Sydney a week after his arrival. I was shocked and flattered but also overwhelmed and confused as to what the hell I was supposed to do.

My plan had always been to finish school and then figure it out after that. But we were in love, and I was afraid to tell him that I didn't want to miss my last year in college and that he would have to wait. I kind of figured since he was so excited to be with me, it might be easier to just play along with his outrageous and irresponsible ideas, move to Sydney, and not finish school, rather than remain an active participant in my own intentions. **So, I stepped aside and for some reason just watched as he began playing creative puppeteer with my future.**

A couple of days after his arrival, I broke the news to my parents that I wasn't going back to school and was moving to Australia. They rightfully lost their minds, and this cockamamie plan of "mine" launched our fighting into World War III. Over the next two weeks, we battled it out. While Rod was whispering, "Come on baby, light my fire,"[3] in one ear, my parents were screaming, "Are you out of your fucking mind?!" in the other.

Even though I knew my parents were right at the time, dealing with their reactions felt like a reverse culture shock after having just successfully navigated foreign languages, international travel, and cultures all alone like an adult. It made me want to prove even more that I was old enough to make my own decisions, plans, and choices, and that they weren't in charge of me anymore.

Needless to say, those two weeks were not the celebratory welcome home I had been anticipating. My parents won some of the important battles, and I went back to school a couple of weeks later to finish my degree.

But the war wasn't over.

1998 - 2002

Throughout my senior year, I went to Australia twice and met Rod in Las Vegas once. He came to visit me four times. Then two weeks after graduation, on August 15, 1998, I moved halfway around the world to Sydney, Australia, to live with him.

My parents were devastated that I had moved so far away and kept telling me that I was throwing four years of an expensive education away for some guy. I didn't quite see it that way and considered the opportunity an extension of my life's experiences beyond the classroom. I wasn't ready to grow up and become an adult yet (clearly), and this opportunity seemed so perfect, so tangible, so outrageous that I knew I had to at least try it. Even if it was only for a few months.

Rod and I were madly and playfully in love. He was a wild thirty-one-year-old child, and I was a naïve, twenty-two-year-young smitten girl attracted to a foreign accent and a six-pack. I moved right into his world, high on a hill overlooking the Pacific Ocean, and stayed blissfully ignorant with him for a while.

My work visa was set to expire in November, but I didn't want to go home (yet), and Rod didn't want me to leave (ever), so with little contemplation (there is a pattern here), at the end of October 1998, we secretly tied the knot and celebrated for the entire weekend like we had the first weekend we met in London. And we didn't tell anyone. The really fucked up part was that, even though I loved Rod and wanted to stay with him (at least for a little while longer), I recall having the conscious thought that if it didn't work out, I could always just get a divorce and go back to the States.

After all, no one really knew, so it wouldn't be a big deal, right?

Like I said, I was a little naïve.

While I was away, my dad kept tabs on my U.S. bank account for me, and one day asked who "Amanda Jackson" was and why was she depositing money into the account. Hoping my dad was as ignorant as I was, I told him it was a logistics idea that Rod's dad had come up with and assured him that nothing serious had happened. Who the hell did I think I was kidding?!

That Christmas, Rod and I went back to the States, and he asked my dad if he could marry me. The look on my father's face was priceless since he already knew we were hitched. And the look on mine was probably equally shocking since Rod hadn't talked to me about asking my dad, and I still wasn't sure if Oz was where I wanted to spend the rest of my life.

Since I had already said yes (twice), we announced our engagement in January 1999. But just like the first time, something about how all of this was happening didn't feel like it belonged to me. Granted, I loved Rod, and I loved being in Oz, but **I still felt more like I was playing a supporting role in a movie, rather than a lead character in my own life.**

I initially took my time sorting out the wedding details. But after a year of planning, Rod's dad told me to get moving and set a date, or he was going to send me back to the States. He was a very smart and intuitive man, and I'm quite certain could see right through the veil of insecurities I was hiding behind. So, with his encouragement (ahem, threat), I kicked the planning into high gear.

Almost two years to the date, Rod and I officially got married (for the second time) in October 2000. Laura, Lori, and a half dozen of my other girlfriends joined us, as well as my parents, brother, and a couple of their friends. Because the 2000 Olympics had just wrapped up in September, there was an incredible buzz around Sydney that made the atmosphere feel even more beautiful and enchanting than the scenery and attitude already were. That electric energy thankfully flowed over generously into the time when everyone was there for the wedding, and for two full weeks, I felt a little more back to normal being surrounded by my family and friends that were part of the life I had curated before Rod entered in and swept me away down under.

—

A year or so later, the honeymoon was officially over, and Rod and I considered starting a family. The biggest challenge was that even though we were married (twice now), I wasn't that thrilled about all aspects of our life together.

I loved the retail job I had at a small family-run store. The owners and other employees became like family as they helped me negotiate the cultural and emotional challenges I faced while living there. I developed and implemented a business strategy plan that quadrupled their sales by my third year and I realized **I loved the aspect of building a business**. But I also knew deep down that retail management was not my ideal career choice.

Conversely, Rod was heavy into gambling on horses and would bet on pretty much anything. I learned how to read the form guide[iii] and got pretty good at wagering on ponies, but I kept my slot kitty small and managed it tightly because I didn't view winning on the pokies as a reliable source of income like Rod did.

Rod kept himself busy as a construction laborer simply to appease his dad's prompting of not "wasting all of his time in the pub." But what his dad didn't realize was that Rod's boss was our coke dealer, and the party scene was always right under our noses. Most of the time I enjoyed the close connections because we never had to look too far for drugs,

---

iii A publication that includes certain information relating to a horse, including its age, pedigree, career statistics and performance history. This is the essential information used by punters (Australian for gamblers) in their bid to predict the outcome of a race.

but sometimes it felt a little out of control. I knew I could do better than staying up 'til dawn blowing lines. I did, however, learn how to squirrel away some each time so I could do a little bump in the morning before work, which would thankfully keep me going throughout the day.

We may have been living together, but our mindsets were worlds apart. Often I would come home midweek hoping to go for a picnic on the beach with a nice bottle of wine, but he preferred to stay inside the pub studying racing stats and slinging back pints of Toohey's New (not Fosters, like most Americans assume of Aussies). When I got a promotion to manager, he lost his job because his employer got arrested for dealing. He eventually found part-time work as a carpenter with another mate who was selling Molly on the side. The party never stopped.

We had a boat—never used it. He owned a Ferrari—never drove it. We had planned on traveling and seeing the country together but never went anywhere. In the four years I lived there, we took four trips back to the States and maybe a half dozen trips up and down the east coast of New South Wales, Australia. His idea of a weekend away was driving forty minutes into Sydney and staying at the casino for two nights. The lifestyle was totally out of sync with what I had dreamed of when I agreed to move halfway around the world to be with him, and after a while I started to realize he wasn't going to change.

For our first anniversary (or third, depending on which wedding you start counting from), he agreed to cut back on the drinking, drugs, and gambling, and we made the decision for me to stop my birth control.

I had been taking the Depo-Provera birth control shot since I moved to Australia and hadn't had a regular cycle in three years. As soon as I stopped taking the medication, however, I went from no period or symptoms to having to buy cases of pads because it showed up, along with everything associated with it, every two weeks. My boobs swelled and didn't deflate each cycle, causing my chest to expand from a "lucky to be a B" straight to a full D-cup in one aggressive month. Rod was psyched because he said I "finally had my figure back," after my three-year-long powder diet had knocked about thirty pounds off me since college graduation. But I wouldn't even let him look at my chest, let alone touch it, because it was so sore and painful.

My adolescent cramps came back tenfold causing me to writhe in pain for three days every other week. I would rage through the neighborhood like a witch on a broom screaming, "Look the fuck out, and get out of my way!" and would have ripped your head off with my bare hands if you said anything out of tune. I couldn't handle what was happening to my body. I couldn't handle life or anything associated with it. **My chaotic hormones had set my physical, mental, and emotional compass on fire, and I was out of control. I turned into a raging bitch overnight.** Literally.

So it came as no surprise that Rod abandoned our deal of cutting back on the drugs and booze and almost immediately went back to the pub and gambling. He said he was trying to get away and hide from me, and quite honestly, I couldn't really blame him.

This went on for over six months. I was miserable—and miserable to be around.

Then one late night, Rod came back to the house to carry on with some buddies after last call. I had already retreated to my estrogen-ridden emotional hell because I had to work the following day and couldn't seem to keep my eyes open, regardless of how much cocaine I had access to. I asked them to take the soirée elsewhere at least a dozen times since it was the wee hours of Wednesday morning, and I needed to sleep, but none of them paid any mind to what I needed and barely acknowledged that I was even there.

As the DJ (Rod) continued to blast mixed tapes and CDs of Jim Morrison, Frank Sinatra, Creed, and Dean Martin all together at full volume, I really started to lose my shit. It was the mishmash between "Fly Me to the Moon" (Sinatra) and "Higher" (Creed) that sent me soaring over the edge and into a silent rage. They were all so fucked up, and the music was so loud that no one even noticed when I walked through the party with hedge clippers in my hand.

They did notice, however, as soon as the power went out.

I had found the electrical box and shut down the main breaker to the house. When a pissed-off Rod came out, raging like a blown-up bull and flailing a torch (Australian for flashlight) around like a lightsaber, I simply showed him the hedge clippers, pointed to the cable coming from the street, and started singing, "This is the end, beautiful friend. This is the end, my only friend."[4] I threatened to cut the power to the whole house if they didn't leave immediately and let me go to sleep.

I had had enough.

Between my hormones, the continuous partying, and the lack of any forward direction in our relationship, I couldn't do it anymore. I gave him an ultimatum: clean up the coke, get a real job, and start living this life the way we had talked about, or I was out.

Initially, he changed. But after the second month, he slipped back into some familiar habits, and by the third month, we were right back to where we started. I had somewhat started to manage my hormones but was still teetering on the edge of losing it more days than not, so that too made our relationship difficult to be in. We both had our work cut out for us, but it seemed that neither of us knew how to adjust enough to make our goal of staying together work.

After the first three months, I reminded him of our deal and said I was done. He begged me not to go, so I gave him another chance. This cycle happened two more times before I booked a one-way ticket back to the States.

"This whole thing is fucked. It's not working. It's not you, it's me. It's not me, it's you. I'm losing my mind. I've lost myself and any form of control, and nothing is going to change. I gotta go," I told him.

I did it my way, whether it was right or wrong. And it hurt like hell.

"Within my heart are memories, Of perfect love
that you gave me; Oh, I remember...
When you are with me, I'm free, I'm careless, I believe...
Above all the others, we'll fly; This brings tears to my eyes...
My sacrifice
We've seen our share of ups and downs; Oh, how
quickly life can turn around, In an instant ..."

~ *Creed, "My Sacrifice" from the album* Weathered, *2001*

In May 2002, at the age of twenty-six, I boarded a plane in Sydney that was headed for Los Angeles and locked myself in the bathroom for the first two hours of the flight. I ranted and cried and fell into a disheveled mess on the floor of that tiny little stall until the stewardess forced the lock open and escorted me back to my seat. Exhausted and in a bit of denial, I settled into my seat next to a large Texan man heading home from vacation. After I poured my heart out to him, he graciously offered me two Vicodin, which I immediately washed down with at least 4 shots of vodka, then passed the fuck out. I slept for ten hours of the fourteen-hour flight and was thankful that, when I woke up, Los Angeles was only ninety minutes away. I was almost home.

But I wasn't exactly sure what home meant anymore, so rather than go straight to Boston and face reality, I traded in my cross-continental ticket for a boarding pass to Hawaii. Flying back over the Pacific to party in the tropical paradise of Maui with some of the same vagabond ladies who were at my wedding seemed to be just the distraction I needed. Or so I thought.

I sofa-hopped for about three weeks until a few of the girls sat me down and told me nicely, but bluntly, that my constant emotional outbursts were a bit of a drag. I was ruining their time in Utopia. They were done with all my crying and politely told me I needed to go home. With their support, I pulled my head out of the clouds far enough to realize that I needed to get my act together and eventually made it back to Massachusetts in early June.

—

My emotional and mental collapse isn't unheard of when women come off of certain hormonal birth controls, especially ones that stop your cycle for months or years at a time. These types of drugs affect everything in our bodies from hormones to bone mass density and can often outweigh the benefits of having a carefree lifestyle at the expense of shocking your system in a very unnatural way. I can't say that a different birth control would have saved my marriage, but I can say from my experience that the results of the one I was on definitely contributed to its demise.

While I was in Australia, I was consumed with the palm trees, drugs, empty value systems, and an overwhelming sense of living the dream "down under." Except it wasn't my dream; it was Rod's. I played a character in the movie I thought I was meant to be in and pretended that everything was okay. But deep within, I knew it wasn't. I wasn't in the right place. I wasn't with the right people. **And instead of seeking out what felt most comfortable, I got into the habit of doing everything I could to fit in where I didn't belong, only to eventually leave and not have any idea where I was supposed to be.**

After four years of surfing, snorting, placating, and pretenses, I had barely started to realize the depth of the emotional and psychological wounds I had inflicted upon myself by not being honest with who I was at my core. Instead, I just kept moving on. I didn't stop to reflect. I didn't take the time to heal my heart, my hormones, or my cloudy head. **I didn't pause to consider that maybe, just maybe, I needed to take a break. Or, better yet, get some help.**

—

Years later, through social media avenues, I found David and reached out in an effort of apology. He confessed to being absolutely crushed when I came home with "that Aussie dude," and I took responsibility for being careless with his heart. I further learned that he had stayed in touch with my family and had spent a couple holidays with them while I was in Australia. No one ever told me that they liked David better than me that whole time, but honestly, I'm not surprised.

Grasping the difference between David's love and Rod's created an even deeper pang of remorse and heartache that lasted well into my early thirties. I knew at twenty years of age I wasn't ready for the unconditional love that David had to offer. And between twenty-one and twenty-six, I was in such a party mode I didn't take time to understand how much Rod's dreams had infiltrated and overshadowed my own. I was so caught up in the exciting romance of heading to Australia, that rather than return home from London to the opportunity of traveling with a partner that I was actually aligned with (David), I ran towards unknown destinations and more adventures, losing the me I had found when I initially set out on my world tour. It took me years and many more relationships before I was mature enough to recognize the rarity and beauty of what David and I once had so many years ago.

"I, recommend getting your heart trampled on to anyone, yeah
I, recommend walking around naked in your living room, yeah
Swallow it down (what a jagged little pill)
It feels so good (swimming in your stomach)
Wait until the dust settles
You live you learn, you love you learn
You cry you learn, you lose you learn
You bleed you learn, you scream, you learn..."

~ *Alanis Morissette, "You Learn" from the album* Jagged Little Pill, *1995*

DEAR DIARY

Have you ever had your heart broken? Have you ever broken someone else's heart? Are you attracted to the same type of person? I'm not talking just height, weight, or eye color; I'm talking about their character, their traits, their background, and their values. If you've never thought about it, maybe now is a good time to see what your relationship patterns are.

1. What are you attracted to? Is it the look, career choice, or sports they play? Is it their way of communicating or how they make you feel? What's your kryptonite?
2. How have these qualities of attraction supported or denied your desires for self-love and respect?
3. Have you ever been in a relationship you knew wasn't aligned with your own values and goals but stayed anyway for the sake of the other person? How did you feel throughout the relationship?

"I asked her if she believed in love, and she smiled and said it was her most elaborate method of self-harm."

~ *Benedict Smith*

5

CAREER MOVES and TRUTH TALKS

Align With Your Truth, and Start Figuring Out Your Path

"The truth is, you don't know what's going to happen tomorrow. Life is a crazy ride, and nothing is guaranteed."

~ EMINEM

SUMMER, 2002

When I finally got back to Massachusetts, my parents encouraged me to buy a house with my divorce settlement from Rod, but I snubbed their advice because I wasn't ready to settle down in any one location, not just yet. Besides, I hated snow and had no intention of staying in Massachusetts for the winter. Instead, I pocketed my divorce money for more travel and put zero effort into thinking about my future.

My brother was nice enough to let me stay with him for a few weeks while I got my bearings straight, but he quickly got fed up with my partying antics and kindly helped me get my act together. Seems I was doing a similar thing to him that Rod had been doing to me by staying up too late and preventing him from sleeping. Who knew the tables would turn so quickly?

I moved into a small, one-room apartment in an old barn and landed a gig waitressing and bartending at the Rockfish Restaurant & Bar in the salty seaside town of Newburyport, Massachusetts. I figured I would take the summer off from looking for a "real job" and relish a little longer in the lack of responsibilities I had. After all, I was just starting my life over. One can't go at these life-changing shifts too quickly. Or can they?

I met a lot of cool people while working at that bar but kept my distance since I was still recovering from my failed Aussie marriage. When the snow came in November, I zoom-zoomed[iv] up and down the East Coast between Massachusetts and Florida in my bright yellow Mazda Protege, stopping in every major city along the way. I kept in touch with a few of those cool people via postcards from the cities I was interviewing as potential places to call home, but we eventually lost touch as I proceeded to drive further away from the salty summer shack I temporarily called home.

I racked up thousands of miles on my odometer over the next few months in a fast and ridiculous attempt to run away from my heartache and figure out where in the world I fit in. I was cruising on the fear of getting hurt again and adrenaline. Once I finalized my divorce, I went skydiving a couple of times just to keep the party alive, then rounded the coast of Key West and skirted up the west coast of Florida before tucking my foolish pride and carefree attitude of "I can do this all by myself" uncomfortably between my heart and soul and moved in with my parents in early December 2002.

I made it almost two months at home with good ol' Mom and Dad before their house started to feel too small for the three of us *and* my adrenaline and whacked-out hormones. My mother politely tacked a note to my door one day that quoted Benjamin Franklin, "Guests, like fish, start to smell after three days."

Taking the hint, I reached out to a few friends in Sarasota, and they suggested I move there. So, at the very end of January 2003, I ventured to the west coast of Florida and did my best at making that posh, artsy, seaside, surfer city my new home.

I got a bartending job at night and worked as an interior design showroom manager during the day. It was a lot, but I was meeting people and having a good time, so I didn't mind the long hours.

---

iv Mazda's "Sustainable zoom-zoom 2030" Vision Part 1: The well-to-wheel concept, August 8, 2017.

My boss lady at the design showroom was the well-known wife of an influential local architect, and although she owned the business, from my perspective she had no clue on how to run it. She would entertain residential homeowners with impulsive decorating ideas and disorganized accessorizing while she only focused on the furniture and not the actual layout of the house (which in my opinion was only half of what *real* designers do). Her business sense lacked direction and leadership. Her merchandising was messy. And she was always complaining that the shop was never busy. There were two other design minions that were kind of useless and just gossiped all day while the boss ignorantly frolicked around town munching on croissants and drinking champagne with her favorite French furniture vendor.

She hired me because she was impressed by the work I had done for the family-run shop in Australia, and it was clear that she desperately needed a manager. I took the position because she paid well, I liked her taste in furniture (regardless of her inability to display it properly), and I enjoyed the challenge of creating vignettes within the store that would inspire clients and random shoppers alike. Plus, she was never there, so once I got comfortable, it felt like it was my own place, and I ran it that way.

Appeasing this woman's desire for success and more design projects, I applied a similar business strategy to what I had created in Oz and set up a sales and marketing campaign. This quickly increased traffic to the store, subsequently raising her furniture sales. And eventually, through my connections at the bar, I brought in a couple of new clients that, for seemingly obvious reasons, only wanted to work with me.

She loved the idea I had increased sales and that the company had more work, but she hated the fact that people were now asking for me by name and not her.

One swampy night in August, I came back to the store late after a client meeting and heard French music as soon as I opened the door. Thinking someone had left the stereo on by mistake, I went straight back to the design library and found Ms. Socialite and Monsieur Frenchie half naked on the conference room table. An empty bottle of Moët was lying on the floor, her pearls were around his neck, and his tie was around her.

I was fired the next day for "invading her privacy." Go figure.

Now with only the bartending job as income, I realized that I was getting more unsolicited phone numbers than tips and knew I needed to find something a little less hot and a lot more stable if I was going to avoid diving deeper into my divorce settlement pool. Plus, this niggling voice (sounding so much like my parents) in my ear (and on the other end of the phone) would not stop telling me to "get serious" and "find a real job."

FALL, 2003

I decided to trade in my flip flops, beach bag, and inconsistent bartending schedule for high heels, a leather purse, and a day planner. Realizing it might be time to pursue the career that I was still paying off via student loans, I found a procurement/design job working for a swanky hospitality interior design firm based in Northern Virginia. It was the "real job" my parents had been strongly suggesting I go after, so I packed up my car once more and headed north in the direction of my alma mater.

My new boss was elegant, passionate about design, and had an incredible portfolio full of five-star hotels and multi-million-dollar residences all around the globe. She showed up every day, on time and dressed to the nines, and commanded a respect that made me want to be a better designer—and invest in a new wardrobe of collared blouses and "dry-clean only" pants. It was here I got my first and most palatable taste for restaurant and hotel design, learned what teamwork really means, and observed firsthand how a strong woman can successfully run *any* company, but especially this incredible international interior design firm.

I traveled to places like Colorado, Texas, Indiana, and Florida. I worked on high-end homes and luxurious resorts. The group of women who were a part of this firm were friendly, driven, talented, and confident. I felt like I had found my new "home." I settled in immediately and felt like I was on the right track and headed in the right direction. Finally.

One of the most spectacular parts about moving to Virginia was that my best friend, Laura, lived there, so I was able to see her all the time. We were finally living in the same place together long enough to hang out on weekends and get together spontaneously like we did when we were in college.

One random Tuesday night, we went out for Italian, and in the middle of dinner, without any warning, I burst into tears. Trying to manage my sobs in between gulps of gin and tonic while spraying spaghetti sauce everywhere, I finally gave up. Looking at Laura with tears pouring out of my bloodshot eyes and snot dripping out of my nose, I asked, "What the hell is wrong with me?"

She started crying too (because that's what best friends do) and said point blank without any hesitation, "Mand, I think you're depressed."

"Well, shit. Now what the fuck am I supposed to do?"

"Go see a therapist?" she half-suggested, half-asked as she gulped her wine and handed me a napkin to wipe the spaghetti sauce off my chin and the snot from my nose.

Her comment, like my outburst, hit me like a wrecking ball. But I knew she was right. I could just feel it within every nerve ending of my fragile emotional and mental states that she was spot on with her sympathetic assessment, and it was time for me to get some help.

Throughout my East Coast travels, I had been "trying" new kinds of birth control when I thought I needed it and skipping it when I thought I didn't. I wasn't able to stay sane long enough to manage any type of long-term romantic love relationship, so the birth control worked the way it was "supposed to," but with my inconsistent dosing schedule, the random influx of hormones was wreaking further havoc on my unhealed hormonal state and my sanity. I determined that being on the move was a blessing because I never got close enough to anyone for them to notice I was a little loopy, and I got really good at morphing into the energy of whoever I was around, so it covered up my insecurities and emotional instability.

My medicine schedule (or lack thereof) was the worst thing I could have done for my body, but I didn't know any better. I had changed gynecologists four times in two years and was self-diagnosing with whatever information I could find on the internet. But between me not being a medical doctor and the fucked-up lingering effects of the birth control shot I took while in Oz, I felt like my body was doing backflips while my mind was trying to hang on by a thread, spiraling out of control.

The last doctor I went to barely made eye contact with me at my only appointment, and instead of taking the time to explain the type of birth control he put me on, he handed me some samples and stated, "Follow the directions on the packet. Don't skip any days." Then he handed me a prescription for Prozac and said, "Try this, it might help with your mood swings." He, like the others, didn't ask me anything about my diet, drinking habits, or if any other drugs were a part of my life. He never suggested my mood swings could be more directly related to something more serious, so I never assumed they were. And he didn't even suggest I talk to a therapist or psychologist. He did, however, attempt to help with my attitude issues with the introduction of the blue happy pills. So, even though I felt irritated with his dismissive personality, I found a glimmer of hope in the antidepressants, took the medications as directed (kind-of), and carried on.

My bouts of instability and waves of mayhem didn't calm down much after that. But that is to be expected since I was haphazardly washing down my birth control and the occasional antidepressant with my daily gin and tonic. Tack on a few years of unaddressed heartache and bar hopping (I mean, tending), along with the increasing pressure of "settling down" and "growing up" coming from my parents, and I concocted my own personal recipe for emotional disaster.

—

With a pounding hangover the day after the spaghetti incident, and with Laura's support, I did a little research and found a therapist I thought would be a good fit for me. I chose this lady because her references declared she had over thirty years of experience and was a consummate professional in the world of women's therapy.

If you're going to engage in therapy, experience is one of the most critical credentials and should be at the top of your requirement list. **The last thing I wanted was a rookie right out of college with little to no life experience trying to advise me on how to pull my head out of my ass and "feel my feelings." I needed tenure. I needed reality. I needed solutions.** And I needed a game plan to heal because where I was in my mind and where I felt I was going in my heart were too dark for me to willingly accept any of it as fate. I needed someone who had been around the block and knew how to address what I was going through. Because I was going through *a lot*.

When I arrived at my first appointment a week later, I noticed that the therapist's office was clean but tired. One of the most obvious indications she had been doing this a while was the grayed-out pathway leading to an ancient, upholstered, wing-back chair in the far-left corner. The carpet fibers were completely flat, and the color was totally faded to white right in front of the chair. Underneath, however, the carpet was still a fluffy bright blue, telling me that the furniture hadn't moved in years. Clearly most, if not all, of this woman's clients sat in that spot when they came to see her. The chair itself had to be at least fifty years old, with tattered floral fabric and matching plaid arm covers. The seat cushion was as flat as a pancake and had a sunken gully in the center. I assumed at least a thousand different asses had probably sat in that chair over the years. Gross. Mine was not going to be one of them.

I opted to sit in the sturdy, clean, wooden rocker across the room. The path to that chair wasn't so worn out, and there was a welcoming view of the park out the window. Rocking back and forth, I pondered why more people didn't opt for this seat over the plaid pancake.

She opened the door and paused with a look of confusion on her face. Then she stiffly wandered over to the floral bouquet across from me. Apparently, I was in her spot. I guess if I was working in this room all day, I'd claim that rocker as mine, too.

When she had answered my initial phone call, the sound of her voice unleashed my sobs and hysteria as if I was witnessing my own death. I told her how upset I was about my life. I think I was still crying from spraying spaghetti sauce all over my new white shirt the night before, and I probably mentioned that I was trying to accept the glaring reality that I may actually be (self-diagnosed) depressed.

My expectations of what she might look like were right on. Older. Tired. About sixty-ish. Graying hair in a low boring ponytail. Pointy, cool looking 1970s-style glasses (one of her only redeeming qualities). And slacks. Like pants, but they were slacks probably made out of 100% thick polyester like what the *Brady Bunch* parents wore. And she had on the token, stereotypical therapist sweater with a patch on one elbow and a button missing off the bottom.

After the typical salutations, she asked some basic questions, and I gave her some basic answers. In a flash, our hour was up. I paid her, made another appointment, and left.

The following week I showed up for my appointment at the same time. We went through the same eyeball routine of her staring me down when she walked in the room as I rocked and relaxed by the window. She asked more questions. I had more answers. I may have cried a little this time. But again, in a flash, the hour was up. I paid her, made another appointment, and left.

For my third appointment, I was five minutes late. She was already in the room, sitting in the rocking chair with a coy smile on her face. I had no choice but to follow the grungy gray path leading to the upholstered pancake—the foreboding throne that stunk of sweat, old stories, and pain.

As soon as my ass hit the cushion (or rather the springs poked my butt), everything changed. My mindset shifted. The energy in the room darkened, and a funny feeling lurched in my stomach. Staring at the woman across the room from me, I noticed she didn't seem so tired any longer. The sun gently brushed her cheek and knocked twenty years off her face.

She smiled and started asking me questions, but this time they were different. This time, I heard her voice coming from a different angle.

There were signs of empathy and compassion that I hadn't noticed before. I wasn't just *listening* to her; I was *feeling* this other voice come up from deep inside me. I was now in the hot seat and didn't like it. But I talked anyway and couldn't stop. I talked and talked and cried and talked and cried some more, then kept on talking. I could not understand why I was spewing this unrelenting verbal diarrhea of secrets and soul-baring truths or where it was all coming from. It was like the fucking chair had magical powers over me and a haze of reality pixie dust was being emitted from those nasty arm covers. I could feel years of memories and truths (God forbid the TRUTH!) seeping through the fabric into my soul and back out of my mouth.

As I was puking my secrets all over the matted-down carpet just about to unload a good chunk of my Australia history, birth control shots, and why I thought I was allergic to gin, she rang a little bell and said, "Time's up." Just like that. Ding-a-fucking-ling.

I was silenced, but my mouth remained open. I focused my gaze on her in strange disbelief that she had interfered with such an incredible part of my story and slowly shut my pie hole.

"When would you like to come again?" she asked.

Aggravated at the interruption but complying like an obedient robot, I picked a date, paid for the appointment, and peeled myself out of the time-warped cushion. Leaving the room, not sure what had just happened or if I had just been manipulated into a Chatty Cathy doll, and not totally convinced I hadn't been drugged by this woman, I stepped outside, started walking, and continued what felt like an insane trip down memory lane. It was one of the craziest experiences I had ever had sober.

With this woman's probing, and my apparent comfort in her empathetic presence, I had finally found a person who was willing to listen to what I needed to say. I felt cared for. I felt like she was supporting and encouraging me to heal. I fell into a vulnerability I had never experienced before. And it scared the hell out of me.

Exposing my frightened younger self by telling my stories to this woman, I was able to develop a better understanding of the darkness and despair that was inside of me. And I hated it. **I quickly became afraid of the demons that lurked in the shadows of my soul and thought if therapy was going to bring out these uncontrollable emotions, then I wanted nothing to do with it.** I didn't want to feel the hurt again. I didn't want to talk about the pain. I didn't want the sensation that I was exposing myself to because I was embarrassed that I didn't know better. I was ashamed I hadn't figured it all out by then. I was afraid that she was going to criticize or judge me. And I honestly hoped it was all just going to go away on its own.

Vulnerability to me, at this point in my life, was a sign of weakness. I had gotten so good at hiding these sensitive parts of myself behind masks of adventure and illusionary smiles that as soon as my vulnerable parts were uncovered with this therapist lady, I feared for my life. This therapy stuff was scarier than jumping out of a plane or traveling halfway around the world alone. It was more frightening than starting over or going broke. So I convinced myself that I didn't have the strength to face my fears, and I didn't *have* to go backwards to heal. I opted to push through whatever this depression thing was and attempted to get used to the sorrows that followed me around. **I had already been doing it for half of my life. Why change now?**

I cried all the way home, promised myself that I would never go back to that filthy, possessed chair ever again, and vowed to figure my shit out on my own.

RESPONSIBILITY IN THE JOURNEY

When you find the right therapist, it can be enchanting. But the most challenging and unexpected part that comes along with a therapist isn't actually who *they* are (although some are better than others), or what kind of questions *they* ask, or even what method *they* use (although that is super important as you start digging and uncover some heady shit). Nope. The most challenging and unexpected part about going to therapy is you. Yup. *You.*

There is responsibility in this journey that can be downright frightening and occasionally horrific if you choose to take it seriously. You *must* show up and take the time to uncover your truth and the root of your issues. **You have to find the strength and learn how to meet the other sides of yourself that you've been burying or ignoring all this time.** You have to create the time, trust in the process, and have faith in the space these guides hold for you. It's your responsibility to reach within the depths of your memory banks and learn how to let go of whatever it is that is vexing or hurting you or making you sad or crazy. You are the special variable that can unlock the vault to understanding what the fuck is going on inside your precious head and your vulnerable heart; the therapist just provides the instruction manual. Just remember to bring your most honest and truthful self to every single appointment because if you don't, you'll be wasting your money and a shit-ton of time.

I am giving you this advice because, despite how great it felt to unburden myself in that magical chair, I didn't do all the things I just listed. I was too afraid. I had been hiding behind my limiting beliefs that I wasn't enough or was too much for so long that I couldn't tell the difference between my real feelings and the ones I had made up. The thought of unpacking my emotional pain and insecurities was so massive, so engrained, so consuming, that one hour (one real, honest, truth-be-told instinctual and soul-cracking, vomiting all over myself with sincere confessions and acknowledgments hour) in the hot seat was enough for me to recognize I wasn't ready to move on or step into the light of vulnerability and change and face my own truth of who I wanted to be. I couldn't imagine unraveling all the me's I used to be to discover the core of who I really was.

What if I didn't like what I saw and couldn't hide it? What if others didn't like it and left me because of it? What if I wasn't able to maintain this new real persona and had to crumble back to where I had been my whole life? I wasn't willing to take the chance and possibly fail, so I simply stopped taking the chance at all.

I continued avoiding help for a few more years and compacted the pain of my disillusioned nonsense. I kept adjusting my dreams and wishes to suit whoever I was with at the timc and repeated the same relationship habits over and over again, convincing myself that depression was just a stupid theory, and I was fine, even though I knew I wasn't. I continued to wash my Prozac and occasional birth control pill down with liters of wine and pints of gin and soda. (I had concluded that I couldn't possibly be allergic to gin, so I switched out the tonic to soda. Seriously. I was that delusional.)

The spaghetti outbursts to Laura would ebb and flow, but I learned how to hide it better. Whenever anyone would ask what was wrong, I reiterated that I was just going through a transition (constantly, it seemed) and was going to figure it all out on my own (what a crock of bullshit), and that I didn't need therapy (HA!). I was fine. (Yup. Cool as a cucumber soaked in gin with a splash of soda to hide the tears.)

Years after my first therapy experiences, I became so irrational and so unbalanced that I realized I couldn't do it on my own anymore and tried again. Through research, interviews, and proximity to where I was living, I sought out and found different therapists who helped me crawl out of the deep sorrows and perpetual pain I had been layering upon myself for years. I learned how to decipher the difference between what I thought was reality and what was just leftover nonsense from my lingering hormonal imbalance. **And I have learned to understand that there is immense power in vulnerability and no strength in avoidance.**

Therapy is an act of self-love. It's a place of self-reflection, discovery, and healing. Through practice, you can learn how to allow yourself to feel the feels and let the emotions come out. There is no shame in therapy. Let the power of the magical chair dust do its thing.

DEAR DIARY

Therapy is a lifesaver. It has genuinely saved me and continues to be one of the most used tools in my toolbox.

1. Reflecting on where you are in your life, consider therapy as a tool to be used to decipher, clarify, and discover some of the emotions that you may not have a deeper understanding of. If you've used it before, how did it help you? What tools did you learn that you still use? Are there any outstanding feelings or new feelings that need more attention?
2. Just like any relationship, taking the time to learn about your therapist is a valuable step in finding one that resonates with your personal communication style and intentions of healing. If you are considering therapy, be sure to research a practitioner. At the very least, review their credentials, what their specialty is, their policy on insurance and payments, whether they conduct both in-person and virtual sessions, and any testimonials available.
3. Be patient with yourself. Sometimes this "work" isn't easy. But it's absolutely worth it.
4. Give yourself a hug; you deserve it.

6

FAIRY TALES

Take Responsibility for Yourself and Your Desires

"Half the world is composed of people who have something to say and can't, and the other half have nothing to say and keep on saying it."

~ ROBERT FROST

APRIL 15, 2006

Fifteen minutes before the sunset ceremony was meant to begin, the wedding coordinator came flying into the bridal suite with a panicked look on her face. She couldn't find him. He wasn't answering his phone. No one had seen him since he had finished golfing at 11 a.m. They had looked everywhere. In twenty years of organizing weddings, she had never lost a groom, and now, rightfully so, she was freaking out.

My heart winced and skipped a beat. Even though I knew he was crazy, I didn't think he'd leave me like this.

Calmly and a little buzzed, I looked the coordinator square in the eye and said with wavering confidence, "He'll be here."

Without another word, she dashed out, leaving a wake of angst and trepidation behind her. I grabbed a new bottle of champagne, popped the top, filled my glass, drank it quickly, filled it back up, let out a little belch, and sat down. Laura, my maid of honor (for the second time), sat down quietly next to me. I stared into space for a few moments and started imagining what I was going to say to everyone in the event this whole party was a bust.

Part of me was concerned and wanted to cry. Another part of me wasn't surprised and was strangely relieved. But most of all, I just held on to the part of me that believed in the fairytale dream that he and I had created and hoped our love was strong enough to conquer his cold feet.

Laura and I gulped champagne in silence until my parents came in a few minutes later. I didn't mention that Colby was allegedly missing because I didn't have the emotional capacity to deal with their potential overreactions (or sighs of relief), let alone the ones I was stifling inside. There was already enough tension around the fact that I was getting married so quickly. Choosing to not mention the elephant that was *not* in the room was the best thing.

I ignored my inner voice of reason that was telling me to take inventory of what was happening and loosely held on to hope instead. I knew, however, that regardless of whatever was about to happen, I would be just fine.

None the wiser about the wedding coordinator's panic, or even Colby's whereabouts, my dad proudly walked me down the aisle twenty minutes later. And there Colby was, waiting for me at the end.

SUMMER, 2004

While I was living in Virginia, I popped up to Massachusetts for my brother's thirtieth birthday in August. Hoping to reconnect with some friends from my 2002 Rockfish days, I randomly reached out to this guy, Colby, to say hello and see if he had received my last postcard.

That connection turned into Friday night cocktails. As Colby and I reminisced about the shenanigans two summers prior, he reminded me of the night he jumped up on the bar and yelled, "AMANDAAAAA! Will you go out on a date with me?"

I recall reciprocating by jumping onto the other end of the bar and yelling, "Only if I'm here when it snows!" It had snowed on Halloween that year, which was one of the reasons I took off in early November. So I owed him a date. Friday night cocktails turned into that overdue date, which led to nonsense at my brother's house where I was staying for the weekend, and ended with awkward introductions of Colby to my brother and my brother's girlfriend (now wife) the following morning. Needless to say, a stranger in his kitchen wasn't quite the birthday surprise my brother had been anticipating.

In Colby I had once again met my match. My exact crazy. It seemed with him, no matter where we were, it felt like home. But there was one major problem: I was living and working in Virginia, and he was running his own company in Massachusetts.

In April 2005, after eight months of airport runs and weekends that felt like honeymoons, I rearranged my life, packed everything into a small U-Haul, and moved back up to Newburyport, Massachusetts, into Colby's house. He convinced me that it would be easier if I packed up my life and moved since I had done it so many times before and that I could get another interior design job "anywhere."

Leaving my swanky job, I looked at the relocation as another opportunity to expand my career and get away from the problems I was having with birth control and Prozac. Not realizing my depression was just getting covered up with the dopamine of a new relationship, I packed all my problems into a bunch of boxes and brought them all with me, only to be left "unpacked" for the next few years.

Colby helped me find a job that offered a lot of potential for growth at an established design firm. He made me feel as if my life was finally "heading in the right direction" (words I adopted from my parents). My new job was about thirty minutes from his house. Not our house. His. He had made it very clear that it was *his* house, and it would always be *his* house, and I would never have any ownership, ever. Okay. Cool. I thought it was a blessing and used my money to pay off my student and car loans. No big deal.

Initially, we both agreed to making changes so we could be fully present in our relationship. One of the biggest agreements was to stop seeing other people. I thought that was pretty obvious, but when I realized he was still sleeping with his cleaning lady a month before I moved in, it seemed only fair to ask that he fire her. I didn't ask for much, but that was kind of a deal breaker. In exchange, he promised me a new garage and a new deck that I would help build.

It was all so consuming, so exciting, so fast, and I just went with it. We both worked in the construction/design industry and shared the dream of riding motorcycles down the coast. He permitted me to plant lilacs (my favorite flower) wherever I wanted. We talked about traveling and even touched upon the subject of marriage and kids, but we never actually had a complete conversation about either one.

I loved him. He loved me. We were equally nuts. And all of it made sense. Almost.

—

Six months after I moved in, I mentioned I wanted a dog. We had come home from a Halloween party and were still dressed in our clown costumes. He said he'd consider it, but his abrupt answer made me feel dismissed. Sensing my agitation, he cracked a joke, and we started laughing about the silly red noses we were both still wearing. I then turned serious again and told him I wanted to practice making babies. That comment was met with an immediate shift in energy as he quickly and quietly walked out of the room.

I yelled in his direction that we never talked about what I wanted and that he *never* took me seriously. When he didn't respond, I gave up trying to talk to him about dogs and babies and climbed into bed, clown suit and all.

When he came back into the room, he had changed the subject and was carrying on about *his* new garage. I sat up and drunkenly interrupted with a loud, "Excuse me, can I say something?"

He paused.

"I feel like you've been acting like a weirdo all night and ignored me at the party."

He stared at me with his big red clown nose, not responding at all. His goofy stare made me giggle while I was trying to stay serious and have an important conversation. I did my best to stay my course, and rather than wait for him to respond, I raised my drunk and aggravated attitude up again.

"Well shit, if you're not going to answer me, I'm going to sleep," I retorted.

As if he didn't hear a word I said, he jumped onto the bed like a monkey, climbed on top of me, shoved something in my face, looked deep into my eyes, and said, "What do you think about this? Is this a serious enough conversation for you?"

I blinked, adjusted my focus, and saw he was holding a giant diamond ring three inches from my face.

Whaaaaat?!?!

"You can't be serious?" I stammered and sat up.

He paused.

"I've never been more serious in my life. Will you marry me?"

Confused, angry, and elated, I looked at him, looked at the ring, looked back at him, and wrapped my arms around his neck.

"Yes, you fucking clown," I replied.

I woke up a few times in the middle of the night and stared at my hand. Was he serious? I mean *really*? It had only been a few months. Was this what I *really* wanted? Did I say yes? I must have because I'm still here, and there is a giant rock on my finger.

My mind wandered (as it did about most things). I was approaching thirty and had stopped taking my birth control when I moved in. However, every time I brought up having a family, he would change the subject. I knew I wanted to have a baby by thirty-five, so I figured we had time. The only conversation I ever got out of him was that he was happy with his life now and didn't want to try. Okay. But what about what I wanted? I made myself believe that I was okay with his answer, that it would eventually happen. I didn't need a solid yes about kids from him, though, because we were getting married now. Naturally, kiddos would be next on the list.

"She didn't want love, she wanted to be loved.
And that was entirely different."

~ *ATTICUS*

After proposing, Colby asked me to hold off on any wedding planning until after the holidays, and I agreed.

A couple of weeks later, he took me to lunch at a golf club he liked. Fifteen minutes after arriving, he asked me if I liked the place as a venue.

"Yeah, it's okay," I said. I wasn't really paying close attention since "we" had agreed to hold off on any wedding planning.

That's when the wedding coordinator came out. I was a little surprised, since "we" had decided to wait, but I entertained her pleasant sales pitch anyway. When she told us the available dates for the following year, I looked at Colby and shrugged since "we" hadn't discussed anything yet. He got excited, picked April 15, 2006, and smiled at me. I unconvincingly nodded yes. I immediately felt overwhelmed and rushed by his eagerness to make these decisions so quickly. Once again, I had let the man take the lead.

Two weeks, eleven hours, and thirty minutes after I agreed to marry him, he had booked our wedding venue and picked the date. I had five months to plan the entire wedding.

"We" (he) decided to forgo an engagement party, and instead, had a few dinner parties with friends and family. That relieved some pressure but ultimately ended up filling most of our weekends for the next two months, leaving us practically no time to talk about all of the other things that were on my mind. Everything was happening too fast, and I didn't take the time to prioritize anything on my agenda. **I didn't know how to speak up in a way that made me feel heard or understood** and felt like he had everything on the outside under control, while my questionable insecurities of what I really wanted started to bubble up on the inside of my heart.

In late February, my Friday afternoon bridal shower turned into a thirtieth birthday party, and the guys surprised Colby with a bachelor party at the Rockfish (of all places). My college girlfriends and I arrived home late, but Colby came home even later, around 3 a.m. The following morning as Colby slept, I quietly picked up the disaster of clothes and feather boas that had been strewn around the bedroom. His jeans were sticky and wet from his party. Curious, but careful, I let the sleeping dog lie and tossed his jeans in the washing machine. By this time in our relationship, "we" had agreed to not ask each other too many questions, so I stifled my curiosity and joined my girlfriends in the kitchen for coffee.

Saturday night, in an effort to keep the party(ies) going, some of the attendees of the shower/birthday celebration and bachelor party joined up for afternoon cocktails. The ladies were all too willing to share the ridiculousness of the previous evening's evolution, but not a word was spoken about what happened with the boys. Not one single word. Nothing. Nadda. Zilch. As if the night never even happened.

The sticky jeans ran around in my mind all night and into the next morning when I noticed Colby was a little uncomfortable as we sat down for brunch. Since we were surrounded by friends and family the entire weekend, I wasn't able to have a private conversation with him about what had *really* happened at his party.

I dropped the girls off at the airport late Sunday night and returned home completely exhausted but still curious. I walked into a dark house and could hear Colby in the other room. I made my way into the living room talking nervously, trying to hide my anxiety about the questions I wanted to ask. As I started to collapse onto the sofa, he jumped up, caught me, and nearly tossed me out of the room.

"What the hell?" I said, looking at him with confusion and annoyance. "Why did you push me?"

He smiled, pointed to the sofa, and said, "Shh. She's sleeping."

Next to him on a blanket was an eight-week-old yellow lab puppy. The cutest ball of fluff I had ever laid my eyes on. The questions about sticky jeans stopped in their tracks and high-tailed it out of my consciousness, replaced with overflowing love for this little sleeping angel.

"We should name her Morgan," I said. Colby agreed.

As I was nuzzling our new member of the family, he told me he booked the honeymoon to Cancun for the middle of June. I thought we had agreed on Aruba in May.

"Happy Birthday, Amanda. I've taken care of everything," he said.

I said nothing. My voice had abandoned me, so I just stared at him and smiled.

—

Monday morning, as Colby got out of the shower, I noticed a bright red strap mark across both his ass cheeks. No wonder he couldn't sit down at brunch the day before. It looked like it hurt.

He saw the inquisitive look on my face. "Things got a little out of control Friday night."

"Define 'out of control,'" I demanded.

"The strippers were a little aggressive, and one ended up snapping my belt in half as she was whipping my ass," he said with a laugh.

Oh. Is that all? WHAT?

Not knowing if I wanted an answer, I asked, "Were you naked?"

"No, I was wearing a thong," he responded.

Oh. Right. Because *THAT* makes sense…

WHAT. THE. FUCK?!

My face turned crimson. I was livid. "Well, then, what the hell happened to your jeans?"

He stopped laughing.

"Oh, that was before the whipping."

I glared at him, waiting for more details.

"They had me wear a strap-on during her dance, and she came all over my pants. Then they poured jelly lube all over us, and she made me get almost naked so she could give me one final spanking before I got hitched."

I didn't even know what I was hearing and could hardly manage the anger erupting inside my chest.

"One *final* spanking?" I heard myself say.

He blushed, paused long, and asked me not to get mad.

Too late, buddy. Too fucking late.

"Yeah, the stripper was my old cleaning lady," he mumbled as he walked into the bathroom.

I almost threw up.

"Pleasure of love lasts but a moment. Pain of love lasts a lifetime."

~ *Bette Davis*

From the outside, I had everything I wanted: a seemingly great guy, a legit great job, a fun and exciting lifestyle. We (he) had a house, we (he) had a boat, and we (he) had an awesome dog. But on the inside, I was overwhelmed.

It had been rapid fire for the past twelve months as Colby handled most everything before I had a chance to wrap my head around it. Whenever he brought something up for discussion, it was more of an opportunity for him to tell me what *he* wanted rather than us talk about what *we* wanted. Whenever I offered an opinion, he would accuse me of always wanting it my way, so I eventually stopped bringing things up.

One night I made a simple suggestion on how to peel the shrimp, and he flipped out. Shrimp went flying, one of the pendants over the kitchen island was smashed, and Morgan ended up with a cut on her nose. When things settled down, he blamed the whole mess on me and called me a control freak.

On another night, I came home from work later than usual to find a life insurance guy sitting at our kitchen table. After the awkward introductions, the insurance guy asked me how much money I thought I would need to maintain our lifestyle if Colby died unexpectedly. I shot him a sideways glance and kind of giggled. It was an interesting question, but I answered honestly.

"Well, a lot more than I'm making. He pays for almost everything, and I'm using my money to pay off my car and student loans."

When he asked Colby the same question, Colby responded with, "She doesn't affect my life one bit. I wouldn't need anything if she died."

I was crushed. His answer expanded beyond the financial question and straight to my soul. With that one statement, I felt totally insignificant, unnecessary, and began to question what I was even doing in the relationship if he didn't feel "affected by me" at all.

The cocktails I had had before I got home must have made me a little woozy, because I passed out when the life insurance guy drew my blood for testing. When I came to, the insurance guy was gone, and I was asked a million questions about why I was *really* late. Not aware I had a curfew, I deflected the interrogation and asked why we were getting life insurance. He dismissed my redirection (tit for tat), laughed, then asked when dinner was going to be ready.

BOUNDARIES

At this point in my life, setting boundaries was as foreign to me as organic vegetables. I was in love and just happy to not be crying in my spaghetti anymore. The thought of telling Colby that his expectations of me felt controlling (let's be honest, they *were* controlling) was more intimidating than the actual control, so I stayed quiet and let my resentment brew.

In relationships, boundaries are meant to be healthy tools to care for and respect yourself and others. They affect your mental health, emotional capacity, physical body, personal space, and often the breadth and depth of your intelligence. By responsibly setting and understanding our own boundaries, we can learn to live in a world with people who value our intentions, protect our personal space, and grant ourselves the freedom to live authentically.

When expressed properly, boundaries can create safe spaces between people, their emotions, and their thoughts, often expanding their partnership and allowing deeper intimacy. When not expressed at all, the lack of understanding can cause confusion and disrespect, amongst many other challenging issues.

I was nine years younger than Colby, and because he had made it abundantly clear he was established within his life, I was the one who had to make the most changes. Initially, I didn't make a big deal of it, but as our relationship evolved, I started to feel like whatever I was doing wasn't enough for him, so I kept changing in the hopes of keeping him happy. When he accused me of not being the same woman he fell in love with, I felt suffocated by his perceptions and didn't know how to turn back into who I had once been. I was living in his life and didn't feel like I had my own. I couldn't win.

For whatever reason, he always said anything he wanted to me, while I felt like I couldn't say anything I wanted to him. So I kept quiet. **We never took the time to listen to each other and learn what each other's actual needs were, let alone how to meet those needs for each other.** We didn't have healthy communication boundaries, and apparently, we both figured it would all just work itself out once we got married.

He had grown up in an Irish-Italian Catholic family where disagreements ended in bloody noses or broken fingers, and I grew up in a stubborn German/Scottish and English/French household where it was easier to brush everything under the carpet than get uncomfortable talking about our emotions.

I'm not saying either upbringing was wrong, but I am saying that the values of our parents that were repeated in our relationship didn't work for us together. We didn't know we needed to discuss how we wanted to be loved, nor how to set emotional or financial boundaries. Actually, I think our habit of *not* talking about our feelings and *not* addressing issues in a healthy manner (I don't consider screaming matches healthy) was the silent boundary that hurt us the most in the long run.

ALMOST A FAIRYTALE ENDING

When the wedding planner told me Colby was missing moments before our wedding, I was too buzzed to fully understand the meaning behind his actions. Yet, as my dad and I walked toward the outdoor altar, and I saw Colby standing there with his heart on his sleeve and a tear in his eye, I pushed the concerns aside and smiled. Then our eyes locked, we joined hands, and I quietly asked him where he had been. He smirked and whispered that he had been in the parking lot with the car in drive, his foot on the brake. I rolled my eyes, squeezed his hands, and with an uncomfortable, yet familiar feeling of the savior behavior addiction I had been chasing around the world since high school, the ceremony began.

Even though I had walked down the aisle with feelings of hope and faith, as soon as he slipped the wedding band on my finger, this symbol of eternal and unconditional love felt more like an invisible noose slipping around my neck.

According to Colby, I had everything I wanted. It was partially true, but we were missing trust and respect in our marriage. A month after the wedding, right before our honeymoon, he said he didn't want to mess up his life by having kids and a family. I was devastated, felt betrayed, and the proverbial noose tightened. The kid question was the most important thing we never talked about, but since we were already living Colby's carefully curated fairy tale life, I swallowed my shattered dream of being a mom. **It felt like a handful of razor blades going down, and I just pretended that his final answer didn't bother me.**

—

Rather than tackle the kid question when we returned from our honeymoon, I threw myself into my career. The more projects I took on, the longer my work days became, and the more neglected Colby felt. But I was angry and felt just as neglected and ignored with his dismissal of my biggest dream, so I didn't think it was a problem.

As I paid more attention to my job, I excelled, and my responsibilities increased. With every new project came a new set of people—architects, contractors, clients. Each time I came home excited to talk about my day, Colby would scrutinize any person I mentioned and tried to convince me that no one was interested in what I was doing as a designer; they all just wanted to sleep with me.

"You need to see it from my perspective. Stand in my shoes for a minute. You're a hot, sexy woman. You don't understand what these people *really* want from you," he would say.

I couldn't grasp his backhanded comments and grew offended that he didn't respect my work.

When Colby learned that I started attending regular construction site meetings, which I loved, and was communicating via cell phone with the contractors for my projects, he flipped. He didn't think it was necessary for designers to be on construction sites. He told me that since I was just an employee, I shouldn't be using my cell phone for work. When I couldn't stop people from calling me, he made me change my number so they couldn't reach me at all. His shitty, controlling attitude started to suck the joy out of the only thing I felt like I had any traction in—my career.

Even after I changed my number, whenever my cell phone would ring, he would hover over me to see who it was. And, if it was ever a contractor, he would go to a place of suspicion and mistrust, insinuating that I was sleeping with whoever was calling. It was fucking ridiculous.

I would retaliate with comments about his cleaning lady "kind of" fucking him right before we got married. But his shit didn't stink, so he would just blow me off and ignore me.

"I've had enough of 'The Amanda Show,'" he'd say. "I'm tired of trying to get you to understand this from my perspective."

All I wanted was to be better at my job and be more available for my teams. I was desperate for positive attention rather than his badgering. But nothing I did or said mattered to him because he just kept slinging a prophecy of his own insecurities and bullshit in my direction.

When I tried to regain a little of my independence, I had to ask permission. If he didn't allow me to do what I asked, I would either fight for it, give it up, or figure out how to hide it.

Eventually, I shut down and kept things to myself, finding ways around his rules. I stopped using my voice and became powerless against his accusations and negativity. The proverbial noose kept getting tighter and tighter, and I started lying just to get out of the house.

Our marriage was suffocating me, but I was so oxygen-deprived that I couldn't see the damaging abuse spiraling me out of control until it was too late. I had morphed into a suppressed version of the free woman he had met all those years ago and was no longer aligned with any of my values or core strengths. I sought out attention elsewhere, which thrust me back into my familiar habits of hazy powdery lines, childish nonsense, and masks of scapegoats. I wanted to be seen for the light that shone within me and not be persecuted or forced to dim my fire. The lies quickly escalated, and about a year into our marriage, I had a convoluted, messy, and torrid affair with one of the contractors I was working with.

Once Colby caught me in my web of lies, **we fought with words so damaging there were times when I just wished he would hit me so I had a "good reason" to leave.** I wasn't able to see that the emotional abuse was doing more damage than any broken bone would have and held on to the abuse as long as I could because I couldn't bear the thought of ending another relationship.

We tried separating for a little bit, but all that did was allow my depression to unpack itself and come back with a vengeance. When I tried to move back in, the war of words got even worse. In an effort to start the healing process, I began to see a therapist. Eventually, Colby agreed to try couples therapy, but the collateral damage had already taken a stronghold of our relationship.

Rather than work through our problems, we would sit there hurt, afraid, and both stubborn as fuck, wasting our money and time. I was willing to take some of the responsibility for my actions but half-assed the sessions with more lies and victimized tears. Colby would just point his finger, blame me for everything, yell about the love notes and baseball hat he had found in my car, and take no responsibility for his role in this mess. I knew in my gut that I was not the entire reason our marriage had fallen apart, but according to Colby, it was all my fault.

Sometime in 2008, after almost three years of calling Newburyport home, Colby kicked me out of his house and slammed the door right behind me. I was crushed. The emotional abuse of that relationship had broken me down. I was a mere shell of myself, without a voice and unable to communicate in a healthy manner. I didn't know where I was supposed to go or what I needed to do. Reluctant to accept the reality that my life was falling apart, I started over again, shattered heart and bruised ego in tow.

DEAR DIARY

We cannot allow others to control or manipulate us. We must ensure that we take ownership of our thoughts, that our opinions matter, and that we speak up for ourselves. We also need to create healthy boundaries to allow space for our mental and emotional well-being.

1. Has there ever been a time in your life when you've lost your voice because of someone else's control? What happened (or didn't happen) because you didn't speak up for yourself?
2. Remember, if things are moving too fast, take time to understand what you need and make certain your partner understands what that means. Don't just go along for the ride.
3. If you are in an unhealthy or manipulative relationship, seeking the help of a therapist or trusted associate can be the first step to healing. We need to take responsibility for our own desires, and it starts with having the courage to stand up for yourself.

7

OPPORTUNITY KNOCKS

When One Door Closes, Another One Opens

"In order to change your life and start living a new one that you've never lived before, your faith in miracles, and yourself, must be greater than your fear. You have to be willing to fall down, get up, look stupid, cry, laugh, make a mess, clean it up, and not stop until you get there. No. Matter. What."

~ *Jen Sincero*

SPRING, 2008

The economy tanked in early 2008, and like many others in various industries, I got laid off. The unfortunate timing corresponded with me serving Colby divorce papers only days after I moved into a one-bedroom apartment, the size of the walk-in closet I had back in Virginia.

With only a few thousand dollars in my bank account, I felt like my life was crumbling all around me. Then I somehow caught the swine flu and was really, really sick. Contagious and trapped in that little apartment for two weeks with nothing but Tylenol, cable TV, and cans of soup, I was convinced that the only thing keeping me company were a crushed reputation and my broken heart.

Solitary confinement and the fear of not getting a job kept me hiding under my sick, sweaty sheets, day after day, leaving me with little to no energy or motivation. As my depression started to wrap its claws around my soul, I clung to my Prozac and bottles of wine as if they were life rings. I truly believed that if it weren't for them, I might have drowned in my own sorrows and never figured out how to float to the surface of my wavering willpower and get out of my own way.

By the grace of God, I started feeling better emotionally and physically after a few weeks. I eventually pulled my head out of my ass long enough to go on a couple interviews and thankfully landed a design job at a firm in Newburyport. Morbidly embarrassed by my actions of the past year, I prayed every day that I didn't drive past Colby or anyone else who knew about my affair, fearing they would just chase me out of town.

There were times when a hangover would magnify my depression, causing me to spend the day in bed and call in sick to my new job. Then there were other days when, if I did manage to crawl out from under the covers, it would take me hours to figure out what to wear, and I would be late for work. So, it came as no surprise when I was let go two months after I was hired. I had trapped myself on my own roller coaster ride of mostly downs with the occasional up and was starting to lose hope altogether.

The compounding issues of getting another divorce, losing my job twice in six months, and living in an apartment the size of a postage stamp were outrageously embarrassing and too ironic to handle. So, I held on to anything that made me feel better, and the closest things were Prozac and wine. I didn't have the wherewithal to consider that *what* I was holding onto might be doing me more harm than good, made the emotional decision that I couldn't afford therapy (but somehow figured out how to buy cases of wine), and called my doctor with another self-diagnosis of hormonal imbalances and depression. Of course, with me crying like a two-year-old having a temper tantrum on the other end of the phone, my doctor aided in my self-induced bedlam by accommodating my requests for more happy pills without even requiring an office visit.

This cycle was exhausting. The longer I submerged myself into an unhealthy pool of alcohol and antidepressants, the more challenging my ability to think clearly and function at full throttle (or even half speed) became. And, regardless of where I was, or who was with me, I cried. A lot. Like all the freaking time. If I wasn't upset about something, I felt like I had nothing, which upset me even more, and the waterworks would flow. I was absolutely miserable and a drag to be around.

One night a friend from back in the marine store days was over for dinner. We had just finished our third bottle of red, about to open another, and as I was fumbling with the corkscrew, the tears started to flow. I was crying about everything and nothing and couldn't stop. My friend, in her supportive and incredibly sympathetic manner said to me, "Amanda, I think it might be time to take a break."

Slightly buzzed and confused, I stopped screwing around with the opener, looked her blank in the face and said, "What, you don't want any more wine?"

"No, honey," she said, gently removing the bottle from my death grip. "I think you need to take a break from alcohol. Maybe just for a little while. Tonight has been fun, but look at you; you're a mess. The booze isn't helping you get any better."

With bloodshot eyes, a bubble of anguish sitting in my chest, and a warmed but reluctant heart, I heard exactly what she was saying and knew she was right. I didn't open the fourth bottle. She went home shortly after that conversation, and I cried myself to sleep.

Needless to say, 2008 was not my best year.

There are plenty of studies concluding the same thing: **Do not drink alcohol while taking antidepressants.** An article from Baton Rouge Behavioral Hospital explains that mixing Prozac and alcohol can actually *lower the effectiveness* of the medication and *increase the severity* of side effects, making everything worse, "...in the longer term, mixing Prozac and alcohol could actually worsen symptoms of your depression."[5] I can guarantee you from years of experience that this article is spot on.

Making it through a year in that pocket of hell proved to be a small miracle, but as winter turned to spring, I relaxed some (not all) of my unhealthy habits (aka, stopped drinking gallons of wine throughout the week and kept the partying to the weekends) and became aware of this relentless underlying feeling that I needed to figure my life out. I mean, I was thirty-three, twice divorced, unemployed, low on cash, and still driving that ridiculous yellow car around like I was a teenager. Something needed to change.

Since the only thing that was sure in my life was my love for design, I jumped on the job-search pony again and eventually secured the Lead Residential Interior Designer position at a local architectural firm. It was a blessing and a curse, like so many other things had been in my life.

At the design company I had worked at from 2006 to 2008, my primary job was the "go-to" designer for a local development group. This developer would receive basic structural and exterior plans from their neighboring architectural firm and would then bring the unfinished plans to the company I was working at (and got laid off from). I would then select and specify all the interior details like trim, cabinets, flooring, paint colors, tiles, stone, etc., and help the developer complete their projects.

During my interview with this *new* architectural firm, I casually informed them that I had been the specifier for dozens of their houses and point blank told them that they needed me. Familiar with my resume, the company I used to work for, and the houses in my portfolio, they knew exactly what I was implying when I pointed to the development group across the street, and hired me on the spot.

This firm was owned by four alpha males who all had their names on the door. There were only five women, including me, sprinkled throughout the thirty-person office, making it a very different environment than any other I'd experienced. Their old-school testosterone-driven protocols were a bit unnerving, so I did my best to stay in my cubicle, settle into their ridiculous sixty-hour work week, and try to make the best of a crappy situation.

About six months into this "more than" full-time job, I asked Mom and Dad for a little help, and with all of my savings and a little of theirs, I purchased my first condo in November 2009. I lived paycheck to paycheck for a while, became a connoisseur of which bread and peanut butter brands were least expensive, and limited my social life to bicycle rides and star-gazing. For additional exercise and entertainment, I would walk the mile to the beach almost every night to smell the salt air and relish in the small wins of starting over. Things were looking up.

Aside from the long hours, I had other issues with my new job. I had been hired to make the finish and fixture selections for their residential projects, but instead they had me computer drafting laboratory layouts for biotech buildings. I told them I didn't know how to use the drafting software, but they had me do it anyway, and then criticized me when I made mistakes and asked why my timesheet was so out of balance. I was fighting an uphill battle with these guys, but I kept trudging along because the economy sucked and "at least I had a job."

So much was misaligned, but I silenced my attitude and kept plugging away. When my initial ninety-day employment trial was over, naturally I expected to get the pay increase they promised in my offer letter. But instead was told that in order to avoid layoffs my pay was *decreasing* by twenty percent until further notice, yet my workload would remain the same. It wasn't fair. *How could they do this and not expect all their employees to revolt?* Their reasoning made me feel totally undervalued, and I started reassessing what I was even doing at an architectural firm in the first place. Afterall, I was a designer, not an architect.

Throughout my professional career (once I started actually working in "real jobs"), I had full faith in the fact that the few things no one could ever take away from me were my education, my motivation, and my drive. I loved interior design from the day I started studying it in college and had unwavering confidence in my skills and creativity. Regardless of any position I held at any firm, I always had this innate understanding of design running through my veins, and I was good at what I did.

By being utilized as a draftsperson in this new firm, I felt like I was trying to force a square peg into a round hole. The more I tried to fit in, the more I knew I did not belong in this men's club. As I struggled to work within their expectations and archaic methods, I had a niggling feeling that there were other, better ways of doing things. This niggle was backed up by a strong and sometimes overwhelming sensation that there was something greater for me, beyond biotech cubicles and negotiating my salary. All I had to do was figure out what I was supposed to do next, and how I could make it happen.

I started to ask myself, *Is this all you've got, Amanda? There must be something better.* Each time I teased the question of if I wanted to work for anyone anymore, my soul would immediately respond with a resounding, "No." I had been molding myself into relationships, job positions, and the expectations of others forever, and I'd had enough. **It was time for me to start thinking about *what I really wanted,* and not just do *what I thought I was supposed to.***

So, I started scheming on nights and weekends with the intention of creating my new future. The words "freedom" and "flexibility" kept popping into my brain, and before I knew it, all that brainstorming turned into a *crazy idea* that took over everything in my life, and I started researching "how to start your own business." Why the hell not?

The economy was in the shitter. Most companies were either going belly up or re-inventing themselves, and lots of people were still unemployed. It was the best time, right? Plus, aside from having confidence in my design skills, I considered myself to be a pretty savvy business person and what I didn't know, I would research and figure out.

For six months, almost every night when I got home and every single Sunday, I immersed myself in as many free courses as I could find on marketing, business planning, insurance, legal requirements, logo designs, and anything I thought I needed to know to open my own interior design company. I dedicated all of my time to this *crazy idea* and transformed myself into something I had never previously imagined becoming: an entrepreneur.

When I was a kid, my report cards always stated, "Amanda is conscientious and diligent. She is very focused when she puts her mind to something." I guess that even through all the emotional follies and personality adjustments I had been making most of my life, I never lost my spark to work hard, and never gave up on what I set my mind to.

"It's about the story we tell ourselves that unfolds in front of us, and if you change your narrative, you change the plot."

~ *Amanda Greaves*

FALL, 2010

On Friday, October 8, 2010, I took an early morning walk on the beach to gather my thoughts. *Was I really doing this? Did I have what it takes to start my own business? What the fuck am I going to do if it doesn't work?*

I checked my only bank account before I went to the office: $3,500 gleamed on the screen. It was enough for three months of mortgage payments and four months of food and gas, as long as I didn't leave the house. My stomach was in knots as I drove to the office, and by the time I got there, I was so nervous it took everything for me to maintain composure and not burst into tears or shit my pants. This was either going to be the biggest mistake or the biggest opportunity I would ever make or create in my life. I walked in and asked to have a conversation with the human resource lady and one of the partners. My heartbeat quickened and my palms sweat for the two long and anxious minutes I waited for them. Then I joined them in the conference room.

Five quick minutes later, I collected my "personal effects" off my desk and danced out the door of that testosterone driven, male-dominated architectural firm, towards my dream of "freedom and flexibility." I vowed to never work for another company again, unless it was my own.

When I talked to my parents over the weekend, I told them I had quit my job and was starting my own business. In my mom's truest style, she flipped out.

"You did WHAT?!" she yelled. "You never think things through! How the hell do you plan on paying your mortgage? This is the worst economy ever. No one is going to hire you. You were lucky to have a job in the first place."

"Well, Mom, if this doesn't work out, and I lose everything, I'll either find a cardboard box and live under a bridge, or I'll move back down to

Florida and live with you and Dad again." I was kidding, of course, but she was already ramped up, so I figured I would try to have a little fun and egg her on.

"JESUS CHRIST, Amanda! You *can't* be serious." It sounded like the phone dropped to the floor as she spewed fire and walked away yelling at my father, "She's *your* daughter. Can you *PLEASE* talk some sense into her?!"

After a short, suspenseful silence, I felt my dad's smile come through the line as he said, "I was wondering when you were going to do this. Congratulations. Let me know if you need any help."

I had changed my story and started designing my new life.

THE COST OF DOING BUSINESS

The following Monday, I started using my new email and changed the signature to read:

Amanda Greaves, President, Owner
AGC Interiors, LLC.

I joined every chamber of commerce and rotary club within a twenty-mile radius. I became a member of four different business networking groups and designer associations. I introduced myself to every builder, contractor and architect from Boston up the coast to southern New Hampshire. I met people for coffee, lunch, afternoon tea, dinner, and nightcaps, all in an effort to get to know them, and to get my name out there. I linked arms with vendors and manufacturer's representatives and said "yes" to every invitation I got. I was sharing my story and my goal of helping people realize their dreams through the power of design. It actually got to a point when people asked me what I did for work, I would respond, "I am in the business of building relationships. I'm a dream designer." It became my tag line.

The more I worked, the more obsessed I became about taking hold of my future. It got to the point where I would wake up and get started at 7 a.m. and still be plugging away at midnight.

My boyfriend at the time, Ken, had wanted me to wait to start "my new thing" (as he called it) until he had secured his next job (for the third time that year), and "we" could save some money. It was a valiant statement on his part, and I know he meant well, but I couldn't wait any longer. I had been waiting for him to get a new job. I had been waiting for my salary to get kicked back up to one hundred percent. I had waited for the right time to do so many things in my life and felt like I had already missed so many opportunities that I wasn't going to wait any longer. I knew that if I didn't make a move now, it might not ever happen.

I was so determined, so intent, so absolutely certain that my dreams were going to become my reality, I stopped at absolutely nothing to attain them.

As Ken and I maneuvered through this drastic new lifestyle change I had tossed us into, our relationship began to suffer. I was hell bent on proving myself to the world that I could do the same thing all these other design companies were doing, but better. I was being driven by an internal need for validation and significance, as well as a selfish desire for acknowledgement, to the point that I lost focus on everything else in my life. **Eventually, my relentless pursuit of success ended up costing me more than just money.**

Ken was a well-spoken and highly educated man, which are a couple of the reasons why I loved him. As the months carried on, he started leaving me little notes around the condo just to remind me that he cared and that he was there.

One night, while I had practically climbed into my laptop, he went out with his friends, and I barely even noticed. Hours went by before I pulled my head out of my screen and realized it was dark outside, and I was all alone. Wandering into the kitchen to grab some food, I found a note on the counter that Ken had left for me before he went out:

To my Custom Made,

I know you are working hard, and I think it's great that you are pursuing your dream. This is a quote by Steve Jobs that I love, and I think it's right up your alley → "*Your time is limited—so don't waste it living someone else's life. Don't be trapped by Dogma—which is living with the results of other people's thinking. Don't let the noise of other's opinions drown out your own inner voice. And most important,* ***have the courage to follow your heart and intuition****. They somehow already know what you truly want to become, so everything else is secondary.*"

I am proud of you and will support you however you need. But I miss you and how we were before all your new business stuff started. Just please don't forget that I'm here, and remember to take a break every once in a while.

Love you,

Ken

I read the note and was aggravated that he didn't ask me to go out with him. But a minute later, I realized that he might have asked me, and I just didn't notice. I hadn't noticed he left and actually hadn't noticed him much at all over the past couple months, except when there were dishes in the sink or the TV was too loud.

We bickered because I worked all the freaking time, and rather than pay attention to him and equally support his endeavors, I chose to call out his shortcomings. He still paid positive attention to me, but he had to tiptoe around because I had set up my office in the dining room. He remained supportive for a while but eventually became aggravated with my businesslike attitude.

"I don't like living with an arrogant guy," he said one night. Apparently I had pissed him off by pointing out another one of his shortcomings. But his statement went in one ear and out the other as I walked right past him, ignoring his comment.

Another night he came home drunk, yapping that I was just like his asshole bosses, and he wanted his girlfriend back. I briefly looked at him, didn't have any interest in arguing, gave him a shrug and an insincere apology, then went back to the drawing board, literally.

I had become more intense, more deliberate, and more stressed than ever. I was wearing every single solitary hat that any new business owner has to don, and it was slowly killing me. The changes in my attitude and complete lack of time to do anything but work drove a wedge between us. And even though I had an inkling of what was going on, I couldn't (or wouldn't) take my eyes off my business goals long enough to do anything about it.

When we had started dating a year prior, I had been doing my best to shine my feminine light whenever possible and supported him while he went through his divorce. After all, I had just been through the exact same situation a year earlier. I was kind, gentle, and patient. But now, while I was trying to prove that I was the right designer/business person for every job, I thought I had to bury that gentle feminine light under a tough outer shell of a masculine business persona. I lost the balance between when I was in work mode and when I was actually living the rest of my life. Those caring and considerate characteristics went incognito while I was grappling my way through a male-dominated industry. And with few to zero female mentors or advisors to tell me otherwise, I may have been gaining momentum with my business, but I was acting like a bitch in the process. No wonder Ken called me an asshole.

Six months into my life as a small business owner, Ken still hadn't found footing in his new job, and we started to get low on cash. I had a couple clients but not enough to generate any sort of financial confidence. Knowing I couldn't possibly live with my parents again (because let's face it, they would never let me live in a cardboard box), I sold the engagement ring Colby had given me and felt a little pressure release. It was a hard day, but I knew the reality of the cash was more significant than the memory of the lost love.

A few months later, in another momentary lapse of reasoning, I succumbed to my old limiting beliefs of me "not being enough," and my fear of failure crept back in. Rather than let failure win, I worked five times harder until I felt like I had won the race against my fear. The next time, however, I started to doubt my abilities to "make it big in the design world" and my limiting beliefs were yelling so loudly that I actually listened and started bartending a couple nights a week in the hopes of making some extra cash.

Half-way through a crazy shift, one of my prominent clients walked in. I turned my back to the customers at the bar and prayed that he wouldn't recognize me. Vacillating between desire and fear, I was playing high-end residential designer by day and mid-level tequila slinging server by night. Ashamed to think I would become better known for crafting cocktails rather than designing dreams, I spent the rest of my shift dodging the eyes of my client. It was exhausting and not worth the anxiety of getting caught. I didn't want to hide parts of who I was anymore, and the sudden realization that I was quite literally hiding behind the bar had me seeing the light that bartending wasn't the answer. I quit at the end of my shift.

When I got home that night, Ken had already passed out on the sofa. While I had been averting awkward glances from a client, he had been out partying and tipping his waitresses and bartenders the same amount I had made that whole night. We got in a huge blowout, and he moved out the next day. My attention hadn't just been divided between success and failure. I had ignored Ken's pleas for affection and neglected my relationship with him entirely. With all of my focus on becoming successful in my business, I left absolutely no room for love.

Exhausted and alone, I convinced myself that come hell or high water, I would figure out a better way. I was going to make this work. **No. Matter. What**. The following Monday, I dedicated even more energy towards my goal of success and adjusted my approach once again. I rewrote my marketing plan, revised my mission statement, and kept pushing forward. Convincing myself I didn't have time to mourn the loss of another relationship, I layered more responsibilities on top of my broken heart and buried my pain in more project proposals. Plus, I didn't want to cry anymore. It had already cost me too much time trying to repair our relationship, and I had a lot of work to do.

I became a relentless networker and proceeded to call, email, and knock on every contractor and architect office door until they responded and gave me the time of day. One local builder finally opened the door and said, "Great timing. My brother and I just bought a spec house, and this would be a great opportunity to try out a new designer. If it works out, great. If it doesn't, too bad."

That first house was about 4,000 square feet in size and located right on the ocean. I had carte blanche on the interior finish and fixture decisions and was tossed right into the project, vowing to do the best I possibly could. The renovation was a huge success. I continued to work with that builder on more projects ranging from restaurants, movie theaters, and office spaces to dozens of residential homes. The spider web of connections that evolved from this single project helped lay the solid foundation of interwoven associations that have solidified my design career, and it's been full steam ahead ever since.

Through my own baptism by fire, I learned just how demanding being a business owner could be and just how much it costs as well. None of what I did was easy. Going out on my own was one of the most terrifying things I have ever done in my life, but it was also the most gratifying. I can't even count the number of times I cried myself to sleep thinking it was the biggest mistake of my life. Or adversely, forgot to celebrate the completion of an amazing project because I had so much more work to do for other clients. I took a leap of faith, combined my previous job and life experiences, embraced the opportunity for change, and threw my heart and soul into building a business. Ironically, the two words that had driven me to start my own company in the first place, "freedom" and "flexibility," were totally elusive as I was working harder and was less flexible than I had ever been in my whole life.

"We must be willing to get rid of the life we've planned,
so as to have the life that is waiting for us. The old skin
has to be shed before the new one can come."

~ *Joseph Campbell*

ANGEL INVESTOR

On the anniversary of my first year in business (still struggling, but with my head above water), I was invited to lunch with the owner of the development company for which I had specified finishes and fixtures between 2006 and 2008. I had always admired him and his companies, so I was thrilled when he reached out as a "Congratulations on making it a year." I had run into him in the parking lot at the architectural firm across from his office just before I quit and had told him about my plans. I was honored that he remembered and wanted to get together.

Throughout lunch he generously offered me advice on how to improve what I had started and what to expect as my network and net worth expanded. He touched on the chaos that surrounded my life for a few years (he knew about the affair since it was with one of his employees) and complimented me on my tenacity to push through it all and start my own business. I blushed, wishing no one knew about any of that, but also thanked him for believing in me.

When we were finished, he handed me a card with a large philanthropic "gift" inside, making me promise that I would use it wisely to invest in myself and my company. He said he planned on congratulating me again when I beat the odds of most entrepreneurs and hit my ten-year work anniversary. I was shocked and overwhelmed by his generosity but accepted the money graciously and agreed to his promise.

I hit that ten-year work anniversary in 2020, but I wasn't able to thank him because he had been killed in a bicycle accident in early 2019. I look up often and feel blessed by my angel investor for believing in me as I continue to blaze trails for other female entrepreneurs and anyone who has been through hell and back again, looking for another chance.

"Here's to the crazy ones. The misfits. The rebels. The troublemakers. The round pegs in the square holes. The ones who see things differently ... Because the people who are crazy enough to think they can change the world are the ones who do."

~ *Steve Jobs*

DEAR DIARY

I took a giant risk, but I had faith in my professional abilities and made the most with everything I had. I didn't let the fear of failing stand in my way and made my dream of becoming an entrepreneur my reality.

1. What do you dream about doing? What would be your ideal job? Write it down, and don't forget to get very specific in the details.
2. When in your life have you been faced with making a decision that would either make or break you? Were you able to rise above the fear and take the leap? Or did you succumb to your fears and stay in a safe position?
3. Change your story, change your life. It's about understanding what drives you and what you need to do to reach your goals. What motivates you, and do you need to change to find or create your ideal job?

When the Student is Ready, the Teacher will Appear.

Part 3

CONTINUING EDUCATION

"It is a lifelong quest for more knowledge, more courage, more humility, and more belief. Because when you summon the strength and discipline to live like that, the only thing limiting your horizons is you."

~ *David Goggins*

In order to maintain a valid certificate for certain degrees or career choices, we are often required to take continuing education courses to stay current with new theories, methods, discoveries, and further developed knowledge available to us within our industries. But I believe we can take that same approach to our lives outside the requirements of our jobs and our careers. We are not born with an instruction manual for life, and there are resources everywhere that can teach us how to do our day-to-day and year-to-year better than just flying by the seat of our pants.

I was exposed to some of these continuing education resources when I started my own business. As my entrepreneurial career progressed and my love life declined, a grand opportunity to learn beyond my own resources presented itself to me in the form of a coach. The lessons that were implemented (and are still being implemented) in my life inside and outside of my business have become integral to creating the life I want. They are part of the connection between the past—and what I've always known—and the future—and what I've always wanted.

We are emotional beings, and learning how to navigate the terrain of your heart and soul, adjust your direction, and redraw your map is how you can excel with your dreams and reach your goals. Courage and belief come from within, and empowerment can be created.

8

THE POWER of COACHING

Adjust Your Perspective to Make Changes in Your Life

"A coach is someone who tells you what you don't want to hear. Who has you see what you don't want to see, so you can be who you've always known you could be."

~ Tom Landry

SPRING, 2012

While waiting for my friends in the back of the room, I was approached by a tall, confident woman.

"Hi," she said, wearing a beaming smile and a navy-blue power suit. "What do you think of the presentation?" We were at a women's symposium about women harnessing our natural gifts to step confidently into leadership and management roles.

Slightly startled by her presence since she came up behind me, I looked up and smiled. Responding in a flurry about how motivating I had found the morning session, I then hinted at my giddy anticipation for the second half of the day. Our conversation flowed easily and naturally until she paused and politely said, "Amanda, it's been lovely chatting with you. Would you mind if I come sit with you for the second half of the program?"

"Not at all. That would be great. Except, I didn't get your name."

"It's Debbie. And it's a pleasure to meet you."

The following week, Debbie and I met for coffee, and she asked me one great question after the next. I hadn't met many other women that were as interested in talking about business as I was, so I was eager to keep answering her prompts. I felt amazing as we hugged good-bye and agreed to meet again in a couple weeks.

Super excited for our next breakfast together, I woke up early that morning, dressed as if I were meeting a new client, and arrived ten minutes before our meeting time. I was never early for anything, but something about this woman had me changing my routine almost instantly. We had so much to talk about. She was attentive and interested in what I had to say. I felt like I could chat with her for days. Towards the end of our meal, it dawned on me that I had done all the talking both times we met and knew nothing about her. After a sip of coffee I asked, "Debbie, what do you do for work?"

She laughed and replied, "Well, Amanda, I'm glad you *finally* asked. I am a business and life coach."

My heart did a little flutter.

I knew I needed someone like her in my life. I'd had a few soccer coaches and college professors that made positive, inspirational impacts on my life, but after college, I never had a consistent or intentionally qualified guide that I could rely on for advice in a time of need. Meeting Debbie was a dream come true.

Curious, I asked her more questions. She elaborated on her philosophical principles and coaching strategy sessions. She explained how every call was based around gaining clarity, recognizing opportunities, and goal setting. She noted that as a coach, her job was to hold her clients accountable for their personal and professional development. I was enamored by her assertive demeanor and wanted whatever she had, so I listened to every syllable she uttered. She got quite specific about incorporating time-management skills and financial improvements into all of her clients' lives (she said all, not some or most, but *all*). When she got to the point of increased self-awareness, confidence, and better relationships, I was in awe. For the first time in three meetings, I was totally speechless.

"So, Amanda, does this sound like something you would be interested in investing in?"

Like a kid about to ride a pony for the first time I was practically jumping out of my seat.

"YES!" I blurted out. "Absolutely! Yes! It sounds like everything I need. But, what does it cost?"

Calm and cool, she stated, "It's fifteen hundred dollars for ten fifty-minute phone calls."

My heart did a backflip. What? Fifteen hundred dollars? For a few phone calls? She had to be out of her freaking mind! That was more than my mortgage payment! And $150 an hour was more than double what I charged for my own services. Her answer felt like a punch in the gut. I wanted her help and insights so badly, but it felt beyond my reach.

Defeated and hopeless, I replied, "Oh. It's THAT much?" I paused to gather my thoughts. "I'm sorry to have wasted your time. I don't think I can afford it."

She gently placed her hand on my arm, "Amanda, you haven't wasted any of my time. I would not have continued to meet with you if I didn't think you were worth it."

"Debbie, even if I were to get another project or two, that kind of expense is just not in my budget right now."

"You are a creative and well-connected woman. I know you have the resources to fund this investment, if you believe in yourself."

Her direct challenge of my self-worth hit a nerve that had me quickly shifting my perspective from I can't do this to I **have** to do this. I *am* creative and well-connected. I wanted to prove to her I was capable of taking on her strategy sessions and better yet, become her best client. However my strong and powerful self-doubt had me questioning the opportunity and wondering if I was worth it. If I could find the resources to start my *business*, why the hell wasn't I able to invent the belief in *myself*? What the hell was stopping me? Why was I so afraid of committing to this opportunity?

I pushed past my doubts and asked, "How quickly does this program start to work? How long does it take?"

Seeing me come around a little, she once again shifted the energy of the conversation.

"We would need to work fast. You'll need to set aside three hours every week for the next two months, and with the results, I guarantee you'll be able to afford it, and so much more."

Calculating all this time and money in my head I looked away from her again because I became overwhelmed with limiting beliefs of lack of time and lack of money. My breakfast started to bubble up inside my gut. I felt ill. My mind vacillated between intrigue and feelings of lack. I didn't know what to do, which was a clear indication as to why I needed her so much. But I just didn't believe in myself enough to have confidence and take action.

Sensing my trepidation, she interrupted my thoughts and said, "Amanda, listen to me. If you do this, and I mean *really* commit to the program and do the work, I guarantee you'll see results long before the ten sessions are up, and the fifteen hundred dollars will be one of the best investments you *ever* make."

"How can you guarantee that?"

"You just have to believe me."

How the hell was I supposed to believe her when I barely even knew her?!

"How about this," she pushed. "After the first five conversations, if you've been doing the work, and you don't start seeing results, I will give you all of your money back. You can keep all of the books that are included with the program and any proprietary information I give you. But you have to *promise* to do the work."

It sounded too good to be true. As I sat there, staring into the eyes of this woman full of grace and certainty, wondering how in the world I was going to pull this off, a tall, older gentleman walked by our table, diverting my attention for a brief moment. From the back he looked like the developer I'd had lunch with a few months earlier. I did a double take, and when he turned around, I quickly realized it wasn't him. But damn—it could have been his twin.

Aware that the universe acts in funny ways sometimes, I took this dobbleganger's presence as a sign to take a chance on myself and was reminded that I actually *could* afford this "investment in myself" with the gift I had received from my developer friend.

Repositioning my energy away from my ruling self-doubt that tried to take over, I determined the potential outcome was worth the risk. I accepted Debbie's offer right then and there.

As I drove out of the parking lot, minus a mortgage payment and feeling a little like I just got swindled by a con artist, a strange sense of peace slowly settled over me. Driving home in silence I started to fantasize about what my life could eventually be like with the help of a professional coach. I envisioned the freedom and flexibility I had been working so hard for within the business that had now taken over my life.

A box of books arrived the very next day, and I had my first coaching session two days later.

Debbie was right. That fifteen hundred dollar check was *the* best investment I've ever made because I invested in myself.

"It is, indeed, a simple task provided one is willing to pay the price in time and concentration until each principle becomes a part of one's personality; until each principle becomes a habit in 'living.'"

~ *Og Mandino*

When I started working in the design/construction world, it was filled mostly with men. Rather than stand strong and assert my intelligence and skills, I felt like I had to dumb down my feminine power and intellect, and prove myself as smart, creative, and "one of the guys." I was afraid of being perceived as weak, inferior, pretentious, and—God-forbid—feminine. I wanted to be accepted and well-respected. My theories back-fired, though, when I realized that trying to be equal to the guys on-site was just lessening my value as a professional and a business owner, causing me to stay in the trenches longer than I would have liked.

Enter Debbie. She educated me on the importance of maintaining polarity in relationships (light/dark, masculine/feminine, the ever illusive push/pull), and defining our purpose in life. She helped me realign my misguided concepts of the strength women embody. And with her guidance, I started reshaping my understanding of how to function within relationships both on and off the job site. I wrote my business mission statement *and* my personal mission statement. I worked on my S.W.O.T. (Strengths, Weaknesses, Opportunities, Threats) for my business *and* for myself. She had me doing market research for a better understanding of what similar business owners were charging for the services I provided *and* understanding what it meant to own my worth. I started uncovering what I really wanted in my life and designed plans on how to get it. Through her coaching exercises and open lines of communication, I started believing in myself more and found higher levels of self-respect, empowerment, and confidence that superseded any expectations I had ever had for myself.

Debbie danced around self-doubt and fear like they were candles on a birthday cake, barely even flinching. With her support, I started to see that I didn't need to prove myself anymore, and that I was doing an amazing job. Her commitment to me provided the encouragement I had yearned for most of my life. With a few gentle yet deliberate nudges, I was able to shift my "women are weak" perception to the growth mindset that, "feminine is ferocious," which led to my self-esteem rising, and subsequently, my company profits increasing as well. It was clear she knew what she was doing, and I was learning the ropes from a pro.

One of the most interesting exercises she had me do was called the "Ideal Partner." I had to create a list of what I did and didn't want in my ideal partner. I also had to consider what my ideal partner did and didn't want in his ideal partner. It was easy listing all the great things I wanted and equally easy listing out all the nonsense and bullshit I'd dealt with in the past that I would no longer tolerate. But when I had to turn the pen around and write out the things I thought this "ideal partner" desired, I saw that I needed to adjust a few (too many) things within my own personality and habits in order to attract him. It was hard.

To turn the mirror back on myself and dig into the source of some of my attitudes, habits, and concepts of what love should be was a tough lesson I wasn't ready to learn back in 2015 when Debbie presented this to me. So, rather than finish the exercise, I completed the first two parts, flaked on the second two, then moved on to the vision board exercise, which was more creative, more entertaining, and certainly not as emotionally challenging as taking ownership of where and how I might not be "perfect."

I knew I was growing as a woman, but self-doubts of my value in business and my personal life still plagued me. Debbie would often use the phrase "How you do anything is how you do everything," and years later, I was finally able to understand what she meant. I knew I was on the right path in my business, but I was neglecting some of my personal relationships, and at times, my health.

As I was learning strategies of how to aim higher and succeed, I could still feel the chains of criticism from other people holding me back. Their judgments about my work ethic would feed into my fear of failure and doubts about whether I was doing the right thing or not, resulting in me making poor decisions, like partying too much, or even business deals that would negatively affect me in all areas of my life. My limiting belief of being too much for others nested in the back of my mind, strangling my forward momentum. I would feel the force of its dizzying impact every day and without balancing out my life's equation, by subtracting the negative influence of others, I single handedly prevented myself from creating the life I *really* wanted.

2015–2016: OPPOSING OPPORTUNITIES

Towards the end of 2015, Debbie invited me to a networking/coaching event in Florida. She told me it would be a motivational experience to excel my coaching career and would enforce the lessons she had been teaching me. When I calculated the cost of the event, airfare, accommodations and food, along with me not working for the entire week I'd be there, it would cost about $12,000. *Jesus,* I thought, *that's gotta be one hell of an event!* My business was doing well, but not spending $12,000 at a networking/coaching event well. So, I politely declined and got frustrated that she even asked me.

Debbie knew my current financial situation. She knew how much I needed to work. She knew I didn't have the time to do a fraction of the things I wanted, let alone take a week away from my business. So why did she think it was okay to put that kind of pressure on me? I didn't think it was fair and was embarrassed that she thought I was ready, when I believed I clearly was not. Unfortunately, at that time, I had no idea what kind of value and impact *that* kind of opportunity could have brought me because I allowed my limiting beliefs, not my empowerment and confidence, to rule my decision.

Regardless of my perceived inability to afford Debbie's offer, my design business was, in-reality, doing well. However, my typical see-saw regulation tactic of if business was great, my relationship was not, and if my relationship was great, the business was not, hadn't yet changed.

At this point in my life, I was starting to feel the tick-tock of my biological clock and was "more or less" on the hunt for a life partner with the everlasting hope that I could still have a family one day. During the first six years of running my business, I had bounced from one unavailable guy to the next, flowing in and out of relationships that were either fleeting or simply not right. In most cases I stayed in the relationship too long because my fear of being alone still haunted me in more ways than I understood, so I would attach myself to any "potential" commitment, whether it was right for me or not.

When the results of the 2015 financial year returned, I patted myself on the back for achieving my most profitable year to date. But rather than spending even more time on my business by attending one of those events Debbie had invited me to, I turned my attention towards "balancing out" my see-saw, and decided to put more time into my personal life instead. I had been dating Eddie for about six months, and I felt like it was time to take our relationship more seriously.

Eddie was an elite soccer coach who matched almost all of my "ideal partner" details. He was motivated, comical, and sexy as hell. And our chemistry together was off the charts. We had a ton of fun, and I just went with it. And, as my typical see-saw would have it, as soon as he came into my life I reluctantly side-stepped a few of Debbie's coaching exercises, replacing the time I would typically spend on coaching with time spent on my relationship. I wanted love so bad that I was willing to put my personal progress on the back burner and go after it one more time.

Ironically, Eddie questioned why I needed a coach. He was impressed with my success and would ask why I kept working to improve myself. He "liked me just as I was." His confusion on coaching confused me, since he was one, but I was so enamored by him and the opportunity for love that I didn't bother explaining my reasons. In fact, I was so deep into our relationship that I wouldn't understand how his unsupportive perception of life coaches impacted the confidence I had towards my work with Debbie until much later. I couldn't see that he felt threatened by my growth as a successful woman.

Eddie had doubts (like Colby) about what I did for my job and how I was working with all the contractors. I assured him over and over that he had nothing to worry about, and I had "cleaned up my act," but his doubts created insecurities in both of us that eventually became toxic. He also challenged my work schedule. He assumed that since I worked for myself, I could adjust my schedule to fit his. But it wasn't that easy, and I didn't know how to make him understand. Debbie questioned why I had let myself fall into a relationship of "in"-convenience with a man who was a little demanding and a lot insecure, and suddenly my see-saw felt totally out of balance and a little out of control.

Over the years, Debbie and I had developed an incredible bond and a significant level of trust. As I became more involved with Eddie, Debbie watched from the sidelines. One day she even leveraged our trust to tell me that she thought I was making some bad decisions with him. She politely observed that my Sunday night outings with Eddie and his boys were negatively affecting how I started my week. She implied I could do better and said I was playing small, which challenged my decision making and my heart. I didn't want to think that she knew me better than I knew myself.

When she suggested I take a step back from Eddie to determine if this relationship was in my best and highest interests, I took a step back from her instead. I didn't like what she had to say and got pissed off by her mothering. I have never liked anyone disapproving my actions, regardless of whether they were right or not, so Debbie's scrutiny of my relationship made me feel like I wasn't smart enough to see it for myself. My old tactic of "I'll show you" had me digging in my heels to prove that I knew what I was doing, and rather than heed the advice of my most amazing mentor, friend, and support system, I "broke up" with Coach Debbie and made the powerful and emotional decision to turn my focus towards Coach Eddie instead.

"It's not what's happening to you now or what has happened in your past that determines who you become. Rather, it's your decisions about what to focus on, what things mean to you, and what you're going to do about them that will determine your ultimate destiny."

~ *Tony Robbins*

DEAR DIARY

Coaching is a powerful tool. When used properly, it can be one of the most effective instruments in our toolbox. The "ideal partner" exercise is below. I have since finished it (a few times) and realized that sometimes the hardest things to do are the most rewarding.

The Ideal Partner Exercise

1. Divide a piece of paper into four sections.
2. In the top left section, make a list of all the qualities you desire in your ideal partner, lover, husband, wife, boss, etc. Things to contemplate could be: sharing the same values, having success and happiness in their career, the desire for travel, their smell, must love dogs, needs to get along with my kids, etc.
3. In the top right section, list all the qualities you do not desire in a partner. Some on my list are bad teeth, drinks too much, financially unstable, "busy" all the time, disrespectful to others, signs of narcissism, and anger issues.

4. The bottom left section is reserved for *your* top qualities. What do you think your ideal partner would want for their ideal partner? My list includes characteristics like being organized, good personal hygiene, loves to travel, genuinely happy, emotionally stable, motivated, and has a growth mindset.
5. Now the bottom right corner is where the work really happens. List out all the things you know your ideal partner doesn't want within their ideal relationship. Believe in the power of perception and do a little examination on what you perceive to be important, worthy, or unnecessary in your life.

9

FIND YOUR "SOMETHING"

Understand Your Driving Force and Renovate Your Emotional Home

"There is a powerful driving force inside every human being that once unleashed, can make any vision, any dream, any desire a reality."

~ Tony Robbins

FALL, 2016

Intending to merge my living space and rented office into one larger house, I sold my two-bedroom condo in the fall of 2016 at a price my realtor told me was fair market value. What I didn't realize was that "fair market value" happened at the lowest point of the real estate market, and I barely made any money on my investment. Since I couldn't find what I was looking for fast enough, I rented a bright, quiet, three-story beach house for the winter while I searched for my dream home.

I thought I would quickly find a place that checked all my boxes, but as spring flourished, my options and my dreams started to fade. The real estate market had skyrocketed quickly right after I sold and then leveled out over the winter with high prices and low inventory. Being slammed at work and having to undergo knee surgery in April (due to a skiing accident two years prior), I had run out of time in my temporary beachside oasis and was quickly losing hope in finding my "perfect house." When I was reminded that the beach house rental rate was tripling in June, I panicked and felt forced to make a quick, misaligned decision that landed me in a less-than-desirable apartment complex on the other side of town.

In late May 2017, I bounced from the beautiful bungalow with views of the ocean and sounds of seagulls to a second-floor, one-bedroom apartment overlooking a parking lot within earshot of the highway. It only had one large window looking out the front and one sliding door looking out the back, which meant it was really dark most of the time.

I hated that place.

I stacked all of my belongings in boxes behind curtains in the living room because I was too cheap to get a storage unit and hoped the boxes would provide a bit of sound insulation from the noisy neighbors.

Over the next two years, I must have attended over two hundred open houses and couldn't find what I wanted or needed. My realtor nicknamed me "Goldilocks" because everything I looked at was either too big or too small, too dark or too old, too expensive or needed too much work, it was missing a garage or a barn, or… something was off. On the rare occasion I would put in an offer, a bidding war would ensue, I'd get scared I couldn't afford it, and I would back out. I felt stuck in hell with little to no help.

Eddie had accompanied me on a few open house tours, but he often wasn't available when I needed him because of his coaching programs. I let his unavailability slide most of the time because our mad love for each other would make up for our lack of corresponding schedules. We had a fiery connection, courageous laughs, and many wild nights. We danced along the misconceptions that we would become a "power couple" and that this status would be enough to keep our love alive. But even with all our fun and heated passion, unhealthy jealousy, competition, and a detrimental lack of trust between us always got in the way.

Our theories on how to reach our individual and relationship goals varied widely, and our schedules conflicted greatly. I was consumed with running my design business, working twelve-to-fourteen-hour weekdays, while his soccer coaching schedule was based on evening training sessions and weekend tournaments. He said I worked too much and gave him too little attention. I rebutted by pointing out he partied too much and that he was around too little when I needed him. We never set out to argue, but we didn't know how to talk through our issues without making the conflicts worse, so when we fought, we fought hard. Not knowing how to honor each other's needs, we avoided the issues altogether and numbed ourselves with bourbon, beer, and Indian food instead.

Something was off between us, and it kept getting more difficult to tolerate as time went on. Our hearts would swoon one week, then our heads would take over, and layers of misunderstanding and arguments would sweep in the next. Nights would be spent drinking and fighting, and days would be lost sobering up and apologizing. The pattern was repeated, and neither of us realized it was a classic case of codependency that needed more heartfelt nurturing than mindless accusations. Whenever the energy of suspicion swirled around us, self-doubt would sabotage my ability to defend myself, and I'd retreat to my emotional home of shutting down. Meanwhile, Eddie would lean into his patterns of anger that I simply could not manage. It wore us both out, and at some point, I realized that something needed to change.

While working with Debbie, I created a large vision board of my perfect life via magazine clippings and photographs that I hung in my crowded living room. It had images of a beautiful seaside house with hardwood floors, swanky architectural details, cozy furnishings, as well as palm trees, diamond rings, and a picture of me with a goofy heart circled around my head. The irony of me being a successful interior designer living in this shit-hole apartment with stained nylon carpet and only two windows looking out to nowhere made me want to punch that fucking vision board every time I walked by it. I was dreadfully ashamed that I put myself in this predicament and felt my goals of an "ideal house" and "ideal relationship" drifting further and further away. My limiting beliefs, feelings of hopelessness, and misperceptions of importance were stacked in the boxes that surrounded me, and I didn't know how to get rid of them. So, instead of unpacking them, I buried myself in work and ignored it all.

—

A year and a half into the all-consuming spiral of Eddie and my embarrassing living situation, I could feel my depression starting to niggle, and I knew that if I didn't do something soon, I would go down that dark rabbit hole again. Looking to shake things up, I searched for an inspirational vacation that might snap me (or us) out of our unhealthy cycle.

An ad for a Tony Robbins event in New Jersey called, "Unleash the Power Within (UPW)," was scheduled for November 2018, and the alluring words "Life Changing… Powerful… Destiny…" grabbed my attention. Even though I had initially envisioned a bikini, cocktails, bare feet on a beach, bongos, and a blanket of stars, I figured this four-day event at a convention center might be the transformative something I was looking for.

I re-read the promises the event offered, thought about it for about thirty seconds, and bought one ticket.

Eddie wasn't able to come with me anyway. He had a tournament that weekend.

NOVEMBER, 2018: UPW

Day one was like a freaking rock concert. Tony exploded onto the stage like a puppeteer and did his marionette magic with all 14,000 people in attendance. When he danced, we danced. When he jumped, we jumped. He told stories that had people oohing and aahing. We were all there learning about life, exposing our vulnerability, and coming up with deeper and more impactful realizations than anyone could have ever imagined. We sobbed through admitting our deepest secrets with total strangers, then laughed at each other until our sides ached. And it felt like it went on for an eternity.

Tony's hour-long guided meditation felt like something out of an exorcism movie. In an absolutely pitch-black stadium, he brought us to our most feared and darkest places. He kept us there, imagining and practically feeling the devastating effects of not changing anything in our lives, never reaching any of our dreams or desires. People were screaming bloody murder from all around the stadium, and even though I couldn't see anything, I was afraid to open my eyes, petrified that my depressed and homeless future would be staring me in the face. It was awful.

Then, suddenly, he changed his tune. His words of hope, encouragement, and guidance pulled us out of the dusty depths of our despair like a vacuum cleaner sucking up cotton balls. The entire stadium went from hell to heaven in a matter of seconds via Tony's enlightening encouragement and promise of change, which shifted the energy so quickly that I could almost feel the breeze of negativity blowing out of the building. We opened our eyes, and through the magic of meditation and the power of visualization, we were able to see our lives transformed into beauty, love, and success in a matter of moments.

Around midnight, Tony told us to leave our belongings and shoes in the stadium and follow him to the park down the street. So, we did. All 14,000 people wandering through the streets of Newark, New Jersey, in the middle of the night with no shoes on.

I could feel the dirt and nastiness of the street on my bare feet as we traipsed through back alleys and fenced-off parking lots. Why I had agreed to leave my shoes behind was now a total mystery to me. This was nuts!

Hesitancy raced through my blood, and all I could do was hope that someone had an idea about what would happen because I had never done this before. The sky was lit up with a smoggy, dark orange haze, and the musical accompaniment was the increasingly loud and out-of-sync banging of drums paired with screams from 14,000 people being drawn like zombies toward some magical light. It felt like craziness was erupting all around me, and it freaked me out a little.

The momentum from the march drew us closer towards the light, and as we entered the park, the frozen pavement turned to stiff grass and then from grass to frigid mud. With the cold-soaked earth now oozing between my toes, I put my faith in the masses, let go of my hesitation and fear, and gave in to the experience once and for all. And I let my concerns of uncertainty and doubt disappear into the cold wintery air with every breath I took.

I could feel the heat of the impending challenge tickle my chilled skin while the rising rhythm of deafening excitement pulsed through my veins. The crowd was advancing in droves, chanting, "Yes, yes, yes, yes!" The volume of the event synced with my rising adrenaline the closer we got to the front of the line. As we got closer, I could hardly hear myself think, but I also knew I didn't need to. It wasn't my head guiding me anymore; it was the combination of my soul, my heart, and this enchanted crowd that kept pushing me towards what I could now see as rows of fire.

As I stood amongst these people, I hadn't known fourteen hours earlier, but who now knew some of my deepest darkest secrets, there was an innate understanding amongst us all. I knew they knew what they needed to know about me, and I knew what I needed to know about them. We were all here for the same reason. We were all here to change. Every single person was there to find their something and break through whatever was holding us back.

Heat from the bright red coals defrosted my mud coated toes as I advanced to the front of the line. Standing on the edge between darkness and light, amidst the roars of encouragement all around me, I paused and looked up at the sky. A couple of stars twinkled down at me, and for a split second, I heard nothing but felt everything. My internal silence had covered me with a blanket of peace and I suddenly felt whole, complete, and perfect.

Everything I needed was in me.

In this moment, I had found my something.

Smiling big and bold, I took a giant breath in, and with passion erupting from my soul, I let out a tribal scream, looked straight ahead, and walked along thirty feet of fiery coals towards the "something" I had come here to discover.

"Cool moss, cool moss, cool moss…" I whispered as I floated above the flames. Reaching the end, the pit crew rinsed my feet with cold water while hot tears of emotional exhaustion soaked my face. I took two more steps forward into the all-consuming embrace and support of my fellow event attendees as we celebrated with joyous screams.

Holy shit! NOTHING was going to stop us now! We jumped up and down, we cried, and we hugged each other tight. It was one of the most outrageous, awakening nights of my life. No drugs. No alcohol. Just pure adrenaline, will-power and the force of thousands of people energizing my path of awareness to who I was about to become.

The next morning, I woke up at 7 a.m. like someone shot me out of a cannon. My eyes felt like sandpaper, my nose was raw from blowing with cheap tissues, and I had lost most of my voice from screaming. I was at the stadium by 9 a.m., high-fiving and hugging my fellow FIREWALKERS like they were long lost besties. I had entered into some freaky energetic bubble and loved every second of it.

I drank Tony's kool-aid through a firehose, and for the next three days I sat on the edge of my seat listening to him and his cohorts talk about Practical Psychology, Driving Forces, and Limiting Beliefs. They touched on topics related to health, and wealth, and science, and business. It was incredible the amount of information they crammed into that event, and I absorbed whatever I could of the vast depth and breadth of resources he's accumulated in his more than sixty outstanding years on this earth. I couldn't believe I had never seen this guy before.

My soul felt like it was waking up for the first time, and I could feel myself evolving. If he had the ability to make me feel this powerful, this amazing, and motivate me to change my attitude and my habits in order to create a better life for myself, then I wanted as much as I could get.

This was the first of ten Tony Robbins events I've attended between 2018 and 2023, and I have stretched and grown and expanded who I am at every single one of them.

YOUR EMOTIONAL HOME

One of the most impactful lessons I learned through Tony's teachings is how the driving forces behind the "Six Human Needs" affect everyone. I was in awe as Tony broke down the science and the art behind what drives all humans, and how he surmised how these needs are similar throughout the world, regardless of culture, race, age, or religion. Once the relationship between our drive and our reactions started to become clear, I opened up to the concept that we all have the ability to redirect our journeys with just a few adjustments here and there. **I found resolution and understanding through it all and finally could see the personal renovations I needed to make within my own "home."**

As children, we are shaped by the effects of our experiences, which become driving forces behind our belief systems and our emotional homes. Both consciously and unconsciously we then prioritize things in our lives (both positively and negatively), and these priorities are calculated based on different levels of needs that fuel our actions, responses, desires, and directions. The importance of meeting each of our needs is the magnet that calibrates our decision-making compass and also shapes who we become during the course of our lives.

We have the power to change the order and priority of these needs *if we want to.* We just need to understand what they are so that we can adjust them according to *how we are* currently living our lives versus *how we want to* live our lives.

I learned that the Six Human Needs include Certainty, Uncertainty/Variety, Significance, Love/Connection, Growth, and Contribution. Each of them relates to our ability and understanding of pain and pleasure; our need for change or variety; feeling unique or special; feeling close or needed; and expanding our abilities and supporting others.[6]

My Six Human Needs order has changed a few times since UPW 2018 (thankfully), but it doesn't mean I was initially wrong or that I'll be right when I'm done. It simply boils down to a better understanding of what I want and who I aim to become. In 2018, this was my original order:

- **Significance.** Once I realized that conformity wasn't really my thing, I oozed my need for significance into everything I did and eventually I got to a point where I *had to be heard* (all the freaking time) and practically paid for recognition so I could *prove to the world* I was good enough. I wasn't loud and aggressive because I thought I was awesome; I was loud because I was *afraid.* I demanded attention because I was *terrified* I'd be forgotten, ignored, or left behind. Significance *was* my numero uno when I started, but as I uncovered the real root of my tattered emotional home, I saw that my need for significance was actually keeping me from reaching most of my goals.
- **Certainty.** "Sure as Shit." One of my favorite sayings. I kept control of whatever I could, whenever I had the chance (although my emotions didn't always know this was the plan). If I didn't know what was going on, I didn't trust what was happening. Because Significance ("Look at me!") and Certainty ("I've got this!") were taking up a lot of space at the top of my list, there wasn't much room left for my heart or soul to grow. What a realization *this* was! I was in my head—all the flipping time.
- **Uncertainty/Variety.** If you like challenges (and I do), and you are willing to take chances (and I am), and are afraid of getting stuck (like a lot of us), then this may be one of your top needs. An adrenaline junkie at heart, variety was always a requirement for me. The quandary of this force is that it can also mean a lack of commitment or conviction or an unhealthy addiction to options and change of scenery. The more I learn, the more I understand, but honestly, this one still trips me up.
- **Love/Connection.** Becoming aware of where we prioritize Love and Connection can be eye-opening and liberating. I wanted love more than anything in the world, but I didn't know how to love myself, therefore I had no idea how to truly love others in a healthy way. My greatest fear was being alone, but my drive for

Significance would often drive people away so Love was flailing behind in the dust of my drive for success and acknowledgement. (This quickly got moved to the top position and has remained there for the past five years. Amazing how adjusting one perspective can shift an entire life.)

- **Growth.** Since I jumped on this Tony train, and since my level of understanding of who I really am has expanded, Growth has become a hot second with the intention of advancement, progress, and learning always being priorities. But when this journey of self-discovery started, I had no idea the importance of leaning into the process and how growing spiritually could heal and empower me.
- **Contribution.** Those of us driven by contribution often feel their best when we are giving rather than receiving. "Giving is Living," and it can come in many ways and means.

Learning the original order of my needs was a slap in the face. I actually consider it to be my initial awakening and learned to assess each of my needs and driving forces so I could reprioritize their levels of importance. I uncovered the intersections of my patterns and problems and started redesigning my lifestyle to become healthier, more fulfilled, and more purpose driven in all areas of my life. **However, this also meant that I needed to clear out old ways of thinking to make room for the new version of me to thrive.**

—

After the intense four day "kick-in-the-ass festival," I had become a *Firewalker* and wasn't going to let anything stop me. When I got home, I saw the world as a very different place. My perspective had acutely changed, and I intentionally set my focus towards renovating my "emotional home" to better myself and my life. I made the following list of what I wanted and needed (more and less of) in my life:

— More self-awareness and self-respect
— Stronger emotional intelligence and a higher self-worth
— More joy and fun
— More comfort, less nonsense
— More love for myself and my journey
— A lot less bullshit

I jumped back on the house hunting circuit, and after a few months, proudly restored my reputation from Goldilocks back to Amanda in early 2019 by purchasing a bright, airy condo in a vibrant neighborhood. I didn't have water views or a garage, nor was there any space for my design office, but it was just the right size, had lots of natural light, had recently been renovated, and was in a great location. For me, it was perfect.

With all this new passion, knowledge, and intention, I continued to integrate what I learned at UPW with research, books, and podcasts, and adjusted my priorities towards a better understanding of Love. However, regardless of all the work I was doing, I still misinterpreted the important value of time, and didn't give myself, or Eddie, enough of it to incorporate the lessons or adjust our habits. I was all about learning but wasn't practicing, and without the respect of time or attention, our relationship continued to suffer.

I didn't adjust my focus far enough outside of my career to balance my life's see-saw, which meant Eddie remained in second place behind my business, always. It wasn't fair, and even though I said I was trying, I knew I wasn't. Driving forces are embedded deep in our inherent nature and psyche, and it takes time to shift the order. Although I had reprioritized on paper and said I wanted Love to be on top, my Significance wasn't stepping back easily, and no matter how many adjustments we said we were making, the fractured love bond between us wasn't strong enough.

This journal entry, like so many others, was one of the clearest acknowledgements that it was time for me to make some big changes.

February 26, 2019 (two days before my forty-third birthday)

"I'm tired of arguing. But I love him. ...

He's right. Shit. Why the hell are we staying together?

Well—I'm afraid of losing a great friend, a lover.

I'm not afraid of being alone

Oh really? That's bullshit and you know it…

Come on, Amanda, wake up*!*

This is so unhealthy.

Fuck... What am I not seeing?! Why can't I CHANGE FASTER!?

I keep getting mad at him for calling me out on my nonsense. I know I'm wrong for some things, but I also know I'm right for others, and he just doesn't agree. Ahhhhh ... I've been acting this way since I was fourteen. Blaming everyone else, rather than taking responsibility for myself.

Dammit Amanda, grow up…

I'm trying to make it all his fault, but I know I have a lot to do with it. Fuck. Same stupid patterns.

Let go of what no longer serves you, Amanda.

Sure. "Let go..." Easy for you to say.

WTF?! Who am I talking to? Who's in my head?

I've been trying to rewrite my story about relationships ***for years****. But I can't because* ***I'm afraid to let go of the ME I've always been.*** *What the hell am I going to do when I let this shit go? Who will I be then? Who will I become and how will* SHE *deal with this? Oh God... that's scary. I don't know if I am ready for all that change*—BUT you HAVE TO!

Pay Attention, Amanda! *If you want to RE-WRITE the story*—RE-WRITE THE FUCKING STORY!! *It doesn't mean copy and paste over and over again with different characters. It means RE-WRITE. EDIT.* ***CHANGE.*** *ADJUST.* ***START OVER.***

It also means it's time to rid yourself of this "depression" crutch. It's ugly. Doesn't belong here any more...

Ugh. I hate feeling like this.

I have to let go. My fears. My insecurities. My self-doubt (where does this even come from??)... Eddie.

I have to let go of him. There is nothing good happening with us anymore. I've been deflecting and projecting my nonsense for too long. WTF! I've been doing this for thirty plus years. Jesus... wow. thirty years? Really? ....

—Let him go. You guys are killing each other...
—Rewrite your story Amanda. All your design work can wait. ..."

Eddie and I broke up (for the last time) in April 2019, and I was single and alone again, at the age of forty-three. The possibilities of having children were getting further and further away from me.

DEAR DIARY

As we discover various ways to recalibrate our compass and adjust our intentions, we must become aware of where we come from and where we go within our emotions whenever we feel sad or pressured.

If our internal compass is off kilter, then our external worlds will follow suit. If we start renovating our space without a plan, it can turn into a big mess without us realizing it's even happening. Learning about the Six Human Needs was a springboard for my understanding of how I prioritize my life and every*thing* and every*one* in it.

1. Where do you go when you feel sad, or scared, or overwhelmed? Do you become defensive and loud, or shy and quiet? When the going gets tough, does your tough get going or do you hide?

2. Delving into the Six Human Needs: can you identify your Driving Forces and put in order your Six Human Needs? This may take a little time to understand, but once we can see what's driving us, we are able to shift gears, and take the steering wheel of our life back. Is there something missing that you need in order to reprioritize?
3. How has your current order of the Six Human Needs affected your life (both positive and negative)? How would you reorder them if you had the chance?

10

NETWORK CONNECTIONS

Surround Yourself with Courage and Empowerment Will Follow

"Surround yourself with the dreamers and the doers, the believers and the thinkers, but most of all, surround yourself with those who see greatness within you, even when you don't see it yourself."

~ *Edmund Lee*

SUMMER, 2019

In June 2019, I found myself atop a telephone pole in Marco Island, Florida. I knew *why* I was up there, but I wasn't exactly sure how I managed to actually *get* there. With a breathtaking view of the beach and sprawling ocean that made me feel like I was on the edge of the world, I held on tightly to the top of the pole, accompanied only by my thoughts, the rapid rhythm of my terrified breath, and a solitary curious seagull. It was a serene moment, devoid of noise and time. I could have stayed up there, alone, for hours.

—

Ending things with Eddie hurt a lot. On the surface, I was secure and confident, but inside I felt a profound and aching emptiness. For the past three months, I had filled my time with unrealistic project deadlines that kept me chained to my office Monday through Friday, too many boat trips out on Beverly Harbor (accompanied by handles of Captain and Casamigos), and a lot of hiking on the weekends (accompanied by copious amounts of weed). I worked hard and played harder in the hopes that I could distract myself and avoid the lonely gaping hole of another failed relationship that had started to engulf my heart.

A lot of what I had learned at UPW a few months earlier had become distant memories buried under my fear of falling apart. The only person keeping me from drowning in my sorrows was Kerri, my new coach. I had been reminded about the importance of coaching while I was guzzling the Tony kool-aid at UPW and knew it was one of the major ingredients I had been missing in my life. Kerri and I started working together in December 2018, and within a couple sessions, I could feel the value, support, and guidance a great coach could offer. I kicked myself for letting my relationship with Debbie sour and realized what it had cost me in time, emotions, and progress.

The Eddie break-up, however, put another kink in my growth momentum as I retreated back into old habits, like skipping meetings with my new coach in efforts of avoiding the truths I knew she would pull out of me. I wallowed in my sadness and resurfacing depression and allowed these defeated "less than" feelings to take over. Even though I only connected with Kerri a few times between December and June, I knew her guidance made a difference. I just couldn't get out of my own way to let it stick.

In late May, a reminder email about the Marco Island trip arrived in my inbox, and I felt a spark reignite where my dark sense of hopelessness had taken up residence. I had booked this trip for myself on day three of UPW while I was feeling utterly unstoppable. So when the email arrived, I was instantly reminded of the energy, the passion, and the sense of accomplishment I had experienced during that transformative event. For whatever reason, I knew, I just *knew* I had to clear my schedule and get my ass to Florida. I didn't give myself the option; I just made it happen.

The irony was that for the past few months, while I hadn't managed to make myself a priority for an hour here or there and push through the coaching sessions with Kerri, I somehow figured out how to move meetings and change schedules so I could take ten days off from my life.

I think I just needed that vacation I had wanted the prior year, and thought, "Well, at least this event is at a hotel on a beach in the summer and not a stadium in an inner city in the winter."

As soon as I confirmed my flights, my soul thanked me with a sigh of relief, and I could feel the chains of my limiting beliefs and self-doubt slowly breaking free.

As I shifted my weight into my "good leg," the one that didn't have the knee brace on it, I felt the harness pinch my inner thigh and a wave of debilitating fear and panic replaced my temporary peaceful space and lack of time. Thankfully, however, the pinch reminded me that I was wrapped in safety gear with a helmet strapped to my noggin and a cable connected to my back. Looking down fifty feet, I saw the sea of people that had motivated my climb, one rung at a time. I want to say I did it in record "spidey" speed because it felt like I had raced up that pole like Spiderman. But in reality, it took me a few minutes. The lines were blurred, and it didn't matter.

Just one more step up, and I'd be on top. With visions of this "one more step" being my last, I cursed my left knee and reflected back on everything that had happened to me in the past few years: the skiing accident; the money I had lost on projects because I couldn't work; the shitty apartment I had lived in for two years too many; and all the time I had spent creating my business resulting in failed relationships. For some reason, everything pissed me off at that very moment, and I cursed it all.

Then, my legs started shaking followed by my core, my arms, my chest, my mind, and finally my soul joined in on the tremble. I thought I was going to shimmy myself right off that big stick stuck in the sand.

With tears streaming down my face, a hot flash of embarrassment ripped through me and boiled my cursing anger into a full-blown bipolar-type argument inside the tight helmet. My inner voice of encouragement was arguing that I *had* to do this, while my fear was trying to stop me from going any further.

Encouragement would say, "What are you waiting for? You can do this!"

Fear would ask, "Why the fuck are you here? This is ridiculous!"

Encouragement would demand, "You MUST do this!"

Fear would question, "What the HELL were you thinking?!"

This argument was interrupted by the shouts of encouragement from below, "STEP UP!"

I looked down and saw all these people hurling cheers of confidence in my direction.

"YOU'VE GOT THIS, AMANDA!!!"

"LET'S GOOOOOOOO!!"

I cracked a smile. These strangers, all circled at the base of the pole like a school of fish, were supporting my voice of encouragement, successfully drowning out my doubt. More than hearing them, I felt them. The unwavering advocacy of these strangers willing to believe in me when I was struggling to believe in myself gave me the encouragement I needed to stop waffling once and for all.

A sense of calm washed over me, and the arguing silenced. Only one voice was left: my heart. And this time I heard it whispering with a gentle force.

"You did NOT come here to quit. You did NOT climb this pole to just climb back down! You came here to defeat your bullshit, break your habits, and kick your depression! You came here to become the best version of yourself, and GOD DAMMIT Amanda, you are going to step up on to the top of this fucking telephone pole and jump!"

I stared out at the ocean and couldn't see anything. The seagull had flown away.

I was all alone.

I listened carefully for more words of encouragement, but it was silent.

Absorbing the emptiness around and within me, I lifted my left foot, which felt like a ton of bricks, and used every ounce of power I had to push my body to the top of that pole. Relieved that my knee didn't explode, and I didn't fall to my death, I stood up straight and screamed a ridiculous, "Wooo Hooooooo!!!"

With a grin etched across my face, I did a micro-wiggle of pride, waved slowly like a queen to the crowd below, and took it all in. Then, I closed my eyes and flew.

For a brief second, I watched my wildest dreams flash within my mind. Then the sharp tug of the safety harness jolted me back to reality, and my eyes popped open as my body adjusted to the sensation of floating down to earth. With the help of the spotters, five seconds later I landed on the sand. The crowd enveloped me with hugs and high fives, and for the next six exhilarating and outrageous days, we were "family" as we supported each other throughout the Tony Robbins' "Life and Wealth Mastery" event (LWM).

COMMUNITY CULTURE

Before introducing myself to Tony Robbins's world, I had rarely felt like I truly belonged anywhere except when doing my work. The business I had created. The place I owned. Around the people I hired. Of course I "fit in" with my family, but I don't think they really understand me, at least not in the way I wish they did. And while my "sister-like" girlfriends from college know me the best, they live states away, so sometimes our closeness is lost over the miles. Through the years, I'd developed a mindset that made me think it was just too damn difficult to find more like-minded people, so I just kept searching for something that felt like "home." But nothing ever did. This constant movement resulted in a worldwide network of arms-length connections, which had left me yearning for closeness and deeper relationships, until now.

Even when I thought I was in the right place with the right people, I continued to feed into the habit of adjusting, changing, and morphing in efforts of conforming with everyone else, while simultaneously trying to figure out who the hell I was at my core. Especially when I was living overseas, I found some of the cultural differences difficult to understand, causing me to feel more like an outcast than part of the group.

Needless to say, I felt lost for a long time, until this "Life and Wealth Mastery" event. The speakers and seminars helped me realize that my struggle to fit in or stand out wasn't because of the external environments; my struggle existed because I had created a knotted up, twisted, and misguided battle of wills within myself. I was seeking love and connection while simultaneously fighting for my independence and significance. Two opposite ends of the scale. Two totally different purposes. All tied up in knots inside my head and heart just trying to untangle themselves.

As soon as I understood that little bit of crucial information (it hit me like a frying pan), I immediately felt a stronger, more congruent alignment with myself, my value, and the people surrounding me. As the threads spun back and forth throughout the event, I could feel the impact of this realization hitting home, and I started to see the fabric of connection, fulfillment, and intentional opportunity unfold neatly in front of me.

As the week expanded our minds, our networks, and our souls at a greater capacity than UPW (which at the time I didn't think it was possible), I could see that by choosing to envelop myself with positive, uplifting individuals who were encouraging my dreams, and celebrating my victories, I had chosen to be accepted into a community *as I was,* rather than trying to conform into a community *as someone I am not.* I didn't have to do anything except be myself, and once that process began, I started to embody and benefit from the love and connections that were naturally sparking all around me. It felt amazing.

Finding a like-minded culture and community that resonates with our soul and our life's intentions is one of the greatest gifts we can offer to ourselves, and it's a blessing when we can give ourselves the chance to look for it.

At dinner one night, the conversation was based on what books people were reading and how each of us interpreted various messages from a multitude of authors and influencers. One of the books that I was able to chime in on was John Maxwell's *Intentional Living.* I had read it back in 2017, long before I joined this Tony Robbins group, and was utterly impressed that everyone at the table had also read it at least once. It seemed that everyone there was following the same principles of intentional living, and I knew I had finally found my tribe.[7]

The more time I spent with these beautiful passionate souls on Marco Island, the more I felt that I was in the right place. This community of strangers was becoming the network and family I had been searching for most of my life. People full of authentic courage, compassion, and willingness to support with faith, belief, and love. Their opportunistic mindsets added to the depth of our conversations, filling me with empowerment, and fueling my desire to live intentionally.

The health guidelines, dietary cleanse, yoga, rhythm dance classes, and educational seminars on alcohol and cannabis, joint mobility and skin care, sleeping patterns, and meditation techniques, all created a bond of positive shared experience between us all. After a week, our values were so realigned and in tune with each other that I knew it was going to be challenging to *not* stay in touch with them. WE had become *one*. This full immersion into a healthy culture of support systems, accountability partners, and lifestyle changes affected us all both in and outside of the event, and we were eager to maintain the connections moving forward.

The most unique thing about the people I meet at the Tony Robbins events is that we get past the surface level shit real fast. We begin by brushing aside the unhealthy stories and walls we've built around ourselves which allows us to openly learn about each other's goals and connect with each other's souls within hours or days. Before this, it would take months or sometimes years to make similar connections with any of the other people I know. **But with this group, I feel seen, heard, and understood.** My Tony Robbins family is unique in their positive affect on my life, and I welcome the continued influence we still have with each other today.

"Life isn't made by what you can accomplish. It's made by what you can accomplish with others."

~ *John Maxwell*

SOUL SOLUTIONS

When I returned from LWM, the first thing I did was call my coach Kerri. Experiencing the effectiveness of full immersion once again, I knew in order to keep the momentum going, she was going to be my most valuable asset.

She customized her coaching approach of working with me, and it was exactly what I needed. With her soulful guidance, we dove headfirst into my relationship history, and although I didn't want to face my typical roller-coaster of emotions associated with my heartache, I pushed through the pain and was eventually able to see the patterns and overlapping confusion I had been carrying with me throughout almost all of my relationships. It sucked but was enlightening at the same time.

With deliberate reflection and raw, honest, and open conversations, I sat through many Zoom calls with tears in my eyes and tissues all over my desk. I had finally cracked the door of the closet where I hid all my scariest secrets and sentiments, sifted through what had gone wrong and what had been so unbelievably right, and was ready to start the healing I had been avoiding for decades.

Though my darkness was deep, Kerri was able to see me for who I truly am, even if I couldn't see myself through my layers of guilt, shame, and doubt. With zero judgment, her empathetic listening created such a safe environment for me that I learned how to express myself in an empowering way, one that is softer, and helped me shift back into my natural feminine state of care and concern versus my typical command-and-control ways of being. We dissected my communication triad, which includes my language or the words I use, the tone I give them, and the pace at which I talk (apparently I talk kind of fast and loud); how I presented myself physically (I talk with my hands and wear every thought on my face before I have a chance to stop any of it); and my focus when in conversation and communication (it can sometimes be fractured and hard to follow).

Kerri also had me take personality tests so I could better understand the science behind "me." She assessed my strengths and weaknesses so we could find ways to intentionally expand and contract parts of me that positively affect my perception of myself, my world, and how I work with other people.

This was beyond me shifting and changing to fit a certain situation. This was me learning how I naturally ticked and how the uniqueness of me was a gift, not a curse. I now fully understand, embrace, and share *me* in a healthy and dynamic way. Moreover, I learned how to radically accept all of my emotions, even the confusing difficult ones, and how to cut through the bullshit cleaner and faster so things don't get messy. I ask better questions to get better answers. I know how to listen and pay attention to what others say, how they say it, and understand their underlying messages. And as a result, my emotional agility has become strong. I've finally started closing the gap between where I was and where I wanted to be.

Before Kerri, **I had become so rigid, so determined, so fucking certain that I had to be significant, that my ego had stifled my heart, and I had no idea that I was suffocating my own creativity and growth.** But through endless practice of reframing my mindset and rebuilding my emotional home, I found her guidance and theory of "being focused on the outcome but flexible in the approach" to be a major catalyst in many turning points in 2019, including successfully breaking through barriers of limiting beliefs and self-deprecating thoughts that are no longer allowed in my vernacular.

In late 2019, I introduced Kerri to my design team, and we expanded the breadth and depth of the company culture beyond my top tier. After a few individual calls with my employees, Kerri came out to our office in early February 2020 for an incredible strategic company collaboration session.

We created a framework of trust, loyalty, and respect by incorporating the value of coaching into the services available for my staff. With Kerri's guidance, we worked through the triad values for the company, did similar personality tests so we could all understand how to communicate with each other, and worked through some personal and significant vulnerable conversations that connected us all on a more united level. Knowing that we, as a team, created a platform where growth and support are the norms, and respect and flexibility are the expectations, has built an incredibly solid foundation for the company.

THE WEBS WE WEAVE

Without realizing it completely, I have been building a network within the design/construction industry for over twenty years now, and my connections with all of those people are what have supported my success and encouraged the growth of the company. I hadn't realized that I was already a part of something great, something wonderful, within the "family" of other designers, contractors and architects that I have intentionally surrounded myself with. They are courageous entrepreneurs and like-minded individuals, similar to me, and I am proud of these connections, knowing my network is equal to my net-worth. In fact, throughout all the failed love relationships and my emotional desire to have a family, I could always rely on the people I had surrounded myself with throughout my industry to support my business, which ultimately supported me. It just became another lesson and observation that the breadth and depth of the relationships that we have in our lives overlap, intertwine, and intersect in the most unassuming and expected places.

For example, on day two of UPW November 2018, as I was entering the stadium, there was a builder I had recently finished a project with back home. It took a split second for us to recognize each other out of context, but as soon as we connected the dots, in sync with the energy of the event, we embraced as if we were long lost family. Now, this isn't something that we do when we see each other in our home town, but the familiarity, the connection, and the understanding that we aligned on another level beyond our businesses gave me a sense of confidence that what I was doing (in or out of my company ventures) was on the right path. What I didn't realize was that my run-in with this builder meant just as much to him as it did to me. Taking advantage of collaborating on a platform outside of the "day to day" meant that our interwoven web of connections doubled for each of us. People do business with people they know, like, and trust, and people thrive when they are given the gift of opportunity and appreciation.

Understanding that I had finally begun to align both my professional network intentions with my personal life intentions allowed me to cultivate the inner strength I needed to unveil my greater purpose. The chameleon-like skin that had calloused over my soul and character started to get washed away at UPW, and the cleansing continued at LWM. The repetition and consistency of me showing up for myself in both my personal and professional lives allows me to reveal the truest version of myself, over and over again.

DEAR DIARY

Creating a network that is a reflection of your belief system and values will only attract more of the connections you seek and more of the life you dream of. As you reflect on your life, going through your history, relationships, experiences, and adventures, remember that it's important to recognize how far you've come, where you are now, where you want to go, and what it all means.

1. Think about the people with whom you spend your time and see how they contribute or curtail your dreams and aspirations. Where are they heading? Are you with them or against them? If they are behind you, determine if they are holding you back, or if you need to reach down and help them. If they are ahead of you, find out how you can catch up.
2. As a suggestion, review your social media accounts and free yourself of any negative or time sucking people that aren't offering you more of what you want or need. (Or maybe put them on silent so they don't keep popping up in your feed).

It's about raising your standards for YOU, no-one else, and surrounding yourself with the minds and bodies that most closely reflect the lifestyle and life experience you genuinely want to have.

11

DATE WITH DESTINY

Define Your Values and Beliefs

"Until we have met the monsters in ourselves, we keep trying to slay them in the outer world. And we find that we cannot. For all darkness in the world stems from darkness in the heart. And it is there that we must do our work."

~*Marianne Williamson*

DECEMBER, 2019

For six days and nights, I felt like Lucy in C.S. Lewis's *The Lion, the Witch and the Wardrobe* as I journeyed through my own healing chronicles of self-love and acceptance at Tony Robbins' event "Date with Destiny" (DWD) in December 2019.

As the legendary story goes, Lucy, her sister, and two brothers are sent to live with a family friend during World War II to escape the bombing and chaos of the Germans. While exploring the new house, Lucy enters the wondrous fantasy world of Narnia through a hidden door in the back of a wardrobe. She discovers an enchanting land filled with fantastical creatures and mythical beings—a world that is not confined to time or limited by reality or belief. The story is an epic adventure of how these four children ally with talking animals in battles between good and evil to defeat a wicked witch and explore themes of courage, sacrifice, and redemption.

My DWD experience was as wondrous as the chronicles in C.S. Lewis's books as I found myself in awe of the opportunities of courage within me that had been hidden for decades behind my persistent struggle of acceptance. Similar to Lucy, I didn't know the door to my soul was there until I practically fell through it. But once I was introduced to Tony's theories and methods at his various events, the thick layers of self-doubt and resistance that had been manipulating my character for years started to fade away.

At the onset of the event, all 5,000 attendees were divided into teams of fifty or so, then we paired ourselves with an accountability partner that we would work with throughout the event. Out of our seemingly massive group, this guy Eric and I immediately felt an energetic pull towards each other, and throughout the event, we shared revelations, snacks, gloves, and tears.

The event was in balmy West Palm Beach, Florida, but they kept the room ridiculously cold to ensure we stayed in "state." The work we each do on ourselves is unbelievably difficult at times, since the event is all about changing your life, so the exhaustion becomes inevitable really quick. When we were short on sleep from the fourteen-hour days but long on motivation, the cold helped to keep us awake.

Leaders prompted us to think about our personal values and core beliefs with difficult question after difficult question. From these questions and answers came realization after mind-boggling realization. Extensive writing exercises required us to think hard and dig deep, then dig deeper, and even deeper again. We aimed at uncovering our most treasured secrets in efforts to reveal who we are at our core. And even with ten-plus years of coaching and therapy under my belt, I had never taken this much time to think about my values, let alone write them down or prioritize them!

I drummed up the Six Human Needs and Driving Force Priority exercise from the UPW event and started to link Tony's curriculum together one message at a time. Our values stem from our belief system, which stems from our childhood and environment. As I uncovered the reality of my core understanding, it became ludicrous to see that some of the values I lived by were old, outdated family concepts that had been passed down through generations and didn't relate to me at all. Some were based on childhood experiences that shaped (and didn't shape) my boundaries and needs. And some were irrelevant and no longer aligned with who I was becoming. **The dissection and investigation of our personal virtues really opened my eyes to an entire universe of self-discovery and understanding.** Eventually I was even able to classify the values that actually belonged to me into two categories: Good/Towards or Bad/Away.

We pushed and we pulled. I scratched and I scribbled on a giant poster board with sticky notes and neatly decorated my list with words in the order I *thought* were accurate and true to me. Proudly I showed my buddy, Eric, and he debated not only some of the words I chose, but the order I put them in. He said it was too robotic and lacked authenticity. I was taken aback. I mean, who the hell was *he* to tell me I was *wrong* about *my* own values and beliefs?! I dug my heels in and explained my reasoning, but he cut me off mid-sentence, grabbed my hands, and told me to close my eyes.

Reluctantly I appeased him, took a breath, and allowed his guidance to pull me out of my tactical designer's mindset back into my emotional heart. As we stood there, amidst a chaotic convention center and in a self-created bubble of silence and calm, he repeated, "Get out of your head and into your heart. Stop playing small. Get out of your head and into your heart. Stop playing small," over and over again. Then something clicked.

I witnessed my heart beating faster and heavier. I felt a sense of empowerment coupled with a new grace of understanding. Letting go of his hands, I stopped *thinking*, embraced him for his guidance, and proceeded to *feel* my way through the exercise. As I reworded and reprioritized my sticky notes, my real life's purpose and newly defined mission came alive.

With everything in black and white (and highlighters and sticky notes), it started to become clear to me that I had been valuing fun and excitement as a driving force but coupling it with instant gratification, rather than integrity and respect. Having fun isn't a bad thing, I had just neglected to look past my adrenaline-fueled pursuit of a good time to see the consequences of my actions on the other side. At the age of forty-three, I was single and without children. This was definitely NOT where I had ever imagined myself being at this age. So, with all this forced reflection, as I was literally drawing it out, I could see my life wasn't the way I had wanted it to be because of my habits, my actions, and my now out-of-date mindset and values that had been driving and affecting me for over forty years. It was like witnessing my own rebirth from center stage. I saw exactly where I needed to shift and suddenly knew how it needed to happen.

It was time to wake up and adjust my priorities if I wanted my future to not reflect my past. As I intentionally reordered my "Towards" and "Away" values and made small adjustments to how I perceived what I needed to do in order to be happy, I could see such a difference and began to believe in a more cohesive, authentic, mature version of myself as it appeared on the poster board. A version that felt and looked like the real me as I believed myself to be—full of love, integrity, and joy.

At the end of the event, my mission statement read, with pride and conviction, **"The purpose of my life is to be loving, fun, and inspirational and to enhance the lives of others with integrity, my voice, and my compassion."**

Performance Anxiety...

The final and ultimate task of the event was to act and personify our top values through words, actions, and anything else that would allow us to embody our top "Towards" and completely rid ourselves of the top "Away" as well. Eric and I simply turned around and paired up with Christine and LJ who were sitting behind us. They were part of our larger, fifty-person tribe, and we had all gotten to know each other pretty well during the previous five days.

The Towards was fun. We were all laughing, dancing, and celebrating. The effort was genuine, easy, and compassionate. I think we all had Love at the top of our lists, so there were similar statements and expressions, but all unique performances.

Christine went first. Her grace and conviction as she screamed her love potion of commitment and faith was incredible. She then flipped the script on her Away value "Fear of Change," but rather than yell and carry on, she got very quiet and proclaimed her courage was stronger than her fear, and she chose to empower her security with pride and love. Her monologue was soft, gentle, and convincing. I was inspired by her and learned to understand the importance of the exercises by remaining present for ourselves and our partners as we worked through these emotional tasks.

LJ was more the strong silent type without any type of acting career in his past or future. But the honesty behind his words and effort was handsome and substantial. We coached him through his Love and Scarcity performances. It took some time, but when he finally got to the end where we all felt his shift, his smile lit up the room.

Eric's Towards and Away were poetic and fun. He was humorous in his approach but deeply devoted to the outcomes. It was almost as if he was in the final practice of his life's speech as he gently tweaked the details. His superpowers become an undeniable confirmation that he is already living a glorious life, and it was refreshing to witness his unwavering belief in Love and elimination of Hesitation.

Love is what I have always wanted, but as I learned through the Six Human Needs exercises, I have been fighting love my entire life. Despite an abundance of love within me, I've perpetually hidden it under all the other bullshit I accumulated in my own wardrobe of codependency, fear, and self-doubt. But now, I had the courage to swing open the heavy door to my own inner-Narnia, where magical-fantasticalism wasn't so mysterious anymore and my theatrical expressions of love were acts of sincerity and reflections of the passion, loving energy, and enthusiasm that surrounded me.

Then I had to do my Away. And for me, my greatest Away value was Lying. And it was a big one.

"He who tells a lie is not sensible of how great a task he undertakes; for he must be forced to invent twenty more to maintain that one."

~ *Alexander Pope*

—

The first lie I remember telling was to my Gramma when I was seven. As a curious child, I attempted to shave my legs with the razor my mom had left in the tub. When the water turned pink from a small sliver I'd cut off the top of my knee, I screamed. Gramma came flying in and asked if I was allowed to shave. Afraid of getting in trouble, I lied and said my friend did so I thought it was okay that I did too. I knew I wasn't allowed, but I didn't know if Gramma knew that. She put a band-aid on my knee, and nothing was ever said about it again. I had gotten away with it, or so I thought.

The little lies, like "I'm fine," when clearly I wasn't or "Nothing is wrong," when everything was totally fucked up, got me out of arguments or having to explain myself. I didn't initially consider it lying, just insignificant deviations from the truth. Afterall, I had been trying to either fit in or stand out most of my life and would lie my way into groups or out of trouble. But I didn't realize I was stifling myself even more by not expressing my honest needs and had no idea the impact these lies were making on my life, as well as other people's.

I lied about driving my mom's car to the store when I was thirteen. I lied about smoking cigarettes and drinking when I was fourteen. At sixteen, you could have blindfolded me with dental floss any night of the week, and I would mumble over and over again "No, I'm not stoned, I just have allergies…" with a squinty, sideways glance towards the half empty peanut butter jar. Then my giggles would bubble up, and I would be sent to my room.

My parents knew. They always knew.

One day, I lied to my mom from behind a locked bedroom door when she came home early from work. "No. No one else is here. I'm just cleaning my room. I don't know whose car that is in the street…" as my high school boyfriend hid naked in the closet and my room looked like it had been ransacked by thieves.

In college, I lied about going to Las Vegas one weekend and told my parents I was in New Jersey. When I thought I got away with that, I lied the following spring break and told them I was in Florida, when I was actually halfway around the world in Australia. Come to find out, they knew about that too!

I lied to boyfriends (and husbands) with a stone cold face, "Nope, I haven't talked to him in ages…" just after I finished deleting the texts and changing the other man's name on my phone. Or I would lie and say "I'll be a little late, I have a lot of work to do…" while I was finishing up my third (or fourth) cocktail at the bar.

I even got crafty at lying to myself. "Yeah, that's fine, it's not that important," I would say to my boyfriend despite feeling devastated that he chose a fucking golf game over attending an important work event with me. Embarrassed when I arrived at the event alone, I lied to everyone and said, "He wasn't feeling well but sent his regards."

A few years back, I got together with my friend from first grade who didn't shave her legs at the age of seven, and she asked me about the leg shaving incident. I had to be reminded of what she was talking about. Apparently, Gramma told my mom, and my mom told my friend's mom, then my friend's mom asked her. And she told the truth—she had never shaved her legs and didn't know why I had said otherwise. But because no one circled back to find out I was lying, she got in trouble. Big trouble.

But her trouble was way different than mine. When her dad found out about this lying leg shaving incident, he went into an abusive rage that ended up keeping my friend out of school for a few days. I had always wondered why she didn't meet me at the corner the following day to walk to school. Or the day after that. Or the day after that. I also didn't know that when her dad got angry, he took it out on her and her younger brother.

I wonder how many things in my life (and others') would have evolved differently if I had understood the truth and consequences of how powerful my statements actually were.

Over the years, the more I lied and got away with it, the more it became an addiction. Sounds a little ridiculous to be addicted to lying, but the adrenaline rush that accompanied the getting away with it part was like a dopamine hit that I loved to hate, so I kept doing it. Problem was, rather than face up to the truth of most things, I would just ignore the darkness that the lies were generating in the hopes that they might all disappear some day. But this darkness started to consume me in the form of anxiety attacks and eventually got so pathetic that I even lied to myself saying the anxiety attacks were adrenaline. Then it got out of control, and my body started to physically react to my absurd diet of toxic lies, and I started getting sick.

At one point, right before my second divorce, I had brainwashed myself so badly that I confused the fine lines between my lies versus reality, and the truth finally caught up with me. A torrid, drug-related, twisted affair and the resulting emotional battle with my husband had me taking off in my car like a convicted felon one day, driving around, denying reality, and bellowing like a baby.

That's when my nervous system shut down completely, and with no warning or control, I shit my pants.

In shock, I slammed on the brakes, which only made it worse. Shit shot up my shorts and all over my back. I pulled over, looked down, and saw it squishing between my legs. I don't know what the hell I had been eating, but it smelled so horrific I started throwing up all over the steering wheel and dashboard. Too embarrassed to get out of the car, because I now had poop and puke all over me, I sat there throwing and going for at least five minutes.

I don't remember what I did next, but if sitting in my own shit and being violently ill wasn't a perfect metaphor for my life at that moment, I don't know what else could have been. That gruesome experience served as a giant sign for me to get my act together.

Soon after that day, I committed to therapy and started working through some (but only some) of the reasons for all the lying. I worked with that therapist for about a year during my divorce, then got laid off and couldn't afford the visits any longer, so the truth behind my lies stayed in the shadows for the next eleven years.

I continued to skirt around the underlying problems of cowardliness, not fully comprehending the extent of damage this obscene lying habit had done to me. Eleven years after that shitty unplanned day of doom, I finally found myself at "Date with Destiny," consciously taking deliberate steps towards defining my values and changing my ways.

—

Naturally, I was nervous when it was my turn to act out my Away value. I had already come clean to my teammates about my habitual lying, and the honesty left me, not with shame but with an immediate sense of relief. I knew it was time to rid myself of the pattern and eliminate my destructive lying monster once and for all.

I felt my energy shift as I stepped into the challenge of enacting the death of a giant misguiding value that had messed me up for over forty years. My performance and authenticity had to be outstanding. I knew I had to play full out 1,000,000%, and I only had one shot at dropping my nuclear truth bomb on top of all the lies to wipe them out completely.

"If you are going through hell, keep going."

~ WINSTON CHURCHILL

As I stood there, amongst these three strangers, who in five days knew more about me than some of my best friends, I could feel the lying monster fighting for his life, hiding in the closet of my soul behind that giant mystical door of secrets and deceit. I could feel its giant prickly hands wrap around my throat in an attempt to choke out my voice and silence my new mission.

This demon had started at such a young age and had grown with me, around me, and inside me for almost forty years. Trying to fit in and stand out, and because I had reformatted myself so many times, I found that lying helped me get through the most uncomfortable costumes and characters I had worn and played throughout my life. The lies were its backbone, and all the other shit and falsities I dressed it in were its armor and tenacity. I now knew what I wanted in my life, and there was absolutely no room for this demon in my new story.

I took a breath, stared at the three eager faces beaming back at me, and broke free. I stated facts. Blurted out reasons and excuses. I came clean about the affairs, the manipulation, and the pain I caused. I flung open the closet door and pushed the skeletons out that had been hiding inside me for years. The verity in the words pouring out of my mouth were life-giving. I talked faster and louder. I wanted it out. I needed to purge this animal, so I dug deep into that dark closet, and I pulled him out by his tail. The ferocity of my energy swirled, and I could feel my face turning red then purple. I felt like I was going to blow up.

I felt him holding on with his claws, and I just kept pulling. My mouth dried up, and I spewed cotton balls like venom from my lips. Molten lava tears ran down my face and burned into my cheeks. I swore up, down, left, right, front, and center and was screaming with every single cell of my existence. I started to shake and felt my body convulse as I just kept blaring the truth and desire to rid myself of this lying demon. He no longer had a place in my life. I yanked him out and swung my arms around in the air then threw the fabricated monster of lies on the ground and jumped up and down on top of it until I felt it crumble.

Sweating profusely, trembling, and enraged, I promised myself that not one more fucking lie was to be spoken from my lips. Then I dropped the bomb. In an explosive detonation, shattering the life of that fucking monster, I stomped and screamed some more as the effects of my radiating performance shriveled those lies into nothing but dust. When it was all done, when I was unquestionably convinced that it was all over, I practically burst into flames and then collapsed on the floor in a shaking heap of pride.

My three cohorts applauded wildly and landed on top of me like a pile of bricks. I'm not sure how it all happened, but it felt like a self-induced exorcism of the most merciless kind. I lay under the weight of this new-found truth and the bodies of my friends, and I cried. I cried tears of release, freedom, and love. After a few moments, and a few hopeful breaths, my friends peeled themselves off me, and I sat up.

With bulging, salty eyes, I could feel an overwhelming peace settle into every cell of my body and felt light as a feather. The strength of my friends' hugs were full of so much unconditional love that I realized in that moment, as I finally came back to reality, that there would never be a space for that lying nonsense in my life ever again. Nothing else mattered. I was finally free.

> *"If you've been up all night and cried till you have no more tears left in you—you will know that there comes in the end a sort of quietness. You feel as if nothing is ever going to happen again."*
>
> ~ *C.S. Lewis*

The Magical Wardrobe...

The further Lucy and her brothers and sister traveled into Narnia, the more complex and convoluted the story became. As they traveled, they fought battles alongside noble characters, saved lands from dark entities, and eventually brought peace and balance to a world far beyond their wildest dreams. As the four of us traveled together through DWD and our dynamic evolution of values were uncovered through battles of willpower and sacrifice, we saved ourselves from our own demons and were all left with a harmony and balance, enriched by our new purposes and missions.

In Narnia, while time carries on, the clocks in the real world stop, and when the children return back through the wardrobe, it is the same day they left. They haven't aged a minute, but they have learned life lessons far in advance of their actual age. At DWD, we had six days and nights of evolution and discovery, and while it felt like we had traveled through space and time, the clocks in our real lives had kind of stopped. We all recognized that when we were to return home, back through the magical closet doors of our own wardrobes, it was going to be similar to the same day we had left. However, *we* knew our souls had changed. *We* had transformed through lessons learned far in advance of our wildest dreams.

The lessons from DWD were the master key I needed to unlock my soul's skeleton closet. At the event, I pulled each limiting belief and element of fear out from behind the door, examined them, and set them free. **The deeper I ventured in, the more veils of defiance and opposition were**

thankfully removed, revealing the breadth and depth of who I really am and allowing my vulnerability to lead me on a guided path of love and self-acceptance. This liberation from shame and embarrassment freed up a massive amount of space, allowing the foundation of my *real* truth to begin again.

Destiny is an incredibly strong word, and it resonates so deeply within my soul because throughout this life changing event, the number of courageous acts of heroism, sacrifice, and personal redemption that occurred were some of the most pivotal encounters I've ever experienced.

Weightless and free, I felt like I levitated and floated right out of that convention center like a cloud on a beautiful summer day. Smiling. Full of abundance, euphoria, and love. Outside, the air was steamy and hot, a complete contrast to the cool coffin I had just buried my worst nightmare in. Gently breathing the muggy air into the new empty hollow in my chest, I thanked the universe out loud and warmed myself with the humidity and heat offered by the Florida weather.

I had accomplished what I didn't even know I had come to do and abolished one of the worst parts of myself. I had Realigned. Reprogrammed. And Restarted. **And I welcomed transformation, acceptance, and growth.**

Adjusting my compass, it was now time to become the best version of me I had ever known. My new destiny was waiting.

"I now see that owning our story and loving ourselves through that process is the bravest thing that we will ever do."

~ *Brené Brown*

FIELDS OF DREAMS

When I returned home, trying to explain my week in Florida proved to be a little difficult to anyone who's never gone through either a near-exorcism or undertaken intentional transformation. So, I adjusted the story and described it like this:

> "It was like I cleared the fields of my soul of all evidence of previous plants, seeds, or undergrowth from the past forty years and am now left with a perfectly empty pasture ready for new crops, new intentions, and a new life. I eliminated all the waste that was cluttering my growth and have started over with a totally fresh opportunity at life."

Some people got it. Although most didn't and thought I had lost my mind. But in reality, it was the opposite. I had found both my mind and my soul! I had just rewired myself and was on a new journey towards love and happiness, and unlike before, I didn't really need anyone to fully understand me.

I came home so fresh, so alive, and so willing to only see the good in anyone because I had discovered the depth of my vulnerability and was finally (almost too) willing to take another chance at love.

The part I missed with my new beautifully prepared, empty, and precious field of dreams, was that I underestimated the importance of planting my own intentional seeds *right away*. In my blissful state of serenity and peace and my desire for love on a deeper level, I unknowingly allowed the wind to blow in a giant toxic seed that quickly took root and eventually invaded every corner of my soul.

Within weeks of returning from DWD, my fresh and empathetic energy fell prey to the rotten and callous games of a charming and manipulative covert narcissist. I had no idea what was happening to me until I found myself playing the unfortunate victim in an exhausting and often debilitating, emotionally-abusive relationship with a man who was leading a double life.

DEAR DIARY

Defining our values and belief systems is one of the keys to opening the doors to our soul. It gives us the ability to understand who we are, where we've come from, how and why we do things, and what the hell we need to adjust if we aren't happy!

1. Make a list of your values. What's important to you? What has been driving your decision-making process all these years? What lights you up and what do you want more of? Without staying in your head too much, allow yourself some space and grace, and listen to your heart. If your mind wasn't always in charge, what would your heart be telling you it wants, and why?
2. Creating a personal life mission statement can seem daunting, but it's totally worth it. Be patient with yourself, and know that it doesn't have to be complicated. Start by writing down what you want your life to mean, and when that feels clear, unpack some of the concepts surrounding it, and expand the intention.
3. Have you ever lied? What's the worst lie you've ever told? What were the repercussions when the truth came out. And if it hasn't yet, how does it feel to live with that lie and have to keep track of it all the time?

Why Did You Do It?

Part 4

EVEN THOUGH

"The loneliest moment in someone's life is when they are watching their whole world fall apart, and all they can do is stare blankly."

~ *F. Scott Fitzgerald*

Even though I had just cleared so much space and was aligned with my spirit and values after DWD, I wasn't able to fully connect with my new core and the integrity principles fast enough. I hadn't had time to imprint the new loving actions onto my soul, so when my desire for a relationship was sparked through an unexpected encounter, my old limiting beliefs kept their stronghold on my heart and kept me on the same path I had traveled for years. **Even though I felt complete, even though I knew my self-worth and value were higher than ever, even though I believed in who I was and what I deserved, I had been a people pleaser for most of my life and naturally forgot to love myself first; and sometimes, to love myself at all.**

The similarities between the lying monster I rid myself of at DWD and the guy I started dating right afterwards are eerily ironic and dreadfully accurate, but I didn't recognize it until it was too late.

The next few chapters are the highlights (or lowlights) of the drawn out *shit*uationship I had with Jay, the guy I introduced in Chapter One, and are the catalyst for why I started writing this book. I was bound and determined to tell the world how much of an asshole I thought he was, but as I wrote, I healed. As I relived the chaos and the stories untangled, so did I.

Part four is thc blatant observation that we often don't pay attention to the red flags around us and end up getting stuck in the same shit even though we should know better. We do all this intentional healing work, have all these tools, and know deep in our gut that we are better than what's happening to us, but we still get caught in the cycles.

Call it ignorance. Call it stubbornness. Call it hopeless romanticism or call it stupidity. Call it whatever you want. But for me, it was a three-year saga that has contributed greatly to my evolution, and I have decided to call it "The *Shit*uationship."

12

FREEDOM RIDES

Forgiveness as the Gateway to Healing

"It's not an easy journey, to get to a place where you forgive people. But it is such a powerful place because it frees you."

~ *Tyler Perry*

SPRING, 2021

I turned the key, and instantly, the boom of the exhaust had my energy swirling. I performed my routine check of the gas, brakes, boots, jacket, and gloves. Feeling grounded, but pausing to register my adrenaline, my heart rate quickened as I pulled the helmet over my head and suddenly felt enveloped in safety from head to toe.

It was one of the first really nice days of spring, making it perfect for a motorcycle ride. I tossed my leg over the seat, clutched the handlebars, and straightened the bike into an upright position. Slowing my breath, I popped it into gear and rolled out of the driveway. As the painful chaos in my mind slowly disappeared, I became one with my motorcycle, and the road ahead held all of my attention. Maneuvering through the scenic back roads and potholed streets of the North Shore, **I didn't have a destination—I had a mission.** Distrust and demoralization had been lingering like a thick fog in my mind for the past couple weeks, and this ride was meant to fix that.

The further I went, the steadier my breathing became. My heart relaxed as feelings of heartache and confusion were left in the dust behind me, and a soft smile spread across my face.

FALL, 2019

I had bumped into Jay at a networking event back in October 2019, soon after I returned from a ten-day vacation to France. I had been off the alcohol for a couple weeks and felt amazing. My energy was bright. My eyes had a twinkle. And everything about me radiated spectacularly. I had come to this event with confidence and the specific intention of getting some new projects, so I made it a point to be noticed.

When I was networking like my life depended on it back in 2010, I had met Jay at a similar event. He is the owner of a high-end residential construction company, which was my target market for networking and design projects. Back then, we met once for coffee, but it never developed into working together. However, he had always found a way to keep in touch either through email or other events, so seeing him at this soirée was a pleasant surprise.

I was excited to talk with him with the intention of collaborating on a project or two, but when he offered to buy me a cocktail, I politely declined saying I was on a health cleanse. Seemingly impressed, he said he had been sober a year, ordered two soda waters and we started chatting.

"Amanda, you look great! How have you been?" he asked with a big smile.

"Thank you. I'm doing *fantastic.* How are you?" I was glowing. I hadn't been to an event in a couple years (because I was too busy wallowing in bourbon and being a basketcase) so I came to this one fully prepared and ready to connect.

"Fantastic?" He repeated, turning all the attention onto me. "Wow. I never hear 'fantastic' anymore. What have you been doing?"

"Well, if you really want to know, I jumped on the Tony Robbins train last year, and it's been amazing ever since."

That was his in.

He lit up like a Christmas tree and told me he used to listen to Tony Robbins tapes back in the 90s, and our conversation flowed like a babbling brook.

Jay had started renovating his condo in Charlestown only a couple months prior to our run-in and asked me for some help with the design. Thrilled at the opportunity to work with him, hoping it would lead to more projects, I eagerly said yes.

When I returned from DWD a couple months later, all glowing, light, and abundantly vulnerable, he entertained me with a potential business deal over coffee one afternoon, and somehow that coffee led to dinner a few days later. And then another "date" a few days after that. I was a little disappointed in myself because after my second marriage blew up, I made a pact with myself to never date anyone I worked with ever again. Seems I wasn't so good at keeping promises.

This guy, however, was so charming, so funny, and so incredibly persistent that the more we worked together, the more I was attracted to him. I was enchanted by his fast mind, his extended social network, his wild and spontaneous adventures and, of course, his vast financial stability. And, to make it even more enticing, he showered me with promises of bigger, more lucrative projects and a romantic relationship once he sorted a few things out with his soon-to-be ex-wife.

A year and a half after our first coffee, his condo was done. He got everything he wanted, and I had somehow become a part of the decor. Regardless of the dating boundaries I had made for myself, I went against my own personal promises, and a few times a week I would race into the city to scoot around town with him, grab dinner, walk the dogs, and hang out.

There were times during those eighteen months that he would disappear for days (sometimes weeks) with no explanation. I would worry myself sick over the fact that I couldn't find him and hoped to God he was alright and not dying in a ditch on the side of a desolate road in New Hampshire. But then he would come back, give me some story about how he was having a hard time with the divorce lawyers (because he was still married), or a project went sideways, or he went to visit his daughters. I would forgive him without asking too many questions, and we would start all over again. He was leading me to believe that he had so much to give, right after this "one thing" finished up. So I stuck around, willing to wait for whatever he had to offer. **But there was always one more thing, and another thing after that, and his compelling offers were always changing. I traveled so far down his rabbit hole that I hadn't noticed he had continued to reroute the exit plan, and kept setting up detours, just to keep me guessing, confused, and intrigued.**

BACK TO SPRING, 2021

One beautiful spring evening, I went into Charlestown to meet Jay for dinner. He had left a note telling me to grab a scooter and meet him at the (Bunker Hill) Monument. He owned a fleet of high-end motorized scooters that made city living feel like an amusement park. Super fun, but also, super dangerous. But that was part of the never-ending thrill with Jay—danger before duty.

It was a little chilly that night, so I headed into the bedroom to grab a sweatshirt. On my way, a little pink dog collar and matching leash by the front door caught my attention. Jay's dog, Tucker, was a forty-pound, white, male labradoodle. This tiny collar was no more than four inches around with little black hairs on it. And it was pink.

Tucker barked at me from the living room sofa, pulling me out of a cloud of questions. I went over to give him some lovin' and attempted to ignore the sudden pang in my gut. After a few wags and a lick, I wandered back towards the bedroom.

Opening the drawer I had seen Jay grab his sweatshirts from numerous times before, I didn't find what I was looking for. Instead, I found more pink things.

Lacy pink lingerie.

Pink leggings.

Makeup remover, and a fucking pink toothbrush.

My world turned upside down in a flash, and son of a bitch, wouldn't you know it, the gummy I had taken on my way into town started to kick in. Now I was high and wasn't sure if I should believe what I was seeing.

Instantly sick to my stomach and desperate to get up to the monument, I slammed the drawer shut and rifled through his closet for anything that might keep me warm. I ripped a jacket off a hanger, causing a few other items to fall out of the closet. And as if the place was bleeding with evidence, a red dress landed softly on the heap of clothes now piled on the floor.

Time stood still. The air in my lungs had been sucked out when I slammed the drawer, and I had an out of body experience. Like a ghost floating above, and in slow motion, I saw myself standing there, motionless, with some other woman's clothing at my feet. Forever passed in a matter of seconds, and I came rushing back to reality when Tucker's tail brushed my legs as he sniffed around the dress.

This wasn't happening. It wasn't real. It couldn't be. Was I tripping? Was the gummy I took cannabis or mushrooms? I just kept telling myself it was all a bad dream. Jay had been acting a little weird lately, but this was too much.

Dammit, Amanda. Why did you take that edible?

Rather than go home and disappear from him entirely (like I *should* have done), I pulled the jacket on in a trance, walked out back, grabbed a scooter, and raced up the hill going about 40 mph (with no helmet) to the monument. I was greeted by Jay and his high, jovial buddies, but when he saw the stoned look of disgust on my face he stepped back, and asked what was up. I just said point blank, in front of everyone, "I found the lingerie, Jay. Who is she?"

Without any hesitation, he laughed. The mother fucker LAUGHED! Then sped away on his scooter yelling behind him, "Be careful what you look for… you might not like what you find…"

I was fucking pissed. I dropped the scooter and started walking. He didn't text. Didn't call. Didn't come look for me. I wandered around Charlestown high, hungry, lonely, and infuriated for a couple hours until the pit in my stomach shrank a little, and I gathered enough courage to go get my things and go home.

Arriving back at his condo, I walked into a cloud of smoke enveloping him and his buddies as they sat around the kitchen table, puffing on joints and blowing lincs. Repulsed, I went in to grab my bag and keys but was stopped by Jay as he peered at me and asked why I was snooping around his place. I pushed him aside and gathered my stuff.

He started yapping, called me crazy, and carried on like he was a hero. His buddies just sat there laughing like idiots as he accused me of going through his shit, spying on him, and disrespecting his privacy. A week earlier he had said his house was "wide open and he had nothing to hide." I *thought* we were in a committed relationship, but it seemed his house was wide open to more women than just me.

Flustered, I found my bag while he kept trying to defend himself and humiliate me. I glared at him one final time, chucked his jacket at his face, and left with wafts of weed following me out the door.

The following day, full of rage, I tried to make all the confusion and pain go away with a spring yard clean-up. I figured a productive distraction might dilute the anger that was boiling over in my heart.

Making significant progress with the leaves, I scrounged for more waste bags behind the shed. In my haste, I knocked over a pile of pots and found a strange, yet impressive, collection of miscellaneous broken shovels. Irritated at the increasing mess, I yelled my anger towards nature, hoping it would rid my heart of the pain. It didn't work. The more I shuffled, the longer my list of stupid shit to do became, and the higher my frustration grew. As I forced myself into near exhaustion, the agony just kept expanding deeper into my soul with every curious spade and busted pot I found.

After a rake shot up out of nowhere and smacked me on the shin, I sat on a bucket and slumped over into a pathetic, disgruntled ball of physical and emotional hurt, totally defeated. I just wanted to light a match and burn it all. Set my entire life on fire so I could walk away and start all over. But instead, through sniveling and profanity, I kept pillaging through the piles of crap hoping to get somewhere. Finally, I got to the back of the shed where I found a surprising distraction covered with a tattered tarp and coated layers of dust, leaves, and cobwebs.

It was my 2014 Honda Rebel 250 motorcycle—a welcomed interruption to my pain and suffering from Jay's bullshit. Years ago, I had been a weekend warrior and loved the clarity and peace I got while riding that relic. Feelings I now longed for. Abandoning all the other projects, I muscled the heavy bike up the driveway and started cleaning her up. As I polished the chrome and pulled leaves from the chain, an undeniable desire was reignited: I wanted my freedom back. But this hunk of tin wasn't reliable and needed more love and care than I was willing (or able) to give it, so I decided to trade it in.

With questions swirling in my head, I drove to the dealership. *Was getting a new bike financially smart? Probably not. Was it something I needed? Absolutely not. Did it even fit into my social activities or travel plans? Not for a second. So why?*

Because I was hurting and wanted to cover up the pain. Because my soul was aching to be filled with love. Because I was yearning for something that brought me joy. Because I needed something that no one could take away from me, and I was convinced that riding was the love, the joy, the *something* that was going to make it all better.

Freedom. Clarity. Peace.

When I learned how to ride, the instructor drilled into me that being present is the most important factor in safe riding. You absolutely *must* be completely aware of the world around you, and you *must* pay attention to everything—every rock, pothole, street sign, car, bird, and bus. Riding a motorcycle forces you to immerse yourself in the moment and compels you to control your thoughts. Losing focus for a second could cost you your life, so connecting with your machine and your mind is the only thing that *must* happen when you ride. Your life depends on it.

On a mission to rekindle my passion for the open road, I wanted to find the symbol that matched my new attitude better than the old Honda. I needed more power, more presence, more control. The top requirements for this new bike were reliability and speed. But I also wanted something I could ride comfortably for hours and look sexy as hell doing it.

Bouncing from Triumph to Honda, Indian to Harley trying to deduce which bike felt best, I did a few sit tests while eyeing the various curves and costs. I took my time and wandered around the dealership for about an hour. As I reached the front corner of the building, I was drawn to a stunning bike that I had subconsciously written off earlier because I thought it was out of my league. The salesman urged me to "try it anyway," and as soon as I lifted my leg over the petite frame, slid my butt into the leather seat, raised my arms to the handlebars, and rocked my hips back and forth, I knew it was meant to be. I looked up at him and said, **"I think this bike was made just for me. My ass fits perfectly."**

Not only did it fit just right, but with the iconic Harley style and low to the ground body, it was exactly the vehicle I needed to change my attitude and get back to my freedom.

One week later, I rode my brand new 2021 Harley Davidson Iron 883 matte black motorcycle out of the lot and right into my new mindset.

"When writing the story of your life, never let anyone else hold the pen."

~ *Harley Davidson*

As I accelerated onto Route 1 North on my mission driven cruise, I could feel the power and potential this motorcycle was bringing back to me. I smiled. God, it felt good to be on the road again.

About an hour into my ride, with a clear head but still a heavy heart, I found myself turning left, then left again. Driving down Low Street, I knew exactly where I was and why I was there. The clarity from this maiden voyage on my new freedom chaser had steered me straight towards a place I hadn't been to for nearly twelve years.

My brain took inventory of the scene as I raced by. The house looked the same. The same boat was up on stilts in the driveway. There was a dog on the porch. A bright orange jeep was parked on the gravel, and I recognized a few characters mulling about in the front yard. It looked like something out of a fairy tale. Beautiful weather. Beautiful people. A few kids.

And it hurt like hell to see it. I had lived in that house and been a part of that fairytale scene back in 2007, but it all got brilliantly fucked up through lies, control, suffocation, and heartache. Now all I could do was speed by in suffering and disgrace. As I rode by, my adrenaline spiked, and though I might have initially bought the bike to get noticed, I now hoped that no one would see me flying by.

I pulled into the farm parking lot down the street, turned off the engine, ripped off my helmet, and did everything I could to not hyperventilate. Panic took over the calm, peaceful awareness I had cultivated during the past hour's ride, and even with the helmet off my head and my jacket unzipped, I felt like I was suffocating. Standing a mere hundred yards from a life I had lived twelve years ago, I gasped for air as an emotional flood drenched me in sweat and images of pink lingerie and red dresses merged with love notes and baseball hats.

Because of the karmic exposure of Jay's secrecy and lies, I was now reliving the events that led to my marriage falling apart twelve years earlier. Shame filled every cell of my body, and I dropped to the ground in a full-blown anxiety attack. For the very first time, I had an understanding of how my ex-husband, Colby, must have felt when he found the crumpled pieces of paper and hat in the trunk of my car. Feelings of guilt grew thick around my heart as I hid behind the lilacs I had planted fifteen years prior and stared through the sweet flowers into the abyss of my former life.

God had taken over my ride and guided me towards the freedom I was seeking in the most unexpected, bass-ackwards way. The voices of reason and empathy whispered into my heart and suddenly I knew what I had to do.

I tried to just say, "Fuck it," but the volume of voices in my head rose above my insecurities and yelled *Come on, Amanda. You made it this far. What do you have to lose? Worst case, he tells you to "fuck off," and you leave.* I appeased my intuitive yearning for humility and stood up to face my fear.

"True forgiveness is an emotional expansion of the heart that must be arrived at honestly and organically."

~ *Katherine Woodare Thomas*

With trembling fingers, I strapped my helmet back on, started up my bike, rode to the end of the driveway, and parked. The woman cleaning her Jeep stood up with a questioning, "Hello?" which sounded more like, *Who the hell are you?*

I asked if Colby was around, and she silently walked me towards the boat. With no idea how my body was moving, I followed along with this Divine plan and took in more details of the scene. There was a new patio set and a large doggie bed under the picnic table.

The woman called up to the boat, and Colby popped his head up from inside.

"What's up?" he asked.

"There's someone here to see you," she replied, turning to look at me.

Adjusting his eyes from the darkness of the boat helm to the midday sun, he eventually focused and saw me for the first time in twelve years. "Amanda?!"

"Hey," I responded quietly. My whole body was quivering.

His buddy Rich, hopped off the swim platform, offered a brief and confused hello, then walked over to the Jeep lady, motioning to the rest of the people on the lawn, and escorting them all to the neighbors' second-floor balcony. I can only assume they wanted front row seats to the throw down that was about to happen.

The air felt thick, heavy, and suppressing. My throat tightened, and I could barely breathe. It took every ounce of will-power and composure to stand there and look at him, looking at me, staring at him. I started sweating profusely under my leather jacket as he climbed down the boat ladder and walked towards me.

"What are you doing here?"

My mind raced. My soul knew what I was doing, but there was no communication between the two, so I just stood there, motionless and silent. Probably in as much shock as he was.

"What are you doing here?" he said again.

Realizing I needed to speak, I blurted out, "I'm here to apologize."

Surprised at the words that came out of my mouth, and scared at what might happen next, I stared right into his face for any sign of whether I should relax or run.

Oddly enough, he smiled. Wiped his hands on a rag. And said "Oh. Umm. Let's go sit down."

Phew. He wasn't going to chuck a wrench at my head. I was always afraid of his anger. I felt my nerves reattach themselves to my body as we walked over to the porch and did the awkward small talk thing for about five minutes. Caught up on where I was living and working, he admitted to bumping into my uncle on occasion and said he already knew what I was up to.

Obviously, he hadn't moved since we were sitting on the same deck we had built together thirteen years prior. He had sold his construction company though and commented that running his own business beat him up too much. It hit home, and I insinuated that it must be so much easier to let someone else be in charge. He smiled as if I took the words out of his mouth. The connection of conversation was still there, and I could relate to his story because I was living his previous reality, just a few years behind.

His girlfriend and her two kids had moved in with him a couple years ago. I wondered how I hadn't noticed the bicycles and skateboard in the driveway. Feeling defeated and looking at the dog bed under the table, I responded with, "Ah, seems you changed your mind about the whole family thing."

"Yeah. I know it's what you wanted, but I wasn't ready back then. I don't even know if I'm ready now, but they come with her territory, and we are making it all work…" He kept talking, and I dropped my gaze as he carried on about kids sports and college plans. The noose of his current reality tightened around my heart, and I started to lose my courage. He caught on and shuffled his feet to pull me back into the conversation.

"Do you want to see Morgan? She's still here."

Looking up at him with a hopeful smile, he took my nod as a yes and hopped inside the house. He came back a minute later accompanied by a beautiful, happy yet gray, fourteen-year-old yellow lab. She was weak and feeble, and he had to help her into her bed, but she was the same pup that stole my heart fourteen years prior.

I couldn't control the flood gates I had been holding back. Colby had given me Morgan for my thirtieth birthday, and I lost custody of her when we divorced. It broke and filled my heart at the same time to see her again and to know she had lived a glorious and loving life. They say dogs never forget, and I believe that, because as I bent down to pet her, she gave a little wag of her tail and looked up at me as if to say, "Hi Mom, I missed you."

When I gained my composure, I stood up and said, "It's nice to see you. I am happy for you and your girlfriend." There was a long awkward pause as I summoned strength and willpower to keep going. "Thanks for not chasing me off your property."

He laughed, and recognizing my energy shift, leaned back in his chair and waited.

Suddenly empowered I blurted out in a long, run-on sentence "I'm sorry for all the bullshit I put us through, and I'm sorry for hurting you the way I did. I now know what it must have felt like to find those things in my car and to hear me lie to you. I was confused and didn't know how to ask for help. Fuck, I didn't even know I needed help. I was in a really bad place and got really fucking overwhelmed with everything. I felt suffocated, and you were controlling. I'm sorry I cheated. I'm sorry for the lies. I'm sorry for the pain I caused. I'm sorry I fucked up the best thing that has ever happened to me. And I am so so so so very sorry that it took me this long to apologize. I was afraid you might kill me if you ever saw me again."

I stood there with rivers of emotions flowing out of my eyes, courage filling my heart, and a sudden rush of air filling my lungs for the first time since I rode past an hour earlier.

He didn't move or speak. My mind begged him silently, *Please say something. Anything! Please, PLEASE say something.*

After what felt like fifteen lifetimes, he smiled and said, "Thank you." He paused and his face changed a bit, "I owe you an apology too."

Wait, what?! ...

"I've been able to reflect back and see how my actions and attitude played a big part in what happened. I was scared about finally getting everything I wanted and wasn't sure what to do with all of it, so I became controlling, didn't know what to do with you, and held on too tight."

Well fuck...

He continued. "I can't imagine what you are thinking about my girlfriend and kids living with me. I was just as surprised as everyone else, but I learned from what we went through and turned some things around. She's great, and we've made it work. But it sucks that it didn't work with us. I'm sorry too."

Fuck again...

The fictitious noose around my neck loosened, and the bindings on my heart released.

With the liberation of my apology and the unexpected offering of his, a dozen years of sadness, pressure, and blame lifted off my shoulders and blew away in the gentle spring breeze. We went back and forth for a little while longer, then realized that forty-five minutes had passed.

I said good-bye to Morgan, and he walked me to my bike. He congratulated me on the purchase and told me he sold his Harley back when everyone moved in. The irony in that alone made me smile. He and I had shared the Harley-dream way back when, so I found it intriguing to see we had both followed through with it, just not together.

FORGIVENESS AS A GATEWAY

I geared up, pulled out of his driveway, and rode straight to the beach. I stripped down to my t-shirt, jeans and bare feet and took a walk, allowing the crisp ocean breeze to clean the tear stains off my cheeks.

Reflecting on what had just happened, I knew that apologizing to Colby was never part of my conscious plan until I found myself gasping for air behind the lilac bushes. I didn't know *how* I got there, but my soul knew exactly *why* I was there. I had wanted to make it all go away but had no idea that "all of it" wasn't just what had happened three weeks earlier with Jay.

"All of it" was a lifetime of bullshit from my past that for some reason I was being forced to face and view from a different perspective. It apparently was time for me to feel the anguish and anger I had caused other people through my own side of the story, standing in their shoes. I thought I had healed all my parts at DWD, but as I stood on the edge of the ocean, vacillating between my current reality with Jay and the destructive affair that ended my marriage to Colby, I had the sudden realization that my continued education on healing had just restarted. I acknowledged the situations weren't equal and could now understand how Colby must have felt.

Staring out into the waves, I felt an overwhelming sensation that it was finally time to make peace with my mistakes, regardless of when they happened, or who they were with.

As my new found gates to freedom opened, I felt so much of my old nonsense, as well as some of the anger and confusion from Jay, dissolve in the form of forgiveness, and I felt lighter. Refreshed. Free.

—

Owning what you do, seeking forgiveness, and granting it to others is a grand act of self-love, self-respect, and growth. It's not always easy to go back and take responsibility for errors or wrongdoings we've made, but knowing that time does help the healing process and mistakes can be remedied is a step in the right direction.

That first really nice spring day was perfect for a cruise, and I rode my motorcycle like my life depended on it, inadvertently healing so many parts of me that I didn't even know were still broken.

"Life's too short to wake up with regrets. So, love the people who treat you right, forgive the ones who don't and believe that everything happens for a reason. If you get the chance, take it. If it changes your life, let it. Nobody said it would be easy, they just promised it would be worth it."

~Dr. Seuss

That June, Jay came back, apologizing profusely for his actions and the other woman and telling me he loved me unconditionally and had made a huge mistake. He promised that all the nonsense was out of his life for good, the drugs and alcohol were gone, and he wanted to work on our relationship. My budding new integrity was still too fresh to fully understand the lack of veracity in Jay's manipulative personality, and because I had started doing the healing work and found forgiveness within myself and Colby, I naively assumed that Jay had been doing the same.

DEAR DIARY

"I'm sorry. Please forgive me. Thank you. I Love you."

Ho'oponopono[v] is a traditional Hawaiian practice of reconciliation and forgiveness. The method of practice is to stare into the eyes of your loved one, opponent, rival, self, or lover and repeat the poem over and over again. Then they repeat it back to you.

1. Try the Ho'oponopono with yourself in the mirror. Sounds quirky, but you just may be amazed at how much lighter you feel when you can forgive yourself, and others.
2. What activity have you stopped doing that you wish you could pick back up again, even if only for a little bit? What kind of joy did it bring to you? Why did you stop doing it?
3. Motorcycles are everywhere. Look twice, save a life (I sound like a bumper sticker). And please, wear a helmet.

---

[v] The Hawaiian dictionary defines ho'oponopono as, "to put to rights, order or shape; correct, revise, adjust, amend, regulate, arrange, rectify (and a few others)." It also means: "Mental cleansing through prayer, discussion, confession, repentance and mutual restitution and forgiveness."

13

FROM SANDPITS to SANCTUARIES

Integrate the Importance and Power of Self-Care

"We are stronger in the places we have been broken."

~ *Ernest Hemingway*

SUMMER, 2021

On the foggy night of July 6, Jay and I were partying down at the Charlestown Marina when it started raining, so we headed home. As we took off on our scooters, the wind picked up and grabbed my hat. In a foolish attempt to catch it, I pulled on the brake, flipped over my scooter handlebars, and broke my right foot in three places. Jay was so wasted (so much for sobering up) that rather than take me to the hospital like I asked, he scooped me off the pavement and took me to his condo instead. Lying on the sofa, realizing this was my fate for the night, I watched my foot swell like a balloon while he and his friends mingled in the kitchen. I attempted to numb the pain and reality of the situation with alcohol, edibles, and one of Jay's Trazadones, but none of it worked.

In the middle of the night, I got up to pee, hopped into the bathroom, and passed out somewhere between squatting and balancing on one leg. I woke to the sensation of repeatedly banging my head on the shower curb and cried out to Jay. I must have been having some sort of seizure or convulsions from the shock of a broken foot and all the drugs. Groggily he came over, and insensitively asked why I was on the floor with my underwear around my ankles. He helped me back to bed, tried convincing me that sex would help us both sleep, and after fending him off for a gross minute, he passed out and snored until 6 a.m., while I laid there in excruciating pain.

The following morning, after Jay took an important call, rolled a joint, and made coffee with weed sugar, he eventually drove me to the emergency room around 11 a.m. He pulled up to the hospital entry, didn't offer to help in any way aside from putting the truck in park, and watched from the driver's seat as I hopped out of his Tahoe. Wishing me luck, he then sped off before I had even gotten onto the sidewalk. I couldn't reach him later that day and had to call an Uber to get home.

Three days after the whole fiasco, and multiple unanswered texts, calls, and emails to Jay, I got a cryptic message from some random number saying my car would be delivered to me by noon. I had left it at Jay's the night of the accident and had no way of getting it back without connecting with him. I waited on my front porch until 6 p.m. when some kid I didn't know pulled up and asked, "Is this your car?" He parked it in the driveway, then pulled a fucking scooter out of the trunk as his new means of transportation.

Quivering from emotional overload, I bumbled down the front steps, crutched over to him, and snatched my keys from his hand. I looked him square in the eye and said,

"You tell Jay that I never, ever, EVER want to see or hear from him ever again. He's dead to me."

"OK, I'll tell him," the kid said blankly, then scooted away.

Fucker.

Hobbling back to the porch through debilitating pain in my foot, I somehow managed to hold myself together while I literally crawled up the steps, into my house, and collapsed on the floor of my front hall. For the next hour, I stayed crumpled in a shivering ball of anguish as I ranted and wailed about how bullshit I was, about Jay's disappearing acts, and the fact that my fucking foot was broken and I had project deadlines to manage. I was crushed in every definition of the word and could not find the energy to pull myself out of this hellish experience. I stayed there crying for hours until my dog, Artie, woke me up with a concerned lick and a wag of his tail.

> *"**Anguish** not only takes away our ability to breathe, feel and think—**it comes for our bones**. Anguish often causes us to physically crumple in on ourselves, literally bringing us to our knees or forcing us all the way to the ground. The element of powerlessness is what makes anguish traumatic. We are unable to change, reverse, or negotiate what has happened. And even in those situations where we can temporarily reroute anguish with to-do lists and tasks, it finds its way back to us."*
>
> ~ *Brené Brown*

It took me a few days, but I taught myself how to drive with my left foot. Rather than stay home like I should have, I went back to work in an attempt to re-route my focus and distract myself from the physical pain and emotional suffering that had taken over my entire existence.

—

At the end of July, it was hot as fuck in New England, and we were in the middle of a drought. Everywhere felt like hell. But that didn't slow me down. I was busy working on a large project in New Hampshire, scrambling towards a deadline to open fifty-six hotel rooms by September 1, 2021.

Ignoring the fact that my foot was broken, I hobbled around that construction site like a warrior princess in a bright blue cast and a strap-on "peg-leg" thing that kept me from toppling over in the sand-pit. I was literally crawling up and down ladders and in and out of unfinished buildings like a kid building a sand castle, not stopping long enough to pay attention to the echoes of insanity that were fogging my common sense, until I absolutely had to.

The opening date for the development had been set at the end of 2019, but then the Covid-19 pandemic ripped around the world in 2020, meaning that in the spring of 2021, we were all still dealing with long-term rippling effects of unprecedented factory shutdowns, supply chain issues, lack of work force personnel, and skyrocketing prices. All of these factors deeply affected the construction and furniture industries and decimated any pre-pandemic expectation. It was clear that the development's schedule needed to be adjusted. However, Howard, the owner of the development, refused to accept reality and kept pushing his ludicrous agenda, regardless of the fact there was no running water, no sewage, no electricity, and no paved roads two months before opening day.

The construction and installation teams worked around the clock under unrelenting stress and unrealistic conditions, doing whatever it took to *attempt* to stay on track. And yet, multiple times a day some sort of emergency would derail the timetable, pulling everyone's attention elsewhere, and obliterating our collective ability to finish anything before another catastrophe blew up.

Like the day a forty-foot furniture delivery truck got stuck in the sand and started to tip over because a road that had been there two hours before had been moved (aka redirected), and no one had been told. After four hours and the help of an excavator, a dozen laborers, and an infantry of carpenters, we were able to get the trailer upright and the truck out of the sand. The next three hours were then consumed with offloading, carrying, and restacking thirty sofas and ninety lounge chairs out of the delivery truck, and into storage containers a quarter mile away. By 7 p.m. we finally finished, and all of us were exhausted. No one got anything else done that day.

This happened in one way or another all summer long.

The following morning I woke up at 5 a.m. with a rash all over my stomach and chest, and I could feel it creeping up my neck and down my legs. My toes were swollen like little sausages ready for the campfire, and my entire body was throbbing. Staring in the mirror, all I could see was a sunburned, exhausted lunatic peering back at me. She was worn out, beat up, and so very sad. The energy surrounding her was fractured and frail. **I hardly recognized myself. I wasn't me anymore, and I think the Velcro on my peg-leg was the only thing holding me together. My final breaking point had caught up with me, and I knew I had to stop.**

Anguish had found its way back to me, and I was in severe pain. Rather than pack my cooler for another day in the desert, I packed up my car to go home. The rash was the final physical sign that my nervous system was unhinging. With my emotions at the base of my throat, it took every ounce of pride to keep them there while I went to the site trailer and told the general contractor that I had to leave.

He took one look at me, promised to handle the rest of the deliveries, and told me to, "Drive safe."

I drove home in silence. No radio. No podcasts. No phone calls. Just quiet.

As I pulled into my driveway, my stifled emotions started to rise. Rather than unpack the car, I got out and sat in a heap on my front porch and allowed the tears to flow. I didn't have any energy to move and by now, the rash had spread to my back, neck, and was teasing my cheeks. I could hardly handle the ache surrounding the hives, the throbbing in my foot, and the pain in my joints as my body was literally shutting down.

Then my phone rang. It was the general contractor checking to see if I made it home okay. His compassion and concern broke me open, and my crying evolved into uncontrollable sobs of defeat and surrender. My relentless determination to remain unphased, emotionless, and detached had been overthrown by one act of gentle kindness.

I spent the rest of the summer sitting on my deck, allowing my foot (and heart) to heal, researching relationship turmoil, and recovering from the anxiety rash that stuck around for over a week. I found a way to manage the project chaos from home and only went back to the sandy job site a couple more times.

Through my research, however, I learned that the back and forth bullshit from Jay, my constant confusion, and the reasons why I was willing to accept his crumbs (even after he would disappear for weeks) were textbook definitions of him having borderline personality disorder and projecting narcissistic abuse on to me. I learned that my empathetic nature and people-pleasing habits had allowed me to be repeatedly lured into his manipulative traps. I was a victim of the whacked out psychological games covert narcissists use to keep their subjects close, but not close enough to understand who they really are.

I didn't want to believe that I had fallen prey to this moron, but whether I wanted to accept it or not, it was the truth. Eventually I started to get over the fact that Jay never called once while my foot was broken. And as my body began to heal, my soul started to ask for some attention as well.

I read that connecting with my soul and spirit would help me regain my values and strength and taking a break from my day-to-day would help with my physical healing as well. By the end of the summer, I had kicked the cast to the curb, was straightening out my limp with some physical therapy, and fully embraced the original message that the Universe had sent me. I recognized that if I didn't slow down, get away from Jay and the chaos in New Hampshire, and take care of myself, I might end up in the hospital (again).

So, I booked a trip to Austin, Texas, and went south to heal.

FALL, 2021

I started my vacation/sanity reset in Austin, Texas, where two of my best friends, Lori and Meg, met me for the weekend. I hadn't seen either of them since the pandemic had started or my *shit*uationship with Jay began. Reuniting with them reminded me of the importance of perspective and quality time with friends.

In true college style (at the age of forty-five), we lit Austin on fire for forty-eight hours! We had cocktails for lunch and soul-filling scrumptious dinners. We rode rent-a-bikes all over the city and shopped till we dropped. Then popped gummies, slung tequila, smoked cigars, and wore ridiculously large Texas hats while we laughed until we peed our pants on the roof deck of a swanky hotel.

I needed it. Every single bit of their love and energy. I needed it. After all the angst, anguish, and suffering I endured that summer, good friends and laughter was exactly what the doctor had ordered.

"There is nothing in the world so irresistibly contagious as laughter and good humor."

~ CHARLES DICKENS

Next I headed for Miraval Resort, located on the outskirts of the city. I chose this lavish hotel chain because they pride themselves on being "*wellness destinations designed to help you create a life in balance.*"[8] And *balance* is exactly what I was aiming for. I had been to spas before, and have had my fair share of massages, facials, and breathwork sessions, but this five day retreat proved to be heaven on earth.

On my first afternoon, I met with this cool Alchemical Hypnotherapist and got energetically reset through a question and answer dialogue that blew my mind. I had been practicing therapy a lot since 2007, so I felt like I was somewhat ready for the hypnotherapy version. But the question, answer, repeat the answer format was an interesting and unique way to experience my own stories through someone else's voice. His recounting of my stories became more soulful, not just factual; and as he did a bit of memory reformation therapy on me, I was able to shift old opinions away from neglect or pain, towards compassion and love. We created spiritual understandings in the name of my parents and identified a few other spirit guides that would accompany me for the rest of the week. His session was so impactful. I walked out of there with a euphoric clarity and, surprisingly, much less of a limp.

The next morning, after a restorative yoga class, I participated in a sound bath meditation led by a master practitioner of Himalayan singing bowls. She filled the small and unique sacred Solidago Sanctuary with bowl and gong vibrations, as well as her etheric and angelic voice. As she traveled through a yoga-Nidra sound-healing journey via the music, her chanting of "Om Namah Shivaya"[9] and the effects of burning sage around the room propelled me to a higher sense of self in a way only the harmonic meditation could have guided me. My newly introduced spirit guides integrated with the session and gently carried my old beliefs and non-essential crap out of me and away from the building. The vibrational synchronization of the instruments and this woman's voice had me crying tears of release as the physical and emotional pain was lifted from my body and years of anger and resentment dissolved, leaving my heart open to the opportunities of this restorative and calming experience and allowing me to feel lighter and more abundant when the session was complete. It was inspiring to say the least.

Filling the rest of my day with a glowing facial and lounge time by the pool, I entered into the sunset Cleansing Ceremony with excitement and anticipation. This cleansing meditation is meant to clear our mind and soul of thoughts and things that no longer serve us, and once I understood that, I settled in, and patiently waited to release all the other built-up crap I had been weighing myself down with that hadn't already been washed away at the sound bath.

As the instructor guided us through the session, I became aware of the ridiculous amount of other people's baggage I had been carrying for years and years. Their problems. Their concerns. Their issues. Their sadness. None of it belonged to me, but yet, I held on to it like it was mine. It was time to let it all go.

When the meditation really took off, we were instructed to pick a door of the building and rid our souls of negative and unhealthy energy in whichever way we saw fit. As I ran west to the door with a whole luggage rack of heavy shit, I flailed and screamed and spat my little heart out towards the setting sun, freeing myself of other people's nonsense as best as I could. It felt almost inhuman, but when I was finished, I felt like I had lost even more weight and walked straight back to my seat, forgetting my foot was even attached to my leg.

After our purge, we all found our way back to our mats, and our guide asked if any of us kept journals. I shot my hand up in the air like the proudest student in class. She smiled, then asked what I wrote about. Was it all good stuff? Or were the pages filled with heartache, aggravation, frustration, and sorrow? Now embarrassed, I meekly dropped my hand. (Pain and suffering was *all* I wrote about!)

She went on to explain how we carry energy around with us, and **when we write about things, we give them energy to remain with us forever.**

I hadn't ever looked at it that way. Taking her concept into consideration, I knew the purpose of my journals had been to liberate my heart and free up space in my mind. I never intended to save the tears or heartache that I wrote about. It all just landed in my journals. I concluded I didn't want to keep unnecessary energy around any longer (or store it in my basement) and contemplated how I was going to use my journals and diaries *moving forward* after this trip. If these books hold energy, and I'm intentionally shifting the type of energy I want in my life, well then, I need to shift the direction of my writing and do something with those damn books.

To further instill the point of the cleansing ceremony, she had us write a few things down that we still wanted to release, then we lit them on fire. As I watched lingering ugly thoughts burn quickly to dust in a little clay bowl, I was instantly inspired and knew exactly what I was going to do when I got home.

After learning about how energy is stored in written words, I shifted slightly and decided to work out any remaining pain and frustration in a physical format via a hatchet throwing class the next day. The physical interrupt to all my zen work and new spiritual patterning helped to balance my week out a bit, and as I chucked the axes at an imaginary face of the dickhead who dropped me off at the hospital, I felt an incredible satisfaction whenever the blade would connect hard and strong on the target. It felt good to know I was leaving my anguish in Texas and going home proficient in hatchet throwing.

My last session was an astrological chart reading. We filled out our information the day before, and as the group settled into class, the instructor asked, "Who's Amanda?"

"Me," I said proudly.

"Oh, you poor thing. How are you doing?" she asked in a concerned tone.

The look of confusion on my face was a clear indication I didn't know what she was insinuating. I had just spent some of the most magical days of my life. I was amazing!

"My dear," she said, "you are water, water, water. It's a wonder you have any grounding at all!"

Ha! Well shit. That explains a lot.

Pisces sun + Pisces moon + Cancer Rising Moon = Water, Water, Water.

As I learned the power of the zodiac and astrological influences, I gained a whole new level of power and understanding of my personality, my empathy, my imagination, and my ability to fall in love so quickly, so naïvely, and so completely, over and over again. It all made complete sense to me, and I was shocked that I had never dug into this aspect of myself before. I quickly digested every single word she said and promised myself I would integrate the teachings into my life, because I now knew that if I didn't, I might drown in my own natural creation.

I embraced every experience for all it had to offer, and I connected with a peace that had been hiding in the shadows for years. The combination of the spirit guides, yoga, meditations, ceremonies, chart reading, therapies, massages, and body work sessions integrated into the greatest understanding of who I knew I was at my core, and I finally, finally felt like I understood *who* I really am, and more importantly *why* I am. It was magical.

The stress wrinkles in my forehead disappeared while my smile became a more natural accessory plastered on my face. This trip was exactly what I needed to heal and let go of the *shit*uationship and nonsense that had been weighing me down for so long. The shifts in me opened up a healed and cleared space that I had been missing since "Date With Destiny."

RISING OF THE PHOENIX

Gifting myself the opportunity to relish in a week of self-care helped me break through some of my unhealthy patterns of ignorance and self-neglect and steered me back on to a course of self-love, dignity, and discovery.

Whatever path we are on, or whatever path we *think* we are on, is one of divine creation and momentum. If you pay attention to what's happening inside while the external world is carrying on with (or without) you, there are messages happening for us, all the time. It's about perceiving our life's experiences as miracles of serendipity or mishaps disguised as messages.

I had become so wrapped up in the narcissistic chaos of Jay and the development project that it took a broken foot and a body covered in hives for me to heed the warning of the Universe and start taking better care of myself. But even when I began to understand what had been happening for almost two years, and I intentionally took a personal health retreat to reset myself, it still took time for me to fully grasp the lingering effects that the abusive relationship had on my emotional and psychological health.

—

A couple weeks after my Miraval experience, I spent an entire weekend going through the boxes of diaries that were packed in my basement. The message of keeping negative energy really hit home, and I decided it was time to go through those books and gift myself more space and more room for self-respect, integrity, and peace.

I read almost every page of every journal I had written from eighth grade to the week before I went to Miraval. Sitting in the basement reliving the experiences and crying through many of the painful emotions was challenging but cathartic. I read through a lifetime of childish impressions and misguided beliefs and recognized a mindset that was no longer accurate nor belonged to who I had become.

With the tools I had learned at UPW, LWM, and DWD, along with all the coaching and therapy I have received over the years, **I began to accept all the characters within the narratives as unique and beautiful parts of myself** in ways I wasn't able to bear at the time of each event. My pain became lessons in strength building. My disappointments shifted into joys of discovery. And rather than beat myself up for misperceived weakness, I reframed the challenges into toughness of temperament.

In pages of insecurity, I found resiliency. I recalled feelings of fear and inadequacy through some of the people-pleasing words in those books, but then gave myself grace and acknowledged how I had overcome some pretty shitty situations along my journey, and was still going. While I read, I started to fall in love with the little girl, the teenager, the young woman, and the grown adult that had written all of these messages. They became reminders of what I've been through and what I thought I wanted. They showed me exactly who I've always been and enlightened me on who I was becoming.

Feeling my way through the pages and critiques of myself, I allowed the pain and joys of the scribbles to have one last moment in the spotlight, then vowed to liberate my heart from the weight of the old energy connected to these books. None of it was black and white. It had all faded to various shades of gray and cream. But it was all mine. My life. My history as I remembered it. And with pride, I knew it was time to let it all go.

I took photos of pages that held positive, encouraging vibes and kept a few of the travel notebooks that included photos, destination logs, and happy memories. Then I burned the rest.

Ceremoniously, I built a bonfire in my backyard, smoked a bowl, and drank tequila. A lot of tequila. I danced around with my spirit guides as I ripped pages out of the little flowery books and spiral binders that represented limiting beliefs, heartache, and drama spanning over thirty years and tossed them in the fire. The closer the dates got to the present moment, the higher the flames rose, and my exhilaration rose with it. I may have been a little high, definitely a little drunk too, and the fire definitely got too big, but I swear when I tossed the most recent book into the fire, I saw the shape of a phoenix rise out of the ashes and fly away into the night sky. I felt like a new woman. Stronger. More powerful. Full of light, love, and limitless potential.

In early October, three months to the day of when I broke my foot, as if he saw a smoke signal or something, Jay reached out and told me he had a huge new project for "us" to work on. With my focus on rekindling my rising qualifications as a prominent designer in the industry, I thought I was now strong enough to keep my boundaries clear and Jay's manipulation tactics at bay. Realizing I should have blocked him, but believing in healed powers more, I foolishly gave in to his tantalizing offer and got sucked back into his devious *shit*uationship once again for another six months.

DEAR DIARY

I cannot stress enough about the importance of self-care. Learning how to integrate it into your routine, in whatever form that is, can truly bring a better balance to your psyche and your lifestyle.

1. The Universe has a very clever way of sending us messages. So clever, in fact, that we often miss them if we are not open to hearing them. Have you ever gotten a clear message to slow down and blatantly ignored it until you were physically unable to move? What *finally* stopped you? What was the proverbial straw that broke your back?
2. If you've never been to a sound bath or experienced the vibrations of a meditation bowl, I strongly recommend it. Music can heal the soul, something fierce. It's beautiful.
3. The burning process can be incredible. I'm not saying go light a fire and toss everything into it, but in small, safe, and manageable ways, burning old letters, books, or notes can be incredibly freeing.

14

YOU'RE DRIVING ME CRAZY

Understand Your Triggers

"Avoiding your triggers isn't healing. Healing happens when you're triggered and you're able to move through the pain, the pattern, and the story, and walk your way to a different ending."

~ *Vienna Pharaon*

WINTER, 1980

When I was four years old, my parents left me at a car dealership by mistake for about three minutes. This event impacted my life profoundly and it took forty years of repeated challenges and a shit-ton of therapy to uncover that this was the root cause of three of my most prominent fears: abandonment, humiliation, and lack of acceptance.

In 1980, it wasn't a crime to leave your kids in the car alone, so they left me sleeping in the back seat while they went in to look at the new Volkswagen Rabbit my mom wanted. Unbeknownst to them, I woke up when they closed the car door.

As any four-year-old might, I panicked at being left alone and jumped out of the car. Seeing my parents enter through a giant glass door, I raced to it in an attempt to catch up and somehow managed to open the incredibly heavy door shortly after them. But they walked through the showroom quickly and left out the back, never turning around to notice I was there.

At three feet tall, I couldn't see over any of the cars; therefore, no one could see me, either. Standing in the bright showroom, afraid I was lost, I turned around to see the taillights of my dad's car as they pulled out of the parking lot and turned onto the street. Terror of abandonment shot through me like a lightning bolt. I lost my shit and became hysterical.

Banging on the showroom window and screaming my little head off, I had no comprehension that they couldn't hear me, but I believed they did when I saw the taillights turn bright red and watched the car spin around like something out of a comic book. My dad must have seen me in the rearview mirror—his little girl behind a giant window, tears streaming down her face, hoping desperately that they would come back to get her.

When they ran back into the showroom, my mother scooped me up and apologized to the salesman. Then, tucking me into the back seat like nothing happened, we all went home with no discussion and I was put to bed.

The next night at dinner, my mom told the story to my brother and his friend. I couldn't believe I had to relive the nightmare; once was enough. My brother thought it was so funny he spewed milk out of his nose, which ricocheted roars of laughter around the entire table. I thought they were laughing at me, and I was humiliated.

Feeling my face explode with heated embarrassment, I ran upstairs crying, wishing I had never gotten out of the car, that none of this had ever happened, and that I could just disappear. The immense depth of shame triggered a temper tantrum, and I trashed my bedroom, throwing stuffed animals and pillows around in a rage until one of them clipped the corner of a lamp which crashed to the floor.

The loud bang snapped me out of my hysteria. When I saw what I had done, I became terrified of getting in trouble and hid under the bed. My dad came up to see what happened, failed to coax me out from under the bed, and left me there to cry it out.

I was mortified that my mother told my brother what happened, but knowing he and his friend were laughing at my expense made me feel like everything I did was wrong. I was even more upset that my dad gave up on trying to pull me out, and I slept under the bed that night—hungry, so fucking confused, and feeling totally alone.

I don't think I ever got an apology from my brother for laughing at me. And I'm pretty sure it was one of the events we just shoved in the emotional closet, pretending it never happened. I would cry every time we drove past that dealership. Eventually, as my parents stopped driving down that road, the memory faded. But it came back in a flash about forty years later.

MARCH, 2022

Jay and I were on vacation in Fort Lauderdale, Florida for the past four days and were meant to be heading home that night. This particular day had started with mimosas for breakfast, then margaritas for lunch. When it got dark, I found myself in the hotel restaurant with Jay and one of his friends, questioning where this new friend had come from and wondering when I had managed to change out of my bathing suit. Nothing made sense, and I kept hearing this voice whisper, "Master. You are a master manipulator. What is wrong with you? Why do you think you're so special?"

Looking around to see if anyone else heard it, I got a sincere sideways glance from our waitress. In an inebriated haze, I excused myself to the lady's room to "powder my nose." I knew drinking all day in the sun was taking its toll, and we had been partying all weekend, so I was slightly numb anyway, but something else felt freakishly off. Staring at my reflection in the mirror long enough to straighten myself out, I realized those fucked up comments had to be coming from Jay.

But why? What the hell was he doing to me?

Disoriented, I returned to the table only to find Jay and his buddy gone. The waitress pointed to the lobby and told me they left as soon as I went to the bathroom. *What?! Where were they going?* The look of astonishment on my face was a clear indication to her I had no idea what was happening.

Buzzed and confused, I raced to catch up with them but stopped at the hotel lobby window when I saw Jay and his friend get into an Uber and speed away. I couldn't understand why they left without me. Where were they going? And weren't *we* supposed to be going to the airport?

Suddenly, an old memory was triggered inside me, and I sprinted after the Uber.

Catching up to the car when the traffic lights turned red, I banged on the window with my fists until Jay got out of the car. Grabbing my arms, he yelled at me to stop and glared at me with disgust. Through drunken fear and bewilderment, I heard him call me crazy, felt him push me away, and watched as he got back in the car. I stumbled as the light turned green and could hear him and his buddy cackling as they drove away, leaving me desperate and alone in the middle of the street.

The honking cars brought me back to reality. In disbelief, rage, and the beginnings of hysteria, I stepped onto the sidewalk and walked back to the hotel only to be met by a policeman.

The policeman warned that I was in jeopardy of being arrested for drunk and disorderly conduct and told me I needed to gather my things and leave the hotel. Apparently, they don't take too well to people screaming like lunatics and chasing cars down the street. Buzzed, baffled, and thinking Jay had left me for good, I heeded the cop's warning and went up to the room to pack my things and get the hell out of there.

Jay's laugh echoed in my head when I entered the room, and as soon as I saw his clothes and iPad on the bed, I launched into another outburst. I didn't even know what I was doing until it was too late. I poured lube all over his iPad then picked up his bag and hurled it across the room. Of course, it knocked the morning's champagne flutes over, smashing them into tiny shards of glass all over the tile floor. The subsequent loud knock at the door wasn't a total surprise, except this time I was greeted by the hotel manager accompanied by *two* policemen. They said I was "0 for 2," and if I didn't leave the room immediately, I was going to spend the night in jail.

What! The! Fuck!

Reality hit me like a truck, and through uncontrollable sobs, I pleaded my case of emotional insanity and begged them to believe me that the broken flutes were an accident.

Magically, the waitress from downstairs appeared out of nowhere and confirmed my story. She concurred the whole scenario was really fucked up and said she was concerned I might be in danger, which is why she followed me outside and was now up in the hallway with them. She told the police about Jay's strange whispers, how the guys had been acting creepy, and that they abandoned me in the restaurant. She said she wasn't surprised I was pissed because the guy I was with was a total jerk.

I ended up with over $2,000 in credit card charges to stay in a separate room for the night, for the damage to Jay's room and broken glasses, for a flight home that I had apparently booked in the middle of the night, and a half dozen Uber rides I never showed up for. But I had no recollection of booking any flights or Uber rides.

The following morning, I woke up with a splitting headache and was totally dumbfounded as to why I was in a different room. I repacked my things and went to catch an Uber to the airport. As the lobby doors opened, I was blinded by the sun and wondered where my sunglasses were. When my pupils adjusted to the light, I looked up to see Jay's rental car pulling out of the hotel driveway.

What. The. Fuck.

My soul lurched. Not only did he *leave me* at the hotel the night before, not only did he *not try to find me* that night or the next day, but there he was, *abandoning me again!*

He must have seen me in the rearview mirror because the brake lights flashed, and he pulled over. Dumbfounded, I watched in shock as the vehicle turned around, slowly pulled into the driveway, and stopped right in front of me. He rolled down the window, and we stared at each other in silence for what felt like eternity.

"Do you want a ride?" he asked.

Like a mute robot, I put my bag in the trunk and got in the passenger seat. Then I grabbed my sunglasses out of the cupholder and buckled up.

We drove for at least thirty minutes before either of us said a word.

The first call I made when I returned home from that fucked up trip was to my coach, Kerri. She listened to my absurd account of the long weekend, made references to me being **triggered**, and suggested I find a **trauma therapist**. *What the fuck did she mean by "trigger," and what the hell did I need a trauma therapist for?* She repeated terms like "abandoned," "emotional abuse," [10] and "gaslighting," [11] and reminded me of the research I had done the previous summer while I was healing my broken foot. Her words flashed me back to flipping off the scooter and ending up on the bathroom floor, and my intuition lit up like Fourth of July fireworks as I fully understood I was once again in the middle of another one of Jay's abuse cycles.

I knew she was referring to the abandonment I felt at the hotel. And I started to acknowledge Jay's ghosting, how he would take advantage of my time, manipulate my resources, and feed off of my empathy, then leave me exhausted and nearly dead time after time after time. He was driving me crazy, but because I had committed so much to him in the hopes of helping him, healing him, and that he would follow through on whatever he kept promising me, I couldn't leave him. Who would I become when I got off the roller coaster ride? I had become addicted to the chaos and didn't know how to stop it.

For some fucked-up reason, I didn't want to believe that the awful and pathetic details Kerri repeated back to me were actually *my* stories. **I didn't want to believe it had happened to me. But, it *was* happening to me over and over again.** I didn't want to admit I had traded my self-respect for love-bombing, and my high standards for manipulative crumbs and hypothetical carrots. **But deep in my gut, I knew the truth.** Not only did I need help with figuring out what had happened in Florida, I needed help getting *all the way out* of this toxic relationship and repairing the collateral damage it had caused over the past two years.

TRIGGERS

By Definition...

To be "triggered" means:

> [To] experience a strong emotional reaction or response often due to an event or certain goading **that reminds you of a past traumatic experience,** negative memory, or personal sensitivity. When someone is triggered, the situation or stimulus has **evoked a powerful emotional or psychological response** that the person may not realize or have control over, sometimes leading to anxiety, anger, distress or other intense feelings...[12]

I wasn't fully aware of any of my triggers until most of them hit their crescendo during that humiliating vacation. Jay seemed to press my buttons constantly, creating waves of confusion, cycles of aggravation, and anger that felt foreign yet strangely familiar. I was never able to demystify my overreactions when he demanded an explanation for them and started to think I was losing my mind. The more discombobulated and infuriated I felt with him about his lack of commitment, random disappearances, and accusations of me lying when I was telling the truth, the more triggered and irrational I became.

It's easy enough to just say my subconscious made me do it, and in reality, it's partially true. Our memories can act out like ignored skeletons in the closet if we stuff them away without working through the incident. The younger versions of ourselves intentionally forget about all this painful shit, and we move on. But once that closet door gets cracked (triggered) by an event or person, a few rickety bones may escape through the chaos, and they become impossible to ignore as they clamber around. In the heat of the moment, our subconscious reacts and pulls forward visceral responses to situations to either protect or defend us without us even being tuned in to the reasoning of our behavior.

These skeletons (unresolved emotions) can have a mind of their own if given the chance. And if we perpetually ignore the signs and triggers, we can end up hurting ourselves and others by not healing the parts of us that are yearning for attention and resolve.

By Experience...

Almost getting arrested for trashing the hotel room in Fort Lauderdale was a vividly clear indication that something in my noggin was sincerely fucked up, and my trigger response was set on high.

Through Kerri's advice, I found Jackie, an EMDR therapy specialist. EMDR stands for Eye Movement Desensitization and Reprocessing, and it is a psychotherapy treatment that was originally designed to alleviate the distress associated with traumatic memories.[13] EMDR allows us to go back into our subconscious, swing open the door to those proverbial closets, and pull the skeletons out, one by one, so we can make amends with the memory, reroute their intentions, and put them to rest, once and for all. This treatment modality is about rewiring our nervous system so those old habits and reactions don't continue to wreak havoc on our lives or emotions any longer.

I shared with Jackie as much of that disturbing trip as I could remember and eventually discussed a lot of the other bullshit I had been dealing with during that entire two-year time frame, like his disappearing acts, how he treated me after I broke my foot, and when it all started way back with the lingerie and toothbrushes.

Jackie and I met every two weeks for about eight months and made significant progress on my abandonment issue and a few other niggling things. However, the first three months were really just a warm-up because, like my first therapy session back in 2004, I was avoiding the hard truth of what was really going on and continued to date Jay.

—

The way of a narcissist can be unheard, unfelt, and unrealized even for some of the strongest of individuals, and unfortunately, I got tangled up with one. During the years I spent with Jay, even with all the Tony Robbins events I had attended, the lessons I had learned, the soul connection I acquired at Miraval, and the growth I had experienced within my own righteousness, I hadn't fully broken through some of my old ingrained patterns. And Jay was able to see and manipulate the cracks.

The dramatic push-pull roller coaster ride of my *shit*uationship with him had taken so much energy out of me that I felt like I had nothing left and became too afraid to do the heavy lifting of uncovering and potentially healing my deepest darkest fears. Over time, the abuse had me succumbing to my childhood belief that I wasn't enough and that I may not ever be loved unconditionally, so I deciphered that holding on to this jackass and his abusive attention was better than being alone.

TEQUILA TALKS

A couple of months into my sessions with Jackie, I was visiting my parents in Florida and wanted to tell them about my Fort Lauderdale experience the previous March and why I hadn't come to visit them (they lived an hour from Fort Lauderdale).

Historically, as a family, we don't discuss negative things regardless of when or why they happen—and we certainly have never talked about therapy. We just shove whatever instance we prefer to forget into the closet of avoidance and ambiguity with all the other skeletons and pretend it never happened. We have functioned on the premise of "don't ask, don't tell" for as long as I can remember; however, I really wanted to get this story off my chest and let them know I figured out one of my issues.

So I suggested we make margaritas early one afternoon. I knew if I brought it up sober, I would most likely be met with uninterested silence. I also assumed that if I brought up the fact that I was in therapy, they may try to change the subject to the weather or something else. But I wasn't going to let this opportunity with them pass me by, so I held my tongue until I felt the energy shift after our second margarita, and while we were lounging in the pool, I started talking. I could tell they were listening because they both smiled when I mentioned the green Volkswagen Rabbit they ended up purchasing after that infamous winter night back in 1980.

I told them I remembered when they bought that car, and my dad shot me a sideways glance that my mom totally missed. She was too eager to remind us all of the time I slammed the door on her fingers, which brought up a whole other set of stories that are still stuffed down in the memory banks of "shit we don't talk about." My dad asked how I could have possibly remembered, and I lightly explained how my therapy with Jackie was working and that the work brought my memories directly to that four-year-old experience.

"Why are you going to therapy? You're okay, aren't you? You haven't talked to us about anything bad. What's wrong with you?" my mother interrupted.

Instantly, I was fourteen again in the passenger seat of the car. The conversations were almost identical, and rather than tackle *that* moment in time too, I just smiled and paused before dismissing her question and continuing with my story. I was determined to move through "*the pain, the pattern, and the story, and walk MY way to a different ending.*"

I breezed through the dramatic incident that had happened in Fort Lauderdale with the police where I almost got arrested, then slowed my storytelling tactics once I got to the part where I had been in an emotionally abusive relationship for the past two years and needed help getting out of it. They stared at me while they floated on their noodles and listened to everything I said. It was a little surreal since we had never talked about anything like this, but it was also encouraging and empowering to see them so attentive and interested in what I had to say. I also knew that I was blocking the stairs, so they were kind of trapped in the pool while I commanded the conversation from the shallow end. But either way, I felt like I was being heard, and they didn't seem to want to get out of the water.

When I was finished with the abbreviated version of Jay, I briefly explained what EMDR is and how my sessions with Jackie were helping me. Then I merged into the abandonment issue that she and I had uncovered because of the car dealership incident and what happened after with the spewed milk. With as much precision as I could, I described what happened that night and watched the tears well up in both of my parents' eyes. With each detail, my father's face changed from surprise to curiosity to astonishment. The more we talked, the more clear our collective perspectives became. Through new heavy and uncomfortable emotions, they asked questions about how I knew so much, so I further explained EMDR and how it was helping me let go of the abandonment trigger and heal old emotions associated with so many other childhood experiences.

When I was done spilling my tequila-tainted heart out in the pool, my father looked at me through his tears and said, "Mandi, I cannot believe you remember all that. The image I saw in the rearview mirror of you standing in that giant glass window ripped my heart out and has haunted me ever since. We never talked about it with you because we had hoped you were young enough to forget about it. We are so sorry."

"Don't forget who you are and where you come from."

~ F. Scott Fitzgerald

DEAR DIARY

When we get to the point of acknowledging who we are, where we've come from, and what might have gone wrong along the way, I truly believe we can get on the path of healing and follow a new vision for living the future differently.

Digging in and finding the reason for your triggers is imperative for healing and moving on. Pay attention to what upsets you and seek to understand the reasons why.

1. As you move through your day and your week, make a list of what pisses you off, what gets you super excited, and what tugs at your heartstrings. Why do you think each of these evokes that emotion in you in the way they do?

2. Try to recall a similar time when you felt a visceral reaction that wasn't quite aligned with who you believe you are. Maybe it was last week, last year, or when you were a child. If you have not yet dealt with the emotions associated with that time, what can you do today to overcome that?
3. If you really want to get into it, find a therapist who is certified in EMDR and parts therapy (inner child work). It's amazing and incredibly effective to go back in time and nurture ourselves from life's past.

Give yourself some time and space for this one. It can be very challenging and often emotionally draining. It can also be painful work to dig into suppressed emotions and seek answers. Have patience with yourself, and you'll reap the rewards. I promise.

15

PIVOT POINT, Part 1–
THE LAST TWO STRAWS

Recognize Your Overlapping Patterns

"Insanity: doing the same thing over and over again, and expecting different results."

~ *Albert Einstein*

SUMMER, 2022

Even though I *knew* I was dating a narcissist, I didn't want to admit I had become that weak, but more importantly, I didn't realize the detrimental effects it was having on me. I was still foolishly attracted to Jay's persona of power, financial freedom, and addictive adventure, so I stayed. I thought I could handle it.

Despite the fact that my confused emotions and feelings were justified, I still wanted to make him happy, so I awkwardly asked for his forgiveness for my actions in Fort Lauderdale. But as always, he avoided the conversation and acted like I made it all up. His blatant disregard had me questioning what was real and what wasn't, and eventually, I gave up trying to figure out the difference.

Then, one day in early May, he changed.

He started making promises about a committed relationship, traveling around the world, taking trips on his fifty-foot yacht, and building a cabin together. He pushed to spend more time with me. And the more I said yes, the greater his exotic plans and enticing ideas would become. I believed in his empty words and tried to reframe his occasional jealousy with misconstrued feelings of desire.

On top of it all, when we fought or something went wrong, I would blame myself for everything so he wouldn't get mad. This just made it easier for him to trample my emotional well-being, then I would respond with more and more in efforts to please him. The cycle was toxic. I became anxious. I depended on his validation. And I wasn't able to find any balance between the truth and his lies, or time with him versus my business. Even though he made all these promises, I still wondered if anything was going to happen with our relationship, so I held on to an unfulfilling hope that he might fully come around *someday.*

Deep down, though, even after everything I'd been through and everything I was learning about myself, I was still really afraid of being alone, so I ignored the niggling voices inside my heart and soul. His gaslighting fully consumed almost every part of me. I lost my self-esteem. I thought he was doing all these things out of his desire to be with me. I didn't realize that he was just distracting me from the other nonsense that was *really* going on in his life, which prevented me from doing the stuff that I was supposed to be doing in mine.

Coincidentally, while I was still on Jay's hook, I was also holding on to a similar hope for a profitable business deal with Howard.

For the past year, Howard had been talking about all these awesome projects—restaurants, hotels, residential houses—that he wanted me to be a part of. He would ask me to attend business meetings that ended up being bullshit dinners with "potential" investors. Then he would end the evening or lunch or meeting with more pledges of work for my design company. I was excited to be a part of the development team, so I tactfully learned to avoid his awkward, disrespectful, and inappropriate sexual innuendos because the project opportunities would have been guaranteed revenue for the next three years. I thought he asked me to these dinners and meetings because he valued my company's high level of project execution and respected my work ethic. I didn't realize until later that he just wanted to get in my pants.

When I started to admit that I was trapped on the same wild roller coaster in the two most important areas of my life, I tried to tell myself to get off the ride. But my old habits and patterns of PUSH—**P**ersist **U**ntil **S**omething **H**appens—overtook my intuitive desire for balance, and I surrendered myself to the selfish intentions of these two men. Rather than embrace faith and everything I knew about my soul, my honest character, and who I really was at my core, I let the ride gain momentum and just held on tighter, praying to God I wouldn't fall off.

Some habits are hard to break no matter how well you know yourself.

I would get excited about traveling with Jay.

I would get motivated about the projects with Howard.

I planned my summer vacations around boat trips with Jay.

I spent days and nights pulling presentations, proposals, and contracts together for Howard.

I reorganized my weekend and started designing the cabin Jay and I were going to build.

I reorganized my company to accommodate all the potential work that was going to start pouring in.

I was lost in a desert of unfulfilled promises chasing mirages created from Jay's and Howard's stories. In my delirium, I believed that my relationship with Jay was on the right track and that Howard wasn't like the rest of the sleazy, conniving developers I knew. I ignored the red flags in both relationships and turned a blind eye to the love-bombing and ghosting cycles of deceit and untrustworthiness while fooling myself that they each had my best interests in mind. But I was wrong. So very wrong.

They were the same person, just dressed in different clothes.

Jay was aggravated when I had to work.

Howard was disappointed when I couldn't join him for a "networking dinner."

Jay picked fights that would derail my focus moments before I had a presentation.

Howard tried to discredit me with half-assed land-bartering suggestions in exchange for my design services.

Explaining myself to Jay over and over every time I went to the development site was exhausting. He kept accusing me of spending "too much time on these projects" as I couldn't get him to understand what these opportunities meant to the success of my company.

Clarifying my company structure over and over to Howard was equally ridiculous, as I had to continuously remind him that my fees were non-negotiable since he had already whittled my pricing down to the bare bones.

The boat trips became elusive and were dangled like potential rewards if I agreed to skip a meeting.

The project proposals went ignored for weeks unless I agreed to adjust my fees.

Jay threatened to not help build the cabin because it was "too expensive."

Howard threatened to decrease the scope of work because he didn't think I could handle it.

I was driving back and forth to Jay's place in Charlestown two to three times a week.

I was driving back and forth to the development in New Hampshire almost every weekend.

I was stuck on repeat. My personal and professional lives mirrored each other, and I couldn't see it until both blew up. I had unknowingly allowed Jay and Howard to devalue me so much over the years that I had lost my ability to rise above their crap and became numb to their synchronized manipulation.

"Be careful what you tolerate, you are teaching people how to treat you."

~ *Various*

The Boat Trip...

At the end of June into the first week of July 2022, Jay and I took a ten-day boat trip around Boston, the cape, and the islands. I naively thought it was the beginning of us really trying to make things work, but quickly realized I couldn't keep up with his pace of living. Every morning started with champagne, then a little food for lunch, and a cocktail combination of booze and blow for dinner each night. It was insane.

I played the part of his first mate, but for the first time in two-and-a-half years, I really got to experience him in action and *finally* saw the writing on the wall. We would have a great morning and make evening plans. Then around midday, he'd randomly start in on me about how I was ruining his vacation and he couldn't stand my neediness. It felt like I was walking on sharp clam shells the entire trip and wasn't sure why he accused me of anything. By the evening, he'd pretend the outburst had never happened, blow a line, pop a gummy, want to have sex, and the cycle would start all over again. I was trapped by a one-man circus with multiple personalities running the show.

His instability, reliance on drugs and attention, and inability to manage anything remotely close to the truth made it increasingly clear to me that I was dealing with a nutcase. The cocaine numbing was just a tool of his to keep me high enough long enough for him to fabricate some other sort of fucked-up reason as to why we weren't staying on course and needed to constantly change our plans to pick up or drop off another one of his buddies. I couldn't believe I hadn't recognized all his nonsense before, but then again, he had never let me spend this much time with him. That was his way. A little here, a little there, a little more, and then poof! Get too close, and he'd scatter.

The night before we returned to port, I'm still not sure exactly what happened. We had such a vicious screaming match that I ended up packing up all my stuff and *almost* slept on a park bench with my dog to wait for the first morning ferry from Martha's Vineyard back to Boston. I remember him cornering me in every angle of the boat and verbally attacking me like a sociopath. I did all I could to remain calm. My internal mantra was on repeat to keep me sane: *It's not you; it's him. It's not you; it's him. It's not you; it's him.* It wasn't until I snapped that he turned coy and quiet and started recording my outburst. That's when I got off the boat.

There was no clear reality. We were numb from all the partying. Like the devil, he coerced me back to the dock, probably because he couldn't handle undocking the fifty-foot yacht by himself at 4 a.m. I knew I was crazy for agreeing to help him, but did it anyway. We threw verbal cannons the whole way back as if we were trying to kill each other. So it came as absolutely no surprise when he implied that he needed a break as soon as we docked in Boston.

I was excited to calm myself down from all the partying and abuse and took advantage of the breathing space back on solid land. Over the next few days, I sobered up and started to dry my nervous system out. I connected with Jackie and did a deep dive on the boat trip chaos, the drugs, the fighting, my increasing self-esteem issues, and how I felt completely out of control with everything in my life.

Then one day, in the middle of one of my rants, she interrupted me and asked, "Amanda, have you had enough yet? Like really. Have you had enough? Aren't you sick of all this nonsense? Aren't you ready to let it all go?"

Love is blind. Especially abusive and manipulative love. It's hard to let go of something when it has its claws wrapped around your heart. I tried to rationalize with Jackie that being in that shitty relationship was better than being in nothing at all, but as I kept repeating the words, I started to hear the insanity. I recognized that I was drowning in my own ridiculous avoidance.

As a water, water, water empath, I unfortunately was the perfect target for Jay's narcissistic deception because I was ready for a love relationship, whether it was the right one for me or not. His manipulation took full advantage of everything I had to offer—my ability to forgive, to see the possibilities in people, to not see the truth, my dreams for a greater company, travel, and excitement. He saw it all in me and took it all whenever he had the chance. Then, when I had nothing left to give, he would leave me exhausted until I filled myself back up. Then he would return once more and siphon it out of me, over and over again. I was a wellspring in his own emotional desert.

That boat trip finally opened my eyes to the fact that I had become a merciless victim to a manipulating, covert narcissist with borderline personality disorder. I *finally* understood that if I didn't do something about it now, I may not ever get the chance to.

About a week later, Jay sent me a text that said, "I can't do this anymore." I wasn't surprised. I figured he would just disappear again. But this time I wouldn't go look for him. So, rather than start a conversation, I simply replied, "I can't either."

I was so done.

There was only one lingering problem: I had left a ton of clothes and personal items on the boat and at his condo in Charlestown and wanted them back. I wanted to get on with my life, and his habit of dragging everything out got under my skin. He must have promised via text to return my stuff "tomorrow" at least six or seven times over the following two weeks, which drove me batty. Now that I had come to the conclusion that I wanted absolutely nothing to do with this nut job anymore, his perpetual lies caused me to have another episode of hives. I couldn't take his bullshit anymore.

"I'm tired of waiting on you. I'm on my way to Charlestown to get my stuff. Marina after that," I texted him, bluffing about the "on my way" part, but knowing it would spark a response.

"Boat's not in the marina. Changed the locks on the condo. You're wasting your time."

We went back and forth on this for a few minutes while I was contemplating getting in my car. His final text read: "You will have your stuff back tomorrow, and then it is over."

That is when I lost it.

"*Then*, it is over? *Then*?! Mother fucker! It was over a long time ago!" I was enraged.

The chaotic push-pull cycle had finally cracked my sanity bubble, and in an effort to rid myself of the anger, I took off in a full-out sprint down the street. With tears pouring down my cheeks and my lungs sucking wind because I hadn't run in over a year, I raced the narcissistic demons in my heart for about three miles. Only stopping a few times to catch my breath, I looked up high into the treetops and bright blue sky and screamed, "Why is this happening to me? When will this all be over? Why the *fuck* is he perpetuating this abuse?"

My knees eventually told me it was time to turn around, so I listened.

Trying to maintain composure at work while my personal life was falling completely apart was an abysmal effort. But I did what I have always done—pushed through each day and succumbed to the numbing effects of wine and television every night for about a week.

Then I started to come around.

I finally got my stuff back three days after Jay's last text, and I didn't hear from him again for the rest of the summer. I tried to convince myself that I didn't want anything to do with him, but that didn't stop me from wondering where the hell he went. So, like anyone who has lost their self-esteem and feels disgraced, discarded, and dismissed, I crept through his friends' Instagram pages in an effort to see what he was up to.

I am totally not proud of that, but it's what happened. When you are hurt and lonely and sad and confused with no answers, no closure, and not a speck of self-worth left in your beat-up soul, social media stalking becomes a self-destructive and unhealthy habit to fill in the void where someone once was.

Obviously, I didn't like what I was seeing, but I kept looking anyway. The whole thing sucked. I knew it was unhealthy. I knew I was just pouring salt into my wounds, but I did it anyway. Until one day it was different. I don't remember what changed, and I suspect the transformation in my heart happened gradually with continued help from Jackie, but eventually, when I saw his face in these photos, I no longer felt loss or pain or love. Instead, I just felt sorry for the guy and became bored with whatever was happening in his life because it was always the same. I had too many more important things to do instead of pine after his stupid ass. So I stopped. And it felt amazing to have that power back.

The Site Meeting…

After the boat trip, I knew I needed to ensure my business was staying afloat in the wavering economy, so once I felt like my nervous system started to level out (kind of), I took a two-hour drive up to New Hampshire at the beginning of August to check on project status and get some of the outstanding contracts and proposals signed by Howard.

I was only fifteen minutes away from the site when he texted, "I can't make it today."

Howard had given me the silent treatment since the middle of May, so setting up this meeting had been a damn miracle in the first place. He had left me hanging with tentative start dates for June and July that had come and gone, but without signed contracts, I had to find other projects for my employees to fill the voids where his projects were supposed to be. Getting these contracts and proposals signed was integral to the success of my company that year, and it felt like the only thing I had left to hold on to since my love life had just exploded.

Howard's lack of courtesy and professionalism was so disrespectful that it irked me right out of my driver's seat. He *knew* I was coming up there specifically to meet with him, and he *knew* it took me two hours to get there! I was still too fragile for this kind of confrontation and deception, so the fake smile I had been practicing on the drive instantly turned upside down. I could feel myself falling apart (again).

I yanked the car into the breakdown lane. This was not happening. I called Howard. No answer. I called again, and it went straight to voicemail. I resorted to texting him back asking when he could reschedule or if we could do it by Zoom or even DocuSign. My phone dinged with a response from him.

"We are not going to be using you for any of the future projects you have sent proposals for. You have become too expensive, and we are handing your projects to a local, less pricey designer. Stop working on all current and potential projects immediately," his message said.

What? We had signed contracts! How was I going to manage the rest of the year without these projects in the pipeline? These were more than half of our projected income! Whatever composure I had left was shattered in a bomb of emotional despair. I couldn't do it anymore. Not this. Not anything. I was done. Nothing was worth this amount of stress.

On the side of a quiet and desolate dirt road in the middle of cow-Hampshire, I got out of my car and proceeded to lose my shit (for the second time in a month). Wandering around the side of the road in a hazy disbelief, I crouched down on my bare knees in the gravel, looked up high into the treetops and bright blue sky, and screamed "What the fuck is happening! Why is this *all* happening to me?! What the *fuck* am I supposed to do *now*?!"

I never went to the project site that day. I figured if I had gone, I would have run him over if I saw him. I decided it wasn't worth it. He and his fucking development weren't worth anything to me anymore. I quit. I did a wild U-turn and made it home in record time after driving through a torrential downpour of tears and anger.

My personal and professional lives had totally fallen apart in a matter of weeks. I was a mess. But I did what I have always done and continued to push through the days, only to fall into the same routine I had just pulled myself out of a mere two weeks earlier. This time, my chemical concoction was tequila, gummies, and Netflix. I was on a mission to numb the bejeezus out of myself. And I did. But only for about four days this time.

Progress, I thought.

HOW YOU DO ANYTHING IS HOW YOU DO EVERYTHING

"How you do anything is how you do everything."

My coach Debbie had tried to explain this theory to me back in 2011 as she pointed out the overlapping patterns in my personal life and my business (both positive and negative). But back then I was too busy doing everything to take time out and understand what the hell she was saying.

About seven years later (in 2018), I heard it again, and then again a few years after that (in 2021). But when the overlap of these two men catapulted me into a spiral of self-reflection and personal and professional assessment that lasted all of 2022, I finally understood *exactly* what Debbie had been trying to teach me.

If I was unbalanced in my personal life, it would flow over into my profession. If I was unhappy in my career, it would affect me everywhere else. It was an internal tug-of-war I had been battling within myself since I could remember, and after the disastrous events with Jay and Howard, I could see that no matter what I was doing, I was hollow inside. I needed to make some significant changes.

I wanted fulfillment. I wanted to feel empowered. I wanted love and joy. And I wanted my courage back. I knew I wasn't going to get any of that doing the same things I had been doing for forty-something years, so I decided to pivot and change it all.

I pulled my head out of my ass and made my therapy with Jackie a number-one priority. She helped to shift my unhealthy thought patterns and start to heal my mental and emotional states. I learned to let go of the co-dependent fear that had clouded my vision for so so so so very long in all of my relationships (even in my business), and I began to redirect my focus in a trajectory that felt more aligned with the person I wanted to be and who I was becoming.

Not surprisingly, and like so many people in their various professions, I began losing my passion for design during the pandemic. And now with all this bullshit from Howard, I was really ready to quit. I had been getting impatient and cynical with most of my clients, and although I still *liked* design, I didn't *love* it anymore. Plus, I had realized that helping people determine which color to paint their living room or which toilet had the best flushing technology did not resonate as deeply as the prospect of helping people avoid all the emotional heartache and bullshit I had endured. **So the shift into something new was inevitable; it was just a matter of time.**

With Jackie and Kerri's help, I committed to my plan of passing on all of the responsibilities of my design company to my business partner so I could side-step and start a new, more soul-centered and purposeful business of serving others, and I got to work.

FINDING YOUR TRUTH

In order for any type of therapy to work, you have to be willing to let it. When I *finally* stopped hiding and started to accept the real truths of what was actually happening in my life, Jackie and I uncovered the root cause of not only my insane outbursts over many years and many relationships, but a plethora of other events that had been stuck to the bottom of my soul for close to four decades. My problems of attracting the wrong kinds of guys and people-pleasing had started way back when I had built so much of my belief system on a rocky foundation of limiting beliefs and thoughts of not being enough that were held together with self-doubt and a serious fear of being alone.

Finally, I stopped resisting everything around me. I stopped pushing against my natural current of trust and fulfillment (what my heart had been yearning for my whole life). I started listening to my intuition respectfully. **And in doing so, my real healing began. Leaning in, I grew to trust Jackie, trust the process, but most importantly, trust myself.**

For the next four months, we dug. I broke down. I journaled until my hand cramped. I cried. I changed. And I cried some more.

Oh my God did I cry.

Sometimes the waves of emotions would crash so hard over my heart that it felt like I was drowning. It was so fucking hard at times that I felt like I couldn't breathe. So hard that I often wanted to stop and give up on all the intentional change, but Jackie wouldn't let me.

"I promise it will be worth it," she said.

Kerri was right there, too, and she promised the same.

They were both right. Eventually, I'd get through each storm and come up for air. Then as soon as I caught my breath, we would dive again. I found places in my subconscious I didn't know existed and worked through decades of fear and guilt that had accumulated inside of my soul. I learned that my stomach aches and niggling feelings were actually my body and soul trying to tell me to pay attention to my intuition. This was also when I realized I had been ignoring important messages of self-respect, empowerment, and self-love most of my life.

Going through this process of purposefully moving through the pain and healing the unhealthy patterns, I began to see the opportunities where I had the chance to change who I am for the better. I started redesigning what I wanted the rest of my life to look like. With the soul channels finally open, I became more willing to listen to whatever the Universe had to say and more capable of changing by following my heart, rather than my head.

"The hard thing about hard things
is they are fucking hard."

~ *Trey Humphreys, Love is Bananas*

I've learned how to exchange resentment and shame with forgiveness and self-acceptance. By going back and sifting through one traumatic experience or relationship at a time, I started to see that all these events happened *for* me, not *to* me. These experiences were the path I needed to travel in order to appreciate the value of the joy and fulfillment I have been seeking my entire life. Eventually, I started to understand that *everything for which I've yearned is just on the other side of different choices.* **I replaced my significant attention-seeking ego with unconditional acceptance of myself and focused on nurturing the most important love of all, my own.**

One day on a walk with my dog, I pondered the question, "Who are you, Amanda, without all the bullshit abandonment triggers and that ridiculous fear of being alone?"

I smiled when the answer bubbled up immediately, and replied to myself (out loud so the Universe could hear me), "I am secure in my beliefs, values, and character, and these values are bursting with fulfillment, empowerment, and joy."

I had turned myself around and navigated onto a completely different course than the one I had been on for so long. It was time to emerge as a new woman.

DEAR DIARY

"How you do anything is how you do everything" has resonated with me for years. Finally being able to see the giant overlapping patterns in my personal and professional life helped me to hone in on some of the habits I'd developed over the years and allowed me to make the changes necessary to break my unhealthy patterns.

The therapy with Jackie and support from Kerri were integral in my ability to get away from these toxic relationship patterns and the key to integrating new and healthy habits.

1. If you are currently dealing with someone who is manipulating, or if you can resonate with any of the characteristics I mentioned about Jay or Howard, maybe it's time to take a step back and think about what's *really* happening. There are therapists, support groups, and coaches that can help you get out of toxic abusive relationships. You are not alone.
2. This may be a great time to make a list of all the habits you know you could adjust (even just a little) and start focusing on one or two over the next couple of months. Then, once you've adjusted those as needed, pick a couple more. Once the habits start shifting, the newly created habit of making changes actually becomes easier.

3. Remember, some of these patterns have been with you since childhood. Trying to unravel thirty or forty years of a habit in one weekend doesn't always work right away. Be gentle with yourself. This stuff takes time.

"The type of human being we prefer reveals the contours of our heart."

~ *Jose Ortega y Gasset*

Where Are You Going?

Part 5

MY RENAISSANCE

"When I let go of what I am, I become what I might be."

~ Lao Tzu

Once I eliminated the bullshit of Jay and Howard from my life and remembered that I had an incredible toolbox of resources available to me at all times, I felt the pivotal shift in my energy and got ridiculously clear with my goals and intentions.

With the lucid understanding that it was time for me to rise above everything that had happened and make some changes to how I was functioning and relating to the world around me, I took the start of 2023 as a prime opportunity to make the second half of my life the best half of my life. This became my mantra as I focused on aligning my values with my reality and connected the love of my soul with who I wanted to evolve into.

The "Rising of the Phoenix" that I experienced at the end of chapter thirteen (Fall of 2021) gained momentum and really took flight a year later in the Fall of 2022. As a result, the stories and messages within the next three chapters are more directed at rescuing ourselves with self-love, appreciation, and action than pushing our limits with self-doubt, expectations, and reactions.

Throughout the development of this book, the cathartic writing changed my pain into awareness and my heartache into empowerment. I began to fall in love with myself the way I *needed* to and the way I *wanted* to because I learned to cultivate patience, acceptance, and self-love that I had never given myself permission to explore before, until now.

16

THE THREE WISE MEN

Connect with Your Spirit(uality)

"To open up to the multitude of resources that lie within you, put yourself in a state of resourcefulness and active expectancy—and watch miracles happen."

~*Tony Robbins*

NOVEMBER, 2022

As I sat on the edge of my seat, listening to Tony Robbins further explain the Ultimate Success Formula and how Neuro Linguistic Programming (NLP) can be the magic ingredient in creating that *ultimate success*, I realized that I had heard it all before but was just now beginning to understand it.

This was my second in-person UPW, but I had also done this event two additional times from the comfort of my own living room during the pandemic. I had always wondered why people would attend the same event over and over. Then, in a conversation with one of my cohorts from Life Mastery in Chapter 10, it hit me. Even though the curriculum and sequence of presentations are relatively the same each time, *I'm* different. I've changed between events, evolving within my own process of uncovering who I truly am. Each time I attend, I show up with a broader perspective and a more intentional purpose. I hear differently. See differently. Learn differently. I *feel* differently every time I go.

There is *so much* to learn, we can't possibly retain it all in one session. As we expand, so does our ability to absorb what is being said. As we get educated on who we actually are and who we want to be, so does our ability to allow the important lessons and messages in.

With Jackie's help, I had removed my mask of denial and started to really dig into my healing between July and November of 2022. This made me feel like a fresh little onion that had just peeled back all its layers. Raw and sweet with a little kick. And very vulnerable. I had opened myself back up to my own personal self-discovery and once again started to actively participate in the redesign of my life.

I had registered for UPW at the end of April when I was grasping at straws with Jay. He had agreed to attend with me, but through all the nonsense that blew up during the heat of the summer, I determined I would go to this alone and not even remind him of it when the date rolled around.

And like all the other events I've been to, it happened at the perfect time.

—

On day two, I ran into my friend, Jake, whom I had met at another event a few years prior. It was spectacular to see him, and as we hugged and high-fived our salutations, I could feel his energy had shifted from our first encounter. He shared his glory of business expansion, and I shared the progress and growth I had prospered through over the preceding five months. I knew running into him wasn't a coincidence and could feel the intention in our conversation.

There was something about the way Jake held the space we were in—focused, purposeful, sincere. He was so grounded and deliberate with his words and presence that when he invited me to an event that he and his girlfriend were hosting the following February, I jumped at the chance to be a part of his uprising.

I wanted whatever he was having. I could just feel in my soul that it was something beautiful.

FEBRUARY, 2023

Jake and his girlfriend, Emily, hosted a two-day branding and communications event in Newport, California, with about two hundred other branding and communications junkies in early February. We were all there to learn how to talk to people and how to make our mark on the world more valuable. It was exactly what I needed to jumpstart my new business.

At the perceived end of the first day, Jake and Emily stepped up onto the stage and were beaming with excitement as they asked us to have patience. They knew they had gone over the scheduled time but invited us to stay for a little surprise. It was 7:23 p.m., and I was starving. But I had faith in Jake and Emily's message and mission, so I got comfortable in my seat and waited for the next speaker.

This surprise guest jumped up from the front row, ran up the steps, and embraced both Jake and Emily like family. He was wearing loafers, cropped plaid pants, a light blue T-shirt, and a tailored navy blue sport coat. They introduced him as Pastor Mark.

I was instantly confused. My impressions of clergy had always been as traditional as the first church I attended when I was a child. I thought all pastors were balding men with glasses who wore long robes and hid behind podiums, telling ghost stories about some guy and his father. This Pastor Mark guy, however, was about thirty-five years young, fashionable, in good shape with a full head of hair, and funny. He was practically dancing around the stage as he interacted with the audience and shared collaborative stories of how he and Jake had found a commonality through golf and beer.

What?! I didn't know pastors were allowed to drink.

He commanded with a presence that excited and entertained while he delivered the most powerful sermon I've ever experienced. He wove the story about Moses and the burning bush into terms that were relatable, and even made a joke about the high-end brand of sandals Moses removed from his feet in the presence of God as he demonstrated respect for the holy ground.

As he spoke, I became consumed with every word on his scroll. I was intrigued by how the details of Moses' internal resistance of worthiness aligned so similarly to mine and how his journey eventually gave way to his ability to take on a role of leadership with the encouragement and support of God.

Partway through the sermon, I felt myself stand up and raise my arms over my head. The energy, the passion, and the messages connected so succinctly with my soul that I heard a few "*Amen*s" exit my mouth in unison with others around me at the request of Pastor Mark. I was so enthralled with this story of overcoming self-doubt and pivotal moments that tears poured down my cheeks and the ratchet straps around my heart loosened. When he finished his sermon with a lively "Amen!" I energetically reciprocated with a boisterous "HALLELUJAH!" After my exuberant experience, I was overcome by such an intense wave of emotions that I collapsed into my chair.

Thanking Pastor Mark, Jake then called "all that had been served" to the front of the room to meet the pastor, but rather than join the line, I ignored Jake's call to action and dropped my head into my arms. I then proceeded to bawl my eyes out through an unexpected emotional release, and the overwhelming feeling that somehow, at some point during Pastor Mark's sermon, I was finally aligned with an energy that *fully* understood me.

That was the exact moment I know He and I had connected.[vi] It was then I started to hear the music in my soul and knew He had been speaking directly to me that entire time.

The woman I had been sitting next to the entire day had ended up standing in the aisle as well. As I collapsed, she calmly positioned herself behind my chair, placed her hands gently on my shoulders, and prayed. She prayed for me with an unconditional love that I could feel through her touch and words. In the name of God, she spoke with messages of

---

[vi] I use the word "He" as a reference to God, or my Divine Sovereign. Because "God" is such a recognized word, it makes sense to use it in this book as a referral to my Higher Power. God could easily be a "She," but I chose to use "He " for simplicity's sake.

love, acceptance, and trust that were directed straight to my heart. With conviction in my honor, she prayed for me. And I felt the creed of her faith and her compassion coming directly from Him. From the Universe. And I broke down even further.

Sobbing hysterically, I let my emotions go without resistance. This woman demonstrated an unwavering patience and remained behind me until my tears slowed and my breathing normalized. A few moments later, I lifted my head, stood up, and we embraced like a mother holding her newborn. The love saturated my soul. Upon thanking her for her support, I looked up and noticed only a few people remaining to speak to the pastor, and I knew it was time.

"Your task is not to seek for love, but merely to seek and find all the barriers within yourself that you have built against it."

~ *Rumi*

HISTORY OF RELIGION

I used to think the only reason I ever went to church as a kid was because it was a convenient, free daycare across the street that my mom was able to shove us off to for two hours on Sunday mornings. I don't really remember learning much, except that I hated having to get dressed up in a cute little dress to just run across the street and sit in a room full of old people.

Those Sunday morning God-sessions were the only connection I had to any type of faith as a child, and they came to a screeching halt when we moved away from the church across the street at the end of fifth grade. At that point, I was eleven, and my brother and I were both into sports, which meant our weekend time was consumed with games and practices in the spring and fall. In the summer, we spent every weekend out on the boat, and we skied as a family during the winter. All this sporty family time didn't leave any time for church, and unless there were Easter eggs or presents under the Christmas tree, religion wasn't a hot topic in our household aside from my parents' occasional "Jesus Christ!" and "What the hell have you done?!"

Marymount University was my next known opportunity to know God since the little Catholic school was located on the tippity-top edge of the Bible Belt in Arlington, Virginia. In the four years, I was there, however, I don't think I ever stepped foot in the chapel. It became a running joke with my friends that I might burst into flames if I went in, so I stayed out.

It wasn't that I didn't like religion; I just didn't know much about it.

One of my favorite classes freshman year was History of Religion. Finally, at the age of nineteen, I was exposed to *all* religions, not just the Christian variations my family kind of held on to. I was fascinated when I felt a pull towards one over the others, but remained somewhat fearful and thought that if the religious direction I was interested in wasn't the same as my parents', I might be disowned or tossed out of school. So rather than rock the boat, I stayed neutral and kind of dismissed God and all His teachings—until much, much later in life.

Back in 1995, however, things changed a bit when I met my best friend Laura, who, unlike me, was a non-alcoholic, virgin Catholic. People often wondered how the hell we were friends, and I just attributed our sister-like friendship to our quirky humor and maybe God's way of sending me a guiding angel. Her vast knowledge of the Bible and the stories within it were the most amazing contributing factor to our trip to Rome together in 1997, and as I mentioned then, I learned more from that trip than all the art history and religion classes I had taken while in college.

I was always curious about the strength of her faith, and although I didn't follow her to church on Sundays (except when we were in Rome), I admired her Catholic beliefs, her devotion to her religious community, and her relationship with God. I just had a hard time grasping the basis of stories that were written in a book thousands of years ago about a guy who goes by Son and Father and Holy Ghost and using those stories as the ruling principle for my life. I've come a long way since then, but for years the whole immaculate conception theory really confused the shit out of me.

THE THREE WISE MEN

After my loving embrace with the angelic stranger at Jake's event, I allowed Spirit to move me. As I walked towards the front of the room, I had this undeniable sense that Pastor Mark was not who I was meant to speak with. Three understudies were working alongside the pastor, so I patiently waited for them as they finished up with one of the other saved attendees. None of this made sense, but I allowed the magnetism of these men to pull my soul closer to their energy, and I walked over.

"As I walked towards the door, toward the gate that would lead to my freedom, I knew that if I didn't leave my bitterness and hatred behind, I'd still be in prison."

~NELSON MANDELA

I had never seen these men before, and they didn't know me from Eve. I told the man in front my name as he took my hands and stared deep into my eyes. Then he started whispering in my ear loud enough for my soul to hear, but quiet enough that no one else knew what he was saying. He talked directly to my fears and woke up the demons that had resided in my darkened soul for decades. In detail, this man addressed my self-doubt and limiting beliefs that had been strengthened by my misguided anger and frustrations in love, and he exposed each one of my nightmares to the light of God. How he knew they were there is a total mystery to me, but they listened and responded. With his words, wisdom, and prayer, I felt a change happening as my spirit opened further, encouraging his gift to dig deeper.

As he continued with unwavering determination to speak to my mobs of negativity, I started to shake. His Reiki master brother stood behind me and coerced love straight into my core, as the third guy hovered on my right praying unintelligible words of justice and faith. They channeled the grace of God into me, making me feel whole, accepted, and unconditionally loved. My chains of resistance were being shattered as they gained momentum and worked feverishly to declare my soul's truth through the light of God.

The whisperer placed his hands on my head, and my arms rose towards the sky as if I were a marionette. With an aching heart, I suddenly felt exhaustion take over, but remained open and allowed each and every word he uttered to seek out the demons and pull them to the surface for final surrender. One by one, he told them they were no longer welcome and demanded they leave me alone.

As the intensity swelled, the force became overpowering, like a dramatic tidal bore. I could hear it. I could feel it. I could sense this wave of eternal release coming from the depths of my existence. Finally, the energy of spirit overruled all of the bullshit, and the transfer of power between the darkness and the light exploded like a giant fifty-foot crashing wave.

On cue, the man in front pushed me into the arms of the Reiki master, and I collapsed backwards. The whisperer grabbed my hands and held my arms in the air as the force of the movement cracked my soul open and allowed the swarm of nonsense to rush past my gut, whoosh past my heart, and out in a ferocious scream that carried all of my atrocious demons to their final abolishment.

When it was finished, I moaned and melted into the floor one cell at a time. The whisperer gently laid my hands over my heart, knelt beside me, and gathered me up in an embrace of love and understanding. The other two men quietly did their Father, Son, Holy Spirit head-heart-shoulder cross thingy and stepped back as I continued to peacefully weep in the whisperer's arms.

For far too long I had unknowingly protected these habits of negativity and depressive emotions, not understanding that they were never mine to begin with. I had adopted them from family, friends, and lovers in the past and carried them with me, afraid to let them go, unsure of who I may become without them. I had subconsciously built a fortress around my heart and blocked out so many opportunities of faith and trust until I allowed these men to come in and knock it all down.

"When healing gets deep there is sometimes an explosion of emotion that occurs to clear out old energetic debris. You feel most agitated right before you settle into a more substantial peace."

~ *Yung Pueblo*

After a few moments, the whisperer helped me to my feet while the Reiki master shared a story with me. Allegedly, on their way to this event, they had received a message of a woman needing exoneration, and they were to stay until she came forward. The muttering brother chimed in and told me he knew I was the woman because he felt my surrender halfway through Pastor Mark's sermon—that must have been when I got excited about Moses' sandals and leapt out of my seat cheering, "Amen!" with my hands in the air.

Thanking them, and totally unsure of what the fuck had just happened, I tried to leave but was stopped in my tracks when I heard "AMANDA!" boom from across the room. It was Jake.

"Are you alright?" he asked when he reached my side.

Through sobs and an unfamiliar stream of consciousness, I managed to calmly say, "Yes. I'm fine now. I just need to rest. These guys whispered the hell out of me. Tomorrow is another day, and I will begin my new journey then." The words came out of my mouth sounding like a foreign language, but both Jake and I knew they weren't necessarily *my* words. They were the words of the Spirit I had just met and that my soul was so very happy to finally have its voice back.

I ran up to my hotel room and wept on the floor until my tears dried up. After baptizing myself with a long hot shower, I climbed into bed and noticed the clock said 10:15 p.m. Three hours had passed since Pastor Mark's sermon started. *Where did all the time go? How long was I crying with that woman praying over me? Was I with the three wise men that long? Was room service still available?* Allowing the questions to disappear as quickly as they entered, and smiling when I realized I wasn't even hungry, I turned off the light, pulled this newfound sheet of faith over my head, and instantly fell asleep.

—

That night with Pastor Mark and his three "brothers" was a phenomenon where I believe God's grace traveled towards me at such a velocity that I was forced to witness the elimination of my demons and the reversing direction of my mindset. I have since created more space for positivity, inspiration, and amazing people and am on a mission to cultivate more meaning in my purpose, create stronger connections, and embrace my empowered self-worth and self-love.

Learning to take my power back with intentional healing practices, lots of coaching, and some great therapists, I can now hear and feel my intuition on a regular basis and know when my Higher Power has something to say.

I've cleared my fields of serenity once again and am now carefully planting the intentions that will lead me towards this new life. Only this time, through the grace of God, I now know to pay closer attention to the thoughts and people I allow into my life. I plan on using the power of the Universe to speak my truth and own my worth and not let the winds of change blow in uninvited or toxic energy.

DEAR DIARY

For the past five years or so, consciously and subconsciously, I have been slowly peeling back the layers of self-doubt, self-sabotage, and limiting beliefs, trying to expose the truth of who I am at my core one itty bitty piece at a time, even if I didn't know what to do with the truth when it surfaced.

Only recently did I grab a shovel and start digging in deeper so I could reach conclusions faster and heal the hell out of myself more efficiently. When my deepest truth was uncovered, I then knew that I was going to religiously and permanently pay attention to my intuition with unwavering faith from this point forward and stay true to my core beliefs of worthiness and integrity.

Having faith in anything takes courage. Courage to believe it's right. Courage to understand the intentions. Courage to bet your life on it. But faith has kept the world turning for God only knows how long, so it must be quite the powerful phenomenon.

Religion can be a sensitive and debatable subject. I guess that's why there are so many of them, and why, over centuries of time, these variations have evolved, creating many opportunities for us to believe in something greater than ourselves and give that greatness a chance to guide or inspire us throughout our lives.

1. Is there a faith, religion, or higher power that you believe in? Take a moment to acknowledge that power, wisdom, energy it offers you and how it has benefited your life.
2. Pay attention to the world around you. There are messages *everywhere.* Let them in and see what they have to offer.
3. And remember, have faith and have fun.

17

ATTITUDE of GRATITUDE

Trade Your Expectations for Appreciation

"If you find something to be grateful for, then you find something to look forward to and you carry on. With gratitude, optimism is sustainable."

~ *Michael J. Fox*

2011 THROUGH TODAY

When I started my interior design business in 2010, I mastered the art of being a chameleon by doing everything all by myself as a solopreneur and wore every hat necessary to get the company up and running and stay alive. Every. Single. Fucking. Hat. From initial meetings, to networking, to drawings, selections, schedules, contractor coordination, presentations, site meetings, marketing, billing, supply orders, vendor relationships, photo shoots, website creation, banking, taxes, strategic planning, etc. You name it; I was doing it. From sunup to sundown and twice in the dark on Sundays, I did everything and anything it took to get the job done and to keep myself from going bankrupt.

As my one-woman band was banging work out, some of my weaknesses reared their ugly heads fast. Computer drafting is one of those weaknesses. I suck at it. As the first year rounded out, I knew I needed help. Although I was great at the archaic and almost lost art of hand drafting, the computer programs took me too much time to learn, and time was not something that I had in abundance. So, I advertised for an intern at the local college, and the very next day I got a call from a confident young lady telling me she was perfect for the position.

On paper, she was one-hundred-percent qualified. However, her interview had me questioning whether I could work with her. She had one of the most placid poker faces of anyone I've ever met in my entire life. She didn't laugh at my jokes. She barely flinched when I swore. And when I mentioned the expectation of doing more personal assistant tasks like grocery shopping and taking my car for oil changes, all she said was, "Of course. I can do all of that."

I hesitated but reminded myself I wasn't looking for conversation or a friend. I needed help and a hard worker, and my intuition told me to trust her. So I did.

With her help, I gained back a ton of time. She *was* good. *Great* even. Her drafting was excellent, her quiet and unassuming demeanor grew on me, and as my company gained momentum, so did she. As she progressed through college, everything about her just kept getting better. When the opportunity presented itself, I hired her as my first employee at the onset of her senior year.

In the spring of 2014, my eyes filled with tears of pride and joy as I watched my young coworker walk across the college graduation stage. After the ceremony, unexpectedly she presented her Stole of Gratitude to me as a symbol of her appreciation for my mentorship. I was astounded. My internal dialogue said, *"Who's mentoring who?"* as I reflected on the incredibly mature manner in which *she* had contributed to *my* life and business over those three years. **In a hug that felt more like family than boss/employee, that embrace became ingrained in my memory as one of the most honorable and precious moments of my career.**

"As we express our gratitude, we must never forget that the highest appreciation is not to utter words, but to live by them."

~ *John F. Kennedy*

Regan came into my life in 2011 and thankfully has never left.

She has grown the business with me so much that she has *become* the business with me. Without question or compromise, she accepts me for who I am (I think) and consistently shows up with grace, gumption, and unfaltering dedication as an employee, friend, and quite honestly the most supportive person in my life.

When I was having a personal identity crisis and couldn't find a place to call home, Regan was my neighbor in that highway apartment complex. We would turn her living room into an office when the roads were closed on snow days, since my place was filled with boxes and a bad attitude.

When we landed our first big hotel project, she was right next to me the entire time, all the way through the opening night.

When I was going through a rough time and left empty wine bottles on the conference table and blankets on the floor of the office, she would clean them up and not ask any questions. Her silence and lack of interrogation became a gentle trust and understanding that I cherish. Her ability to keep personal and business separate is a trait I sincerely admire.

When I made a (fucking GIANT) mistake and had to learn the hard way how to write off sixty-thousand dollars, she helped tighten up our contracts.

When we started to grow the company, we interviewed as a team. After all, whoever was joining AG&Co was going to work with both of us equally, not just me.

When she asked me to be a bridesmaid in her wedding, I naturally said yes.

And when I told her I wanted to go fulfill my dream of writing a book, she said "OK, what do we need to do to make it happen?"

One of the most interesting parts of how Regan and I function is that on paper (and in real life) we are polar opposites, a classic case of Yin and Yang.

I'm a Pisces: emotional, erratic, and a little insecure, sympathetic, a dreamer, big-picture gal, and intuitive.

Regan is a Capricorn: serious, calm, and confident, stoic, practical, detail-oriented, and analytical.

I jump into radical ideas headfirst, eyes closed, ready for whatever the adventure creates; she needs time to process the situation, gather the pros and cons, and prefers to be fully prepared for all possibilities.

She has been with her husband for about ten years, and I, well you know I have not been with anyone (except for her and some girlfriends from college) that long.

Over the years, we've learned how to navigate our contrasting personality traits and varying methods with style and grace, balancing out my wild and crazy with her steadfast and strong. My intuition was spot on the first time I met her, and with respect and gratitude for all that she is, I am truly thankful she is still in my life.

FEBRUARY, 2022

One snowy Sunday night in February 2022, Regan insisted she come over with brownies. She said they were the best she had ever made, and I had to try them right away. I thought, *these must be some brownies for her to come out on a night like this.* And when she arrived all cheerful and smiley, I started to wonder if there was weed in them and got a little excited.

"Hi," she said, walking in with the pan of brownies. "Stay where you are. I'm going to make brownie sundaes." She went straight through the kitchen, and I nestled down into my blankets on the sofa.

"Hey," I said as she went past. I took a sip of wine and turned my attention back to the movie I was watching. A moment later, beaming with joy she walked towards me and said, "Surprise!"

I looked up to see her holding not sundaes, but a little baby onesie over her belly. It was cute and had the company logo on it.

It took a second to register, but when it did, I spat out my wine.

"What is *that*?" I said, staring at her stomach. Obviously, I knew what it was, but fuck, I wasn't ready for it.

Exploding with excitement, and a trace of trepidation, she said, "I'm pregnant! We are going to have a new employee!"

It was two weeks before my forty-sixth birthday, and although I was super excited for her, I wasn't ready for the news. It broke me apart inside a little. With my waning enthusiasm for the design firm, *I had planned* to pass her more of the business responsibilities that upcoming summer and *I had planned* to start writing this book in the fall. Her unexpected announcement of an October 2022 due date fucked up *my plans* by almost a year. This was definitely not the brownie sundae I had anticipated when she said she was on her way over.

As soon as she left, I ate half of the brownies (they were regular fudgy brownies, no weed, so you can imagine my increased disappointment), finished the bottle of wine, then collapsed and went through my typical birthday "I still haven't had any children" anguish a little early.

GREAT EXPECTATIONS

"Trade your expectations into appreciation and your whole world changes in an instant."

~ *Tony Robbins*

A loose, generalized definition of ***expectation*** could be *the anticipation or belief about what might happen in the future based on past experiences, assumptions, or desires of outcome.* I believe that the word *expectation* is a nicer way of saying that there is a contingency on how we want things and people to show up. The greatest challenge behind it all is when we *expect* something or someone, and the reality is different from what *we want*, or it fails to *meet our expectations*, we are often left feeling let down, disappointed, discouraged.

However, on the flip side of expectations, as I've learned over the years, when we open ourselves up to being more present, more understanding, and more accepting, **we can learn to trade *expectations* for *appreciation.***

Somehow learning this shift from what *should be* to what *actually is* releases the pressure and allows us to enjoy each moment for what

it brings, rather than hanging on to potential moments that may not bring anything at all.

With all the therapy and coaching I was doing, by the early part of 2022, I started to accept that many things weren't meeting my expectations, and I had started to be okay with it all.

I had *expected* to be in a solid relationship and have a family. But instead, I started to *accept* that my biological clock was almost done ticking and that having children of my own may never happen.

I had *expected* to have passed my business on to Regan and to have already started something new. But instead *accepted* the fact that I wasn't ready to let it go yet. After all, the business was my "baby," and letting go of it meant I would have to remove all my expectations and put my full trust in her. I wasn't ready for that.

I had also *expected* to be living in a beautiful house on the water and traveling the world on a regular basis. But I have *accepted* that I live in a cute condo in the suburbs and look forward to my yearly trips to see my parents in Florida.

I certainly did NOT *expect* to be in an abusive relationship or to be struggling with a waning desire to stay motivated in my own company. I did not *expect* to be shifting careers at the age of forty-seven. I did not *expect* to be exposing some of my deepest secrets and stories in a memoir/self-discovery book. And I absolutely did NOT *expect* Regan to get pregnant. Not yet, anyway.

But, I also didn't *expect* that the young, placid, budding designer I met back in 2011 would become my most trusted business partner, would have unconditionally supported me in ways no one else could have for more than a decade, and would also become one of my closest and most honorable friends.

So, even with all my unmet expectations of what I *thought* my life was supposed to be, I started to understand that the Universe had a greater plan for me. I accepted the reality unfolding before me and around me and shifted my mindset. My writing and new business ventures could wait. My existing company still needed me. And now it was my turn to support Regan in her dreams by way of pausing mine.

Because I had been so distracted by the drama of my own personal life during the past few years, I had lost sight of what was even happening in my company. While Regan was out on maternity leave, I would have to step back in, clean up whatever wasn't working, and commit to working more than full-time to cover her jobs and the ones I was still responsible for. Needless to say, with one foot already out the door, I was not looking forward to jumping back into a company I had lost my motivation for.

But, as history has trained me, I could not have expected what ended up happening.

While I had been out dealing with the effects of an emotionally abusive relationship, Regan had taken over many of the day-to-day tasks within the firm because someone had to take care of the business. She nurtured relationships with clients and contractors and practically doubled the size of our vendor list. In my absence, she had already been doing all of the things I had hoped to transition to her, but I didn't realize just how much she had been doing, or how well she had been doing it, until she was gone and I was standing in her shoes.

During her maternity leave, I realized there wasn't much I needed to do aside from show up and support my team of four employees. So, instead of working a ton, I took the time to pay attention and remain present with my staff and clients. I started to enjoy the process again and learned that Regan had been running a tighter ship than I ever had, creating an easier, more efficient, and less stressed company. She had been managing all the people, projects, and schedules with ease, and had set up tasks and projects for all the employees to do while she was out. I stepped into what I *expected* was going to be an overwhelming and busy time and found myself blessed with a company so organized, my presence was barely needed at all.

Regan had been taking care of my business like it was her own. She was caring for what I had built from scratch with the same passion and dedication that I started the company with but had lost over the years. I wouldn't have been able to see it if I hadn't had to step back in while she stepped out to start her family. My *expectations* shifted towards the *acceptance* that it really was time for me to start letting go more, which in turn created an even greater *appreciation* for Regan. Although her timing may not have lined up with my original plan, the divine timing of it all filled me with a gratitude I had never before experienced, which not only strengthened our professional bond but also deepened our friendship.

THE GIFT OF GRATITUDE

Reflecting on all of the unexpected turns of events throughout my life and the continued support provided by the networks and people I surround myself with, I couldn't help but acknowledge the transformative power that gratitude has. **I've realized that being thankful and appreciative is not just a fleeting emotion, a smile, or a thank you card, but a complex gift that extends beyond all immediate circumstances.**

Gratitude has the remarkable ability to reshape our perspectives and enhance our well-being. It can be a powerful force, inviting positivity into our lives even when faced with unmet expectations or challenging situations. By shifting our mindset to an attitude of gratitude rather than an unknown cauldron of expectations, we can shift our energy, and in turn, shift our life.

The more I practice the gift of gratitude, I've found that it extends into each area of my life and has a profound influence on all of my relationships. Being thankful for who others are, what they do, and how they show up—all expectations aside—helps to secure connections and foster a sense of unity, reminding me that acknowledging the efforts of those around us can be a fulfilling source of joy and abundance, not only for me, but for them as well.

The idea that cultivating an attitude of gratitude can contribute to improved mental health, reduced stress levels, and an overall sense of happiness has been explored for years through various studies and articles.

One notable source is an article published in the journal *Psychological Bulletin* in 2011 titled, "Gratitude and Well-Being: A Review and Theoretical Integration," by Robert A. Emmons and Robin Stern. In this paper, the authors discuss how practicing gratitude is linked to positive outcomes such as increased life satisfaction, positive mood, and overall psychological well-being.[14]

Without getting too technical, I personally believe that it also helps to improve our outlook when we become intentionally thankful for the experiences that life has to offer, whether they are what we expect or not. By viewing life as a gift, and being thankful for the presents we receive (even the shitty, confusing ones) we can develop a stronger, deeper connection with our values and consciousness and understand that life is happening *for* us, not *to* us.

As a prime example, even though I have endured extreme heartache, a crushed ego, broken promises, and suffered severe disappointment and loss within so many of my relationships, I am thankful for all of those people and experiences. If it wasn't for the hell I have been dragged through (or brought upon myself), or the storms that I've weathered, I wouldn't have such a great appreciation for the opposite of all that anguish and despair. I wouldn't have anything to which I could compare the good or great things. I wouldn't have learned just how tenacious and courageous I really am. And I may not have been able to align my heart, my soul, and my mind together as one without all the ups and downs and roller coasters that spun me into who I have become today. With all of the loves and likes and random situations, all of those people, and exposure to the vast whirlwind of emotions I've had the pleasure to encounter, I have been able to experience so much reality, so much love, and so much opportunity that is now helping me to navigate the remaining complexities of my life.

In the midst of altered timelines and unanticipated responsibilities, appreciation for Regan's job-well-done became my guiding light, and it illuminated the hidden blessings that I initially thought were disruptions to my overall plan. Adjusting my expectations to appreciation encouraged resiliency and empowerment in my business journey and in my personal perspective of everything happening in my life. I started to see how the benefits of slowing down and remaining present within my company, rather than running off and starting something new when I honestly wasn't even ready, positively influenced my mood, my mission, and my mantra of, "How you do anything is how you do everything." Life started to become more balanced, and I could feel the effects warming my soul.

It's taken me years, but I've learned how to develop a gift of gratitude and recognize its ability to turn challenges into opportunities and unexpected detours into avenues of growth. **The journey of life may not always unfold according to our mapped-out plans, but with gratitude as a constant companion, and optimism as our navigator, every step gracefully becomes a more meaningful part of a larger, beautifully orchestrated tapestry.**

DEAR DIARY

Shifting our mindset into an attitude of gratitude can bring even more love and abundance into our lives. When we are thankful for what we have, rather than focusing on what we don't or what may not have happened the way we expected, we can raise our vibration towards more of the good and less of the bad.

1. Take this opportunity to practice gratitude by cultivating a habit of writing out three things for which you are grateful every night before you go to bed. Ideally, this will help to shift expectations into appreciation and adjust any negative mindsets into more positive ones.
2. Is there someone (or some people) for whom you are grateful for their support, love, encouragement, or friendship? Have you ever considered writing them a letter, thanking them for being in your life? Now might be a good time to do so.

3. Take a few moments to look back at situations that, possibly in the moment, felt like they were the worst things to ever happen to you. Can you reframe the expectations of what you thought was going to happen to appreciating what actually happened? Is there good hiding within the perceived bad of the situation?

18

LEAN INTO LOVE

Make the Best of YOU

"For what it's worth... it's never too late, or in my case too early, to be whoever you want to be. There's no time limit. Start whenever you want. You can change or stay the same. There are no rules to this thing. We can make the best or the worst of it. I hope you make the best of it. I hope you see things that startle you. I hope you feel things you've never felt before. I hope you meet people who have a different point of view. I hope you live a life you're proud of, and if you're not, I hope you have the courage to start over again."

~ *F. Scott Fitzgerald*

FALLING IN LOVE

I have fallen in love a lot (like a lot, a lot…). I'm not sure I have fallen out of love as many times, however, because some of the outs were more like a crawl, or a sprint, or even a jump out than a fall. But I consider all that loving to be a blessing and believe I am fortunate to have shared so many life-shaping memories with the people who have woven the fabric of my life with their common threads.

When my most disruptive pivotal moments happened in July and December of 2022, I knew in my soul I was long overdue for a life redesign. I could see that critical changes were necessary in order for me to *not* repeat the same mistakes I had been making for decades. So, with the intention of discovering exactly who I am, who I want to become, and where I want to go, I started searching. And by searching, I mean looking inward and focusing on the work that I've outlined in this book.

I meditated a lot (like a TON). My goal with this tactic was to calm the voices in my head (because there were many) and understand what my true soul intentions were lying underneath all the noise.

There was one meditation that blew my mind as it unraveled, and I'd like to share it with you here:

> *I sat in the darkness with my eyes closed. My subconscious presented puzzle pieces of my life falling all around and landing gently on the path in front of me. I watched as the pieces fit together one by one, then stared as the images started to appear one by many, creating a masterpiece—a skillfully curated map. I felt my history lessons weave into my ambition, and my future intertwine like threads as the course ahead became more clear. The anticipation of my new epic adventure became a gorgeous flowing fabric, leading me towards my destiny.*
>
> *As the cloud of my experiences dissolved from my vision and a new avenue of promise presented itself at my feet, I held my compass of integrity and resonating values high above my head and started on my journey.*
>
> *This marked a time when I began to relish in the power of my voice, found courage in the presence of my spirit, and exposed the vulnerability of my soul to the world.*
>
> *A time when I felt I had finished all my research, applied all the lessons, and completed all of my tasks. A time when I knew I was ready because I felt fueled with healthy passions and armed with a shield of personal evolution. A time when I set out on my next chapter and vowed to trust in the process, but more importantly, believe in myself.*

I desired acceptance, but began to recognize my own unconditional approval was all that really mattered.

I had been yearning for fulfillment, but when it presented itself as abundant experience, I discovered joy.

I was seeking alignment, and as I took better care of myself, I became more congruent in my mission.

I embraced the changes as they presented themselves in this meditation, and with them I found self-respect and courage.

I reached for the truth, and when I found it, it set me free.

I had longed for love, but when I embraced myself at the end of my long journey, I was gracefully reminded that love has been within me the entire time, and I no longer needed to look for it.

Opening my eyes, tears of joy gently washed down my cheeks as I felt a radiating light coming from my soul and filling the room. My integrity felt replenished. My heart revived. The message from this meditation was so clear, so precise, so real that I knew it was mine. And all I had to do was go out and live it.

Up to this point, I had been going through life refusing to take other people's words for anything because I was convinced that I had to experience everything on my own in order to understand it. But as time has proven to be the greatest teacher, I really didn't need to experience *everything* once my enormous pivotal events sent me careening over the edge of emotional tolerance right into a world of intentional healing.

As I evolved into this new mindset, new emotional environment, and new patterns, I started to feel the dignified alignment with my new destination of personal truth and fulfillment, and see the course I needed to navigate in order to get there. The further I ventured down this fulfilling highway of self-love, the more I could see that I didn't have to go through so much pain anymore. I didn't have to endure so much heartache. And I felt the importance of sharing my messy monologues with you, knowing you might be able to relate, hoping you can learn from my mistakes on your own personal journey of living out your dreams—without all the pain, tears, and suffering I crammed into this book.

It has taken courage to unmask all the versions of me and share them with you. It has taken determination to understand the reasons why and why not. And with all the twists and turns and mysteriously convoluted back alleys and pathways I have wandered down during the course of my life, I knew that part of the process was to go back and accept each and every step I've already taken. But, holy hell, were some of those pathways dark!

Backtracking through some of my most painful moments and most difficult times was a *giant* undertaking. But I needed to heal those parts of me so I could rebuild my foundation, raise my standards, and move on. Even though I was resistant at first, the value, purpose, and healing exposed themselves once I got started. **And through it all, I became filled with the wholehearted and deeply-rooted belief that I am enough, I am worthy, and I am so very lovable.**

I have made peace with the fear that had me changing constantly and have created new habits that now encourage me to adjust in real-time before the limiting beliefs take over. I started to understand that the morphing of my personality had actually offered me a freedom and flexibility that created valuable opportunities over the years, but that the unhealthy habit of people-pleasing is no longer necessary.

I'm not perfect. But I know that every time I've been knocked down, I've gotten back up. I continue to work on myself every day to be the best I can be, and that is all I can ask of myself. I am proud of the adventures I've been on and the results of the battles I've fought. I've stopped looking for the lost time I wasted and have come to accept that I am the one who allowed the distractions to take away my focus in the first place. I'm not going to allow it to happen anymore. I've detached from the things that no longer serve me, allowing more space for the things that do. I've learned to lean into the discomfort of my fear and stay uncomfortable until the lessons are imprinted on my heart. And I have learned to do the next right thing for the right reasons, owning my choices, right or wrong—all on a mission to love myself unconditionally.

Through it all, after breaking down my walls of resistance and allowing the messages from the Universe to sink in through an outrageous (slightly awkward) spiritual awakening, I finally saw the value in all the therapy, coaching, journaling, events, classes, courses, meditations, medications, and maneuvering. All of it combined brought me the fulfillment I was yearning for in the expression of self-acceptance, honor, and joy. All I need is within me now. The love I have been searching for this entire time was already a part of me—I just needed to pause long enough to recognize it.

So, to all of you who are patiently waiting to shine: it's your turn. You are beautiful, courageous, and bright. You are everything you are meant to be, with the strength and tenacity to become anything you wish. You are bound to make it through whatever this life has to throw at you; just learn to listen to your gut and trust your intuition. It knows exactly who you are and will lead you down the right path.

When you get started, the world will open its arms and encourage you to step further into your own truth. Resiliency will come along and be your guide as you conquer your trials, command your tribulations, and rejoice in your successes. And that is when you will expand into the greatest version of yourself.

DEDICATION TO THE PROCESS

The process is about many things, but mostly it's about finding the courage to dedicate time to yourself through intention, perseverance, and planning. It's about pushing through the pain and the challenges, and digging deep to uncover the hidden parts of ourselves that we may not like, and working through the hard stuff anyway. It's about recognizing what belongs to you and what does not. It's learning how to listen for the messages and generating the patience for them to come to you. It's about speaking up for yourself and believing in your voice. And it's about making the intentional changes towards greatness, knowing you are meant to be an outstanding and unique individual.

You must surround yourself with others who support, encourage, and respect you as you create a network that reflects your self-worth and enhances what it is you've already done. Hold yourself accountable for the success and fulfillment you so desperately wish to have, but also let go of the things that prevent you from becoming the most beautiful and empowered version of yourself.

It's about doing the fucking work, and then doing it again, and again, and again until the change happens, and until you feel the shift inside.

Lean into gratitude.

Fall in love with yourself.

And design a life that you know is worth changing for.

"The more you retrain yourself to choose happiness over fear, the more blissful you will be."
~ *Gabrielle Bernstein*

IN THAT MOMENT

Years ago I began compiling a poem that had been left unfinished, until now. I've pushed and pulled it apart. I've added and subtracted lines here and there. I worked and reworked it so many times that I am not even sure where the original inspiration came from, but I know the energy of all the people I have crossed paths with over the years are the reasons it has now landed in this book.

IN THAT MOMENT

It was in that moment,
I knew.
I truly knew
in the depth of my soul
that I am enough,
more than enough,
and I am right where I'm supposed to be.
I am surrounded by all the right people,
by all the right resources,
and by love, opportunities, support, and magnificence.
It was in that moment,
that clarifying moment,
when I was transformed into enlightenment,
and the world suddenly presented itself anew in all its glorious abundance.
In that moment,
my life's painted canvas wiped itself clear
and begged me to create a new masterpiece
with brilliant colors and mesmerizing imagery—
an artwork that transcends beyond me.
In that moment,
my history lessons were complete,
my challenges were logged as epic battles,
my insecurities became cherished wisdom,
my unreachable dreams evolved into my new reality.
That moment is here—
savor it,
embrace it,
step through it and never look back.
I wasn't brought into this world to fit in;
I was created to stand out.
It was in that moment,
I knew
in the depth of my soul
that I am enough,
and I am right where I am supposed to be.

DEAR DIARY

As the world communicates loudly, how do you filter what you take in? Are you allowing the right messages in? Are you telling yourself the best messages about who you are and how you want to show up?

1. Take some time to reflect on how you speak to yourself. If you have moments of negative self-talk or unhealthy thoughts that perpetuate, what are they? How can you change them? What can you do to increase your positive self-talk?
2. Are you facing a pivotal moment and are ready to either start over or give up? First, allow yourself grace. Acknowledge that something needs to change. Congratulate yourself for making it this far. Then gain clarity by jotting down what it is you want to do, or even, what you don't want to do anymore.
3. Congratulations! I hope my messages were helpful in your self-acceptance journey, and I hope to see you soon.

You are

Enough.

You are

Worthy.

You are

Loveable.

Afterword

"To be or not to be, that is the question..."

~William Shakespeare

GETTING INTENTIONAL

Adapting and nurturing a mindset where you actively and consciously shape your life according to *your* values, dreams, and desires is what *Designing a Life Worth Changing For* is all about. You must make deliberate choices and take purposeful, massive action to live out those choices. It's not always easy, but I can tell you from experience, it's totally worth it.

Throughout my journey, I've realized how crucial it is to move from a place of playing the victim (life happening *to* me) to a place of being the victor (life happening *for* me), and how going through the processes of working through the pain and reorganizing the habits can help lead you to living a life full of purpose and heartfelt desire that is way better than just letting your life happen and playing with the cards you *think* you've been dealt.

Here are the skills I've learned that will ideally help you along your journey of joy and fulfillment:

— **Learn what is limiting you.** Discovering what your limiting beliefs are and where they come from can be an incredibly effective first step to determining how you need to move forward. Some of us have fears that are more difficult to work through than others, but without taking the time to understand what they are, the rest of the work may be built on an unhealed, unstable foundation.

- **Set goals.** Be specific. Set meaningful and direct goals, and get clear on where you want to go and who you want to be regarding your personal growth, career, relationships, health, etc.
- **Take responsibility for yourself.** This means taking time out to understand who you are, what your habits and patterns are, and how they are affecting you. Some habits are hard to break, but they are even harder if they remain unidentified. If there's something you don't like about yourself, seek ways to change it.
- **Take a chance.** If there is hesitation in your journey, have faith. By taking chances in this world, we get to explore and experience different opportunities and figure out what works for us and what doesn't. You don't know until you try.
- **Get some help.** Coaches and therapists are abundantly helpful when it comes to intentional creation. They come equipped with tools and methods. Gathering the right mentors and advisors can significantly advance your journey and your life.
- **Practice mindful and intentional decision-making.** Assess where you are (mentally, emotionally, physically) and learn what type of external factors are influencing you. Take time to look within to see how these factors align (or don't align) with who you are and who you want to become. The more aware we are about the environment we spend our time in, the better we can make decisions based on a place of self-awareness.
- **Define your values and set your boundaries**. Write them down. If they don't feel good, make adjustments until they do. Knowing what you stand for will keep you moving forward. Not knowing will keep you sitting on your ass, going nowhere.
- **Surround yourself with awesome people.** Because if you're doing this life thing on purpose, you're going to need a great cheering squad and respectful support. (And awesome people are fun, so fill your life with them!)

— **Learn forgiveness.** I'm not suggesting you become a pushover, but the value in forgiveness and letting go of anything that may have pained you is a valuable lesson in self-preservation. Holding on to what no longer serves us is a waste of energy. Let that shit go.

— **Take care of yourself.** As a society, we get so wrapped up in the mental rush of work and life. We must remember to nurture our bodies, hearts, and spirits. The value of self-care goes beyond the occasional massage or walk in the park. Give yourself a long and much-needed, relaxing break.

— **Change your habits, break the cycles.** Change the bad habits for better ones, and cultivate routines that contribute to your overall well-being and forward momentum. Figure out what lights you up, both good and bad, and work on reformatting the patterns towards healthier responses and routines.

— **Clarify your purpose.** What do *you* have that no one else does? What is your *why*? What *really* matters to you? Clarity equals power.

— **Take the initiative.** No one else is going to do this for you. It's up to you to take control of *your* life. Seek the opportunities. Take the risks. ***DO THE WORK.***

— **Connect with your spirituality.** In a religious sense or not, there is an energy that moves with us and is a guiding force that is integral to our lives. Taking the time to understand, connect, and contribute to that energy can be the source of understanding you've been searching for.

— **Be thankful.** Gratitude is a gateway to healing. When we can let go of expectations, and look towards appreciation, a shift happens, and the world becomes a more resilient and pliable space.

— **Get creative and embrace change.** This whole intentional living thing doesn't have to be hard. Have fun with it. It's your life, after all. Change it up and embrace what's happening *for* you.

And most of all, ***be intentional with the design of your life***. When you start to live a life full of intention, things are bound to enhance your abilities and experiences in ways you've never seen or known possible. Embrace it. Not everything has to change, but your intuition knows what does in order for you to live your best life.

Endnotes

Chapter 2

1. Nicole Celestine, Ph.D. "How to Change Self-Limiting Beliefs According to Psychology." PositivePsychology.com, October 13, 2023. https://positivepsychology.com/false-beliefs/.
2. *The Italian Job. YouTube*. YouTube, 2010. https://www.youtube.com/watch?v=KfcrM7ukzCU.

Chapter 3

3. The Doors. "Light My Fire." The Doors. Elektra Records, 1967. Record.
4. Morrison, Jim. "The Doors - The End (HQ)." YouTube, June 20, 2015. https://www.youtube.com/watch?v=eqgXGMAS__M.

Chapter 7

5. Contributor, Digital Team. "Prozac and Alcohol: Why Drinking and SSRIs Are a Dangerous Combination." Baton Rouge Behavioral Hospital, January 28, 2022. https://batonrougebehavioral.com/tag/prozac-and-alcohol/#:~:text=Unwinding%20with%20a%20glass%20of,must%20be%20taken%20every%20day.

Chapter 9

6. Tony Robbins. "Discover the 6 Human Needs." tonyrobbins.com, January 18, 2023. https://www.tonyrobbins.com/mind-meaning/do-you-need-to-feel-significant/.

Chapter 10

7. John C. Maxwell. Intentional Living: Choosing a Life That Matters. (New York, NY: Center Street, a division of Hachette Book Group, Inc. 2015).

Chapter 13

8. "Miraval Resorts and Spas: Luxury Inclusive Wellness Retreats." Miraval Resorts, November 28, 2023. http://www.miravalresorts.com/.
9. "Om Namah Shivaya." Wikipedia, November 4, 2023. https://en.wikipedia.org/wiki/Om_Namah_Shivaya.

Chapter 14

10. "Psychological Abuse." Wikipedia, November 29, 2023. https://en.wikipedia.org/wiki/Psychological_abuse.
11. Staff, Newport Institute. "How to Tell If Someone Is Gaslighting You." Newport Institute, December 4, 2023. https://www.newportinstitute.com/resources/mental-health/what_is_gaslighting_abuse/.
12. Pedersen, Traci. "Triggers: What They Are, How They Form, and What to Do." Psych Central, April 28, 2022. https://psychcentral.com/lib/what-is-a-trigger.
13. Shapiro, Francine. "What Is EMDR?" EMDR Institute - Eye Movement Desensitization And Reprocessing Therapy, October 20, 2022. https://www.emdr.com/what-is-emdr/.

Chapter 17

14. Heim, Dr. Christian. """The Science of Gratitude (Part 1), December 9, 2019. https://www.drchristianheim.comblog/2019/12/7/1h7r3gsed6xqtuni1r7hjlz6befpsn.

Acknowledgments

To all the people I've crossed paths with: all the ones who have remained; all the ones who have passed through; and all the ones I have yet to meet. You've made (or will make) an impact on my life and this book, and for that I thank you. I am so very fortunate to have lived the life I call my own and am truly blessed to be surrounded by an army of warriors, a tribe of lovers, a gaggle of comedians, and all of the members of my divine council. You are my past, my present, and my future. Without all of you, none of this would have ever happened, and now with all of you, it will continue to. Thank you.

To my editor, Marianne Evans, and the team at StoryBuilders. As a first-time author, I can't thank you enough for walking me through my first rodeo and having the patience to advise and steer this carousel ride through my clunky and awkward creative process and into the delicate hands of my readers. Your undeniable expertise and compassionate guidance brought me the confidence and support I needed to make this all happen.

To Lori Apicelli. You are a solid rock in my life, a friend I cherish and hold the tightest in my heart. I am eternally blessed with your ride-or-die friendship and unwavering acceptance of everything I've ever done and plan on doing. You've been a part of practically every single story in this book, and you know me better than anyone. I can't wait for our next chapters. They are going to be epic! Love you, Sister.

Regan Couto. I am so proud of the woman you are. If it weren't for you, so much of the past twelve years would not have been possible. You have become the yin to my yang, and I value every single solitary thing you do with and for me and AG&Co. You've stepped into a role that was incredibly challenging for me to relinquish. Still, as I watch your continued success, I am ridiculously proud to call you my business partner and dearest friend. Thank you so very much.

Kerri Krell. Your soul has enlightened not only my world, but also the universe that surrounds my team and the energy we all bring to the table. Your consistency, support, patience, and power in the pause have expanded my horizons, helped me to acknowledge my successes, and made me appreciate the journey even more. I am grateful for everything you are and how you have so positively impacted my life.

Renee Linnell, Tony Dufresne, and David Richards. Thank you for reading my manuscript (sometimes in bits and pieces) and supporting me through your experience as authors and friends. Your continued encouragement fueled my final 20% (the most challenging part for me) and helped me get over this finish line. I appreciate you and the beautiful world of words that we all find comfort in.

Brand Builders Group and all your associates. I started writing this book in March of 2023, and with your incredible mentoring, formulas, and strategies, I was able to complete one of the biggest dreams of my life, in under a year, with your momentum and resources to keep going and do it again and again.

Friends (old and new). You have all added such tremendous light and dimension to my day-to-day life. Through laughs, tears, adventures, and fears, I am so thankful our paths have crossed. Some of those who I must mention because of your generous support while I wrote this book include Laura N., Mark A., Jackie K., David R., Larissa S., Brendan F., Jesse D., the AG&Co Team, Austin & Hannah, my awesome Beverly neighbors, Stephanie R., the entire Empower Pilates community, Vanessa, Lori's tribe in NJ, and of course, Artie Mac.

To my lovers, boyfriends, friends, and even my two ex-husbands. Thank you. You are why this book exists. You have been the lessons I've learned, the heartache I've overcome, and the tonic in my gin. You are what has made up so much of my life. Without you, our ups and downs, the ins and outs, the roller coaster rides, and world-won, I mean whirlwind romances, I never would have evolved into the educated, experienced, loving, headstrong, empathetic, understanding, and courageous woman I am today. All of the time I spent with you has led me directly to this point in my life, and for that, whether our relation- or *shit*uationship ended on good, bad, or indifferent terms, thank you. May we all find the love we deserve in the lifetimes we serve.

And, of course, Mum and Dad. You've never given up on me through all the shenanigans I've pulled, the wild dreams I've chased, and the emotional ride I've kept you on for all these years. Your love and support have always been the true north of my compass, whether I want to follow your lead or not. Whenever I've needed a recalibration, you have constantly and relentlessly been there for me, to guide me on righting my wrongs and help me to repair any damage that happened throughout my journey, no matter what. I am the perfect blend of both of you. And for that, my pride rings strong. The balance between who you both are has taught me patience, acceptance, determination, encouragement, wisdom, and faith. As well as business savviness, creativity, compassion, and common sense. Your influence is deeply ingrained in my values and beliefs, and I am proud to have come from such a loving and beautiful family. For all those gut-wrenching nights you stayed awake wondering where in the world your daughter was or what the hell was going on and if I'd be okay, I'm sorry. I hope you can sleep better now by having some light shed on those mysteries and mishaps that pulled me around the world and back again. Hopefully, the stories weren't much of a surprise, and if they were, at least now you understand what really happened. Your unwavering presence and investment in me as your daughter and as the woman I have become have had an incredibly positive impact on me, and for that, I am exceptionally grateful. I love you both unconditionally, and I am so incredibly thankful that you are both still here to commemorate this next chapter of my life and for me to continue to celebrate yours.

And to you, the holder of this book. There is beauty in change—we all just do it differently. For that difference in all of us, thank you. For more information on the lessons within this book, please visit my website: www.amandagreaves.com for tips, additional publications, speaking engagements, and courses.

Thank you for joining me on this journey.

I am honored to be a part of yours.

About the Author

Amanda Greaves, armed with a Bachelor of Arts in Interior Design, a decade of global adventures, and over twenty years in the design and construction sectors, recognized a deeper calling beyond aesthetics. Fueled by a passion for self-development, coaching, and meaningful connections, Amanda intentionally shifted from a successful design career to embark on a journey of writing, speaking, consulting, and coaching.

Her innate creativity and commitment to cultivating purpose led to the establishment of The Amanda Greaves Group, a personal development consulting firm dedicated to guiding individuals towards authentic self-discovery and intentional living. Additionally, Amanda founded Two 29 Publishing, a partnership publishing company providing tailored support and strategies for aspiring authors seeking a more curated journey in their writing endeavors.

Discover more about Amanda's transformative work at:

www.amandagreaves.com and www.two29publishing.com.

Made in the USA
Middletown, DE
26 February 2024

49921401R00166